D0322467

SHAKESPEARE IN PRODUCTION

KING HENRY V

This is the first stage history of Shakespeare's *King Henry V* to cover the play's theatrical life since its first performance in 1599. Staging this play has always been a political act, and the substantial introduction traces its theatrical interventions into conflicts from the Napoleonic Wars to Vietnam and the Falklands crisis, offering a complete account of the play's fortunes: from its absence in the seventeenth century to its dominant position as historical spectacle in the Victorian period, through twentieth-century productions, which include the popular films by Olivier and Branagh. Together they raise vital interpretive questions: is *Henry V* an epic of English nationalism, a knowing and cynical piece of power politics, or an anti-war manifesto? The volume also includes the playtext, illustrations and detailed footnotes about major performances.

SHAKESPEARE IN PRODUCTION

SERIES EDITORS: J. S. BRATTON AND JULIE HANKEY

This series offers students and researchers from A level Theatre Arts to postgraduate dissertation the fullest possible stage histories of individual Shakespearean texts.

In each volume a substantial introduction presents a conceptual overview of the play, marking out the major stages of its representation and reception. In this context, no single approach to the play can be described as more 'authentic' than any other. The extrapolations of Tate, the interpretations of Dryden, the upholstering of Charles Kean and the strippings-down of Marowitz are all treated as ways of reading and rewriting Shakespeare's text and understood in terms of contemporary audiences, tastes and sensibilities.

The commentary, presented alongside the New Cambridge edition of the text itself, offers detailed, line-by-line evidence for the overview presented in the introduction, making the volume a flexible tool for further research. The editors have selected interesting and vivid evocations of settings, acting and stage presentation and range widely in time and space.

The plays of Shakespeare are a particularly rich field for such treatment, having formed a central part of British theatrical culture for four hundred years. Major stage productions outside Britain are also included, as are adaptations, film and video versions.

ALSO PUBLISHED:

A Midsummer Night's Dream, edited by Trevor R. Griffiths
Antony and Cleopatra, edited by Richard Madelaine
Hamlet, edited by Robert Hapgood
Much Ado About Nothing, edited by John Cox
The Tempest, edited by Christine Dymkowski
Romeo and Juliet, edited by James N. Loehlin

KING HENRY V

EDITED BY
EMMA SMITH
Hertford College, Oxford

PUBLISHED BY THE PRESS SYNDICATE OF THE UNIVERSITY OF CAMBRIDGE
The Pitt Building, Trumpington Street, Cambridge, United Kingdom

CAMBRIDGE UNIVERSITY PRESS
The Edinburgh Building, Cambridge CB2 2RU, UK
40 West 20th Street, New York, NY 10011-4211, USA
477 Williamstown Road, Port Melbourne, VIC 3207, Australia
Ruiz de Alarcón 13, 28014 Madrid, Spain
Dock House, The Waterfront, Cape Town 8001, South Africa

http://www.cambridge.org

© Cambridge University Press 2002

This book is in copyright. Subject to statutory exception
and to the provisions of relevant collective licensing agreements,
no reproduction of any part may take place without
the written permission of Cambridge University Press.

First published 2002

Printed in the United Kingdom at the University Press, Cambridge

Typeface Ehrhardt 10/12 pt.   *System* QuarkXPress [BTS]

A catalogue record for this book is available from the British Library

Library of Congress Cataloguing in Publication data

Shakespeare, William, 1564–1616.
King Henry V / edited by Emma Smith.
p.   cm. – (Shakespeare in production)
Includes bibliographical references (p. 237) and index.
ISBN 0 521 59428 6 – ISBN 0 521 59511 8 (pbk.)
1. Henry V, King of England, 1387–1422 – Drama.   2. Henry V, King of England,
1387–1422 – In literature.   3. Henry V, King of England, 1387–1422 – In motion
pictures.   4. Shakespeare, William, 1564–1616 – Film and video
adaptations.   5. Shakespeare, William, 1564–1616 – Stage history.   6. Shakespeare,
William, 1564–1616. Henry V.   I. Smith, Emma, 1970–   II. Title.   III. Series.
PR2812.A2 S49   2002
822.3'3 – dc21   2001052892

ISBN   0 521 59428 6   hardcover
ISBN   0 521 59511 8   paperback

CONTENTS

ILLUSTRATIONS

SERIES EDITORS' PREFACE

It is no longer necessary to stress that the text of a play is only its starting-point, and that only in production is its potential realised and capable of being appreciated fully. Since the coming-of-age of Theatre Studies as an academic discipline, we now understand that even Shakespeare is only one collaborator in the creation and infinite recreation of his play upon the stage. And just as we now agree that no play is complete until it is produced, so we have become interested in the way in which plays often produced – and pre-eminently the plays of the national Bard, William Shakespeare – acquire a life history of their own, after they leave the hands of their first maker.

Since the eighteenth century Shakespeare has become a cultural construct: sometimes the guarantor of nationhood, heritage and the status quo, sometimes seized and transformed to be its critic and antidote. This latter role has been particularly evident in countries where Shakespeare has to be translated. The irony is that while his status as national icon grows in the English-speaking world, his language is both lost and renewed, so that for good or ill, Shakespeare can be made to seem more urgently 'relevant' than in England or America, and may become the one dissenting voice that the censors mistake as harmless.

'Shakespeare in Production' gives the reader, the student and the scholar a comprehensive dossier of materials – eye-witness accounts, contemporary criticism, promptbook marginalia, stage business, cuts, additions and rewritings – from which to construct an understanding of the many meanings that the plays have carried down the ages and across the world. These materials are organised alongside the New Cambridge Shakespeare text of the play, line by line and scene by scene, while a substantial introduction in each volume offers a guide to their interpretation. One may trace an argument about, for example, the many ways of playing Queen Gertrude, or the political transmutations of the text of *Henry V*; or take a scene, an act or a whole play, and work out how it has succeeded or failed in presentation over four hundred years.

For, despite our insistence that the plays are endlessly made and remade by history, Shakespeare is not a blank, scribbled upon by the age. Theatre history charts changes, but also registers something in spite of those changes. Some productions work and others do not. Two interpretations may be entirely different, and yet both will bring the play to life. Why? Without setting out to give absolute answers, the history of a play in the theatre can often show where the energy and shape of it lie, what has made it tick, through many permutations. In this way theatre history can find common ground with literary criticism. Both will find suggestive directions in the introductions to these volumes, while the commentaries provide raw material for readers to recreate the living experience of theatre, and become their own eye-witnesses.

J. S. Bratton

Julie Hankey

ACKNOWLEDGEMENTS

I have accrued debts to numerous institutions and individuals during the writing of this book. All Souls College supported my research at the Folger Shakespeare Library in Washington D.C.: I am grateful to the Warden and Fellows for this opportunity, and to the staff of the Folger for their welcome and efficiency. Colleagues in the Bodleian Library, Oxford, the Shakespeare Centre Library in Stratford-upon-Avon, the British Film Institute, the Theatre Museum, Covent Garden, the Irish Theatre Archive, the Maison Française, Oxford, and the University Library, Cambridge, have answered my queries and helped in different ways. The book is obviously built on Professor Andrew Gurr's New Cambridge text, and I have relied implicitly on his meticulous scholarship. I would also like to thank Andrew Gurr for allowing me to view video recordings of the Globe production from the collection at the University of Reading, Rebecca Breuer for lending materials relating to the new Globe, Kate Clark and Josie Rourke for the stimulus of supervisions for the 'Shakespeare in Performance' paper in Cambridge, Clotilde Morhan for translating French reviews, members of the Renaissance Graduate and Drama in Performance seminars in Oxford for inviting me to present earlier drafts of the book, readers of Oxford's *North Oxford Association News* for talking to me about their recollections of Olivier's film, and Philip Schwyzer for reading the Introduction and making constructive criticisms. Linda Squire has read it all several times for large and small points. Students at New Hall and Newnham, Cambridge, and at Hertford and Pembroke Colleges in Oxford have stimulated my thinking about the play and about issues of performance, and I have been extremely lucky in my English colleagues at New Hall and at Hertford. Jacky Bratton and Julie Hankey have been patient, encouraging and eagle-eyed: their share in the good parts of the book is a considerable one. I am glad to have had Sarah Stanton as editor at Cambridge University Press and am grateful for her support of the project, and her tolerance of my elastic definition of the deadline. The book is for Linda Squire, with love.

ABBREVIATIONS

1 Henry IV	Herbert Weil and Judith Weil (eds.), *The New Cambridge Shakespeare: The First Part of King Henry IV* (Cambridge: Cambridge University Press, 1997)
2 Henry IV	Giorgio Melchiori (ed.), *The New Cambridge Shakespeare: The Second Part of King Henry IV* (Cambridge: Cambridge University Press, 1989)
BBC	BBC, *The BBC Shakespeare: Henry V* (London: 1979)
Beauman	Sally Beauman, *The Royal Shakespeare Company's Production of Henry V for the Centenary Season at the Royal Shakespeare Theatre* (Oxford and New York: Pergamon Press, 1976)
Bell	*Bell's Edition of Shakespeare's Plays, As they are now performed at the Theatres Royal in London; Regulated from the Prompt Books of each House By Permission; with Notes Critical and Illustrative; By the Authors of the Dramatic Censor* (London and York: 1774), vol. IV
Branagh	Kenneth Branagh, *Henry V by William Shakespeare: A Screen Adaptation* (London: Chatto and Windus, 1989)
Calvert	*Shakspere's historical play of Henry the fifth, arranged by C. Calvert, and produced under his direction at the Prince's theatre, Manchester* (Manchester: 1872)
Calvert pbk	Charles Calvert (1872), Folger Shakespeare Library (Shattuck, *Henry V*, 3)
Coleman	John Coleman, *Shaksper's Historical Play, Henry V* (London: 1876)
Cooper	Roberta Krensky Cooper, *The American Shakespeare Theatre: Stratford 1955–85* (Washington D.C.: Folger, 1986)
Coursen	H. R. Coursen, *Shakespeare in Production: Whose History?* (Athens, GA: Ohio University Press, 1996)
David	Richard David, *Shakespeare in the Theatre* (Cambridge: Cambridge University Press, 1978)
Davies	Anthony Davies, *Filming Shakespeare's Plays: The Adaptations of Laurence Olivier, Orson Welles, Peter Brook*

	and Akira Kurosawa (Cambridge: Cambridge University Press, 1988)
Eckert	C. W. Eckert (ed.), *Focus on Shakespearean Films* (Englewood Cliffs, NJ: Prentice-Hall, 1972)
ES	The *Evening Standard*
F	Folio
Fitter	Chris Fitter, 'A Tale of Two Branaghs: *Henry V*, Ideology, and the Mekong Agincourt' in *Shakespeare Left and Right*, ed. Ivo Kamps (London and New York: Routledge, 1991), pp. 259–75
Foulkes	Richard Foulkes, 'Charles Calvert's *Henry V*', *Shakespeare Survey* 41 (1989), pp. 23–34
FT	The *Financial Times*
G	The *Guardian*
Geduld	Harry M. Geduld, *Filmguide to Henry V* (Bloomington: Indiana University Press, [1973])
Gurr	Andrew Gurr (ed.), *The New Cambridge Shakespeare: King Henry V* (Cambridge: Cambridge University Press, 1992)
Henry 1780	*King Henry V. A Tragedy. As it is Acted at the Theatres-Royal, 1780*
Holland	Peter Holland, *English Shakespeares: Shakespeare on the English Stage in the 1990s* (Cambridge: Cambridge University Press, 1997)
I	The *Independent*
Johnson	Arthur Sherbo (ed.), *The Yale Edition of the Works of Samuel Johnson, Volume VIII 'Johnson on Shakespeare'* (New Haven and London: Yale University Press, 1968)
Kean	*Shakespeare's play of King Henry the fifth, arranged for representation at the Princess's theatre, with historical and explanatory notes by C. Kean* (London, 1859)
Kean pbk	Charles Kean (1859), Folger Shakespeare Library (Shattuck, *Henry V*, 6)
Kemble pbk	John Kemble (1811), Shakespeare Centre Library 50.01 (1806) (Shattuck, *Henry V*, 1)
Kiernan	Pauline Kiernan, *Staging Shakespeare at the New Globe* (Basingstoke and London: Macmillan, 1999)
Leiter	Samuel L. Leiter (ed.), *Shakespeare Around the Globe: A Guide to Notable Postwar Revivals* (New York: Greenwood Press, 1986)
Loehlin	James N. Loehlin, *Shakespeare in Performance: Henry V* (Manchester: Manchester University Press, 1996)

Macready pbk	William Macready (1839), Folger Shakespeare Library (Shattuck, *Henry V*, 8)
Mansfield	*The Richard Mansfield Acting Version of King Henry V* (New York: Maclure, Phillips and Co., 1901)
Masterworks	*Masterworks of the British Cinema* (London: Faber, 1990)
Moment	Gary Taylor, *Moment by Moment by Shakespeare* (London and Basingstoke: Macmillan, 1985)
Noble pbk	Adrian Noble (1984), Shakespeare Centre Library s.3410.
O, Fol	Laurence Olivier (1944), shooting script, Folger Shakespeare Library (Shattuck, *Henry V*, Folio 1)
Odell	George C. D. Odell, *Shakespeare: From Betterton to Irving* (London: Constable, 1963)
Phelps pbk	Samuel Phelps (1852), Folger Shakespeare Library (Shattuck, *Henry V*, 9)
Players	Russell Jackson and R. L. Smallwood (eds.), *Players of Shakespeare 2* (Cambridge: Cambridge University Press, 1988)
Q	Quarto text
Quayle pbk	Anthony Quayle (1951), Shakespeare Centre Library, OS 71.21 (Shattuck, *Henry V*, 35)
RSC	Sally Beauman, *The Royal Shakespeare Company: A History of Ten Decades* (Oxford: Oxford University Press, 1982)
Shattuck	Charles H. Shattuck, *The Shakespeare Promptbooks: A Descriptive Catalogue* (Urbana and London: University of Illinois Press, 1965)
Shaughnessy	Robert Shaughnessy, *Representing Shakespeare: England, History and the RSC* (New York and London: Harvester Wheatsheaf, 1994)
Smallwood	Robert Smallwood, 'Shakespeare Performances in England (1997)', *Shakespeare Survey 51* (1998), pp. 219–55.
Sprague	Arthur Colby Sprague, *Shakespeare and the Actors* (Cambridge, MA: Harvard University Press, 1944)
SS	*Shakespeare Survey*
SSt	*Shakespeare Studies*
STel	The *Sunday Telegraph*
T	*The Times*
Taylor	Gary Taylor (ed.), *The Oxford Shakespeare: Henry V* (Oxford: Oxford University Press, 1984)
Tel	The *Daily Telegraph*

TLS	*Times Literary Supplement*
Wars	Michael Bogdanov and Michael Pennington, *The English Shakespeare Company: The Story of the Wars of the Roses 1986–1989* (London: Nick Hern Books, 1990)
Williamson	Audrey Williamson, *Old Vic Drama 2* (London: Rockcliff, 1957)

SIGNIFICANT PRODUCTIONS

This list includes major productions discussed in detail in the Introduction and Commentary. Dates refer to the first date of performance.

Director	Theatre (London, unless otherwise specified)	Date	Henry
	Globe	1599	? Richard Burbage
	Court	1605	
	Covent Garden	1738–82	Dennis Delane, Spranger Barry, Thomas Hull, William Smith, Richard Wroughton
John Kemble	Drury Lane	1789 1806, 1815	John Kemble Edmund Kean
William Macready	Covent Garden	1819 (revived 1825, 1837)	William Macready
William Macready	Covent Garden	1839	William Macready
Samuel Phelps	Sadler's Wells	1852	Samuel Phelps
Charles Kean	Princess's Theatre	1859	Charles Kean
Charles Calvert	Prince's Theatre, Manchester	1872	Charles Calvert
	Booth's Theatre, New York and touring	1875	George Rignold
John Coleman	Queen's Theatre, Long Acre	1876	John Coleman
Charles Calvert	Drury Lane	1879	George Rignold
Frank Benson	Shakespeare Memorial Theatre, Stratford-upon-Avon and touring	1897–1916	Frank Benson
Lewis Waller	Lyceum	1900	Lewis Waller
Richard Mansfield	Garden Theatre, New York	1900	Richard Mansfield
William Poel	Shakespeare Memorial Theatre, Stratford-upon-Avon (outdoors)	1901	Robert Loraine

Director	Theatre (London, unless otherwise specified)	Date	Henry
John Martin-Harvey	His Majesty's	1916	John Martin-Harvey
William Bridges-Adams	Shakespeare Memorial Theatre, Stratford-upon-Avon	1920	Murray Carrington
Nigel Playfair	Lyric, Hammersmith	1927	Lewis Casson
Robert Atkins	Shakespeare Memorial Theatre, Stratford-upon-Avon	1934	Robert Atkins
	Ring, Blackfriars	1936	Robert Atkins
Ben Iden Payne	Shakespeare Memorial Theatre, Stratford-upon-Avon	1937	Clement McCallin
Tyrone Guthrie	Old Vic	1937	Laurence Olivier
Lewis Casson	Drury Lane	1938	Ivor Novello
Robert Atkins	Regent's Park	1941	Patrick Kinsella
Milton Rosmer	Shakespeare Memorial Theatre, Stratford-upon-Avon	1943	Baliol Holloway
Laurence Olivier	Film	1944	Laurence Olivier
Dorothy Green	Shakespeare Memorial Theatre, Stratford-upon-Avon	1946	Paul Scofield
Glen Byam Shaw	Old Vic	1951	Alec Clunes
Anthony Quayle	Shakespeare Memorial Theatre, Stratford-upon-Avon	1951	Richard Burton
Michael Benthall	Old Vic	1955	Richard Burton
Michael Langham	Stratford, Ontario	1956	Christopher Plummer
Michael Hayes	BBC television production	1960	Robert Hardy
Douglas Seale	Stratford, Connecticut	1963	James Ray
John Barton and Peter Hall	Royal Shakespeare Theatre, Stratford-upon-Avon	1964	Ian Holm
Joseph Papp	Delacorte Theater, New York	1965	Robert Hooks

Director	Theatre (London, unless otherwise specified)	Date	Henry
Michael Langham	Stratford, Ontario	1966	Douglas Rain
Michael Kahn	Stratford, Connecticut	1969	Len Cariou
Terry Hands	Royal Shakespeare Theatre, Stratford-upon-Avon	1975	Alan Howard
David Giles	BBC television film	1979	David Gwillim
Adrian Noble	Royal Shakespeare Theatre, Stratford-upon-Avon	1984	Kenneth Branagh
Wilfred Leach	Central Park, New York	1984	Kevin Kline
Michael Bogdanov	English Shakespeare Company touring	1986	Michael Pennington
Michael Croft	Regent's Park Open Air Theatre	1986	Hakeem Kae-Kazim
Christopher Selbie	Theatre Clywd, Mold and touring	1987	Colin Hurley
Kenneth Branagh	Film	1989	Kenneth Branagh
Matthew Warchus	Royal Shakespeare Theatre, Stratford-upon-Avon	1994	Iain Glen
Douglas Hughes	Delacorte Theater, New York	1996	Andre Braugher
Edward Hall	Watermill, Newbury	1997	Jamie Glover
Richard Olivier	Globe Theatre	1997	Mark Rylance
Ron Daniels	Royal Shakespeare Theatre, Stratford-upon-Avon	1997	Michael Sheen
Jean-Louis Benoit	Avignon Festival, France	1999	Philippe Torreton
Edward Hall	Royal Shakespeare Theatre, Stratford-upon-Avon	2000	William Houston
Jeannette Lambermont	Stratford, Ontario	2001	Graham Abbey

INTRODUCTION

First performed in 1599, and, according to its first appearance in print, 'played sundry times' by 1600, *Henry V* fell out of the theatrical repertoire after a single revival in 1605 until the eighteenth century. By the mid-twentieth century, however, a skit on Shakespeare in the theatre included a weary Henry alongside Hamlet and Juliet begging audiences to 'give us a rest'.[1] Popularity and unpopularity both tell a story about the play and its audiences, and the fluctuating fortunes of *Henry V* in the theatre are instructive in reminding us that stage history can only be understood in a broader cultural and historical context. The political and emotional distance, for example, between George Rignold's heroic Henry entering the stage in 1879 on a white horse called Crispin, and Michael Pennington leading a ragtag hooligan army with placards proclaiming 'Fuck the Frogs' (1986–9) is as much a measure of changing British attitudes to leadership as it is of the changing cultural role of Shakespeare, changing scholarly opinions or changing theatrical styles. It could be argued that the Napoleonic wars, the Festival of Britain and Vietnam have been at least as important to the history of *Henry V* in production as have Hazlitt, Kemble and Stanislavsky. Gary Taylor notes that the popularity of the play in the nineteenth century owes more to 'English foreign policy than to English theatrical taste',[2] and this association between stage and politics is a perennial feature of the play's life in the theatre in other centuries too.

The play's serial topicality emerges as one of the most pressing features of its life on the stage, as it reflects, recalls and participates in military conflicts from the Crimea to the Falklands. To stage the play has always been a political act, and most often consciously so. The politics to which the play has spoken have most commonly been British or, more specifically, English ones: no other Shakespeare play has been so ignored outside the English-speaking world, and it is both a cause and an effect of the insularity of its performance history that it has been seen to be so inescapably engaged with

---

1 Sandy Wilson, 'Give Us A Rest' from *See You Later* (1953), reprinted in *The Shakespeare Revue*, eds. Christopher Luscombe and Malcolm McKee, (London: Nick Hern Books, 1994), pp. 23–4.

2 Gary Taylor (ed.), *The Oxford Shakespeare: Henry V* (Oxford: Oxford University Press, 1984), p. 11.

changing and contested definitions of English and British national identity.[3] In addition there are, however, specifically theatrical questions in the history of the play on the stage: star versus ensemble playing, realism versus epic, historical pageant versus contemporary *realpolitik*, the issue of roles for women. The Introduction to this volume aims to discuss these in the chronology of *Henry V* in the theatre and to trace the interventions which have shaped this ongoing narrative.

All stage histories are inevitably structured around the necessary absence of their object: the director Richard Eyre has suggested that the theatrical performance has the same ephemeral beauty as the snowman sculpted by Michelangelo during rare wintry weather in Florence.[4] All available sources of information – promptbooks, reviews, interviews or recollections or stated intentions of theatre practitioners, photographs, and, for the most recent productions, video recordings of live performances, are partial, sometimes contradictory, and often potentially misleading. Stage history is as much an account of reception as it is of production, and often audiences do not experience what directors intended them to experience – as when to the professed surprise of the cast, some audiences at the play in the new Globe theatre in 1997 cheered the English and booed the French. Of course neither productions nor audiences are homogeneous, although stage history has tended to prefer the pragmatic singular 'production' over the bewilderingly multiple 'performances'. Sometimes a long-held assumption about a play can be sustained in the face of a production which attempts to dismantle it: a number of reviews of Terry Hands' quizzical 1975 production maintained that the play was a patriotic epic despite the director's attempt to interrogate, rather than reproduce, this dominant interpretation.[5] In the Commentary I have preferred to quote from rather than paraphrase or interpret promptbooks and reviews so as to allow readers to reconstruct something of these performances and form their own judgements on their significance. Unless otherwise identified, commentary on the productions by Adrian Noble, Ron Daniels and Richard Olivier is based on my own experience as an audience member; so too are the comments on the filmed versions of the play directed by Laurence Olivier, Michael Hayes, David Giles, Michael Bogdanov and Kenneth Branagh. Because not all

3 See, for example, 'What Ish My Nation' in David Cairns and Shaun Richards, *Writing Ireland: Colonialism, Nationalism and Culture* (Manchester: Manchester University Press, 1988).

4 Richard Eyre, *Changing Stages: A View of the British Theatre in the Twentieth Century* (London: Bloomsbury, 2000), p. 10.

5 For example, the *Daily Express* review, quoted in Beauman: 'This is a gutsy, reviving production at a time of national adversity. And boy, do we need it' (p. 253).

productions of a play are radical reinterpretations, and because we mis-represent theatre history if we leave out the standard productions in favour of those which pioneer different approaches, I have tried to give space to periods when stage productions do not change as well as those when innova-tive practitioners transform the theatrical possibilities of the text. The Introduction takes a broadly chronological approach to the stage history of the play, although it will be clear that this does not imply a linear narrative of development.

I have also made extensive use of filmic examples, particularly from the films of Laurence Olivier and Kenneth Branagh, largely because these are still widely available for individual viewing and discussion unlike the melted snowmen discussed elsewhere in this book. There are, however, significant differences between stage and film versions of a play: not just the specific differences of interpretation for the different languages of the two media, which can be traced in the example of Branagh's very different stage and film versions of the play discussed below, but more fundamentally in the posi-tioning of the audience. Plays do not control the focus of an audience in the ways that films must do: in the theatre, we always have the choice to look elsewhere. Sitting with other audience members in the theatre watching a live performance played out on a stage in front of you is very different from sitting in a cinema watching the constructed sequence of shots put together by the director, and both these are different again from the small-screen, often solitary, or domestic experience of watching Shakespeare on television or video. There are also methodological problems in this distinction: live per-formance exists, as Walter Benjamin put it, in 'time and space, its unique existence at the place where it happens to be',[6] but film's material existence allows its repeated viewing and analysis by audiences far removed from the original viewers. For example, in an article first published in 1984, Graham Holderness proposes that to interpret Olivier's 1944 film as offering a ' "straight" patriotic version of *Henry V* is to interpret selected parts' and 'to seriously underestimate the subtlety of the film's aesthetic devices' by which, he argues, a traditional reading of Henry's character is seriously destabilised.[7] This retrospective reinterpretation constructs meanings from the film text which do not seem to have been available to cinemagoers who saw the film in its historical context at the end of the war. I have tried to take account of film's original audiences and situation as well as recognising its

6 Walter Benjamin, 'The Work of Art in the Age of Mechanical Reproduction' in *Illuminations*, ed. Hannah Arendt (London: Fontana Press, 1993), p. 214.
7 Graham Holderness, *Shakespeare Recycled: The Making of Historical Drama* (Brighton: Harvester Wheatsheaf, 1992).

particular and fruitful ongoing life in the pedagogy and scholarship of Shakespeare in production.

RABBIT AND DUCK: THE PLAY'S
INTRINSIC AMBIGUITIES

The relationship between academic criticism of Shakespeare and the plays in performance often seems slight. One seminal article, however, Norman Rabkin's 'Either/Or: Responding to *Henry V*' can be used to frame the major dynamic of stage interpretations of the play. Rabkin argues that, like the familiar optical illusion showing a creature that can be perceived as either a rabbit or duck, *Henry V* is either a heroic play about a 'mirror of all Christian kings' (2.0.6) or a cynical play about a ruthless and hypocritical Machiavellian tyrant. The force of the analogy, however, is in that, like the rabbit-duck, it is both of these things at the same time. Rabkin thus identifies *Henry V*'s 'ultimate power [as] precisely the fact that it points in two opposed directions, virtually daring us to choose one of the two opposed interpretations it requires of us'. Rabkin describes Shakespeare's 'terrible subversiveness' in undermining the play's ostensible message, in a view of the play which has its theatrical counterpart in Trevor Nunn's account of the 1964 production at the Royal Shakespeare Theatre as an interpretation 'which saw a play-within-a-play, a hidden play which amounted to a passionate cry by the dramatist against war'.[8]

As Nunn's comment acknowledges, Rabkin's view of the interpretive dichotomy which animates the play's critical history – whether it is a celebration of Henry's rule or a scathing analysis of bellicose powermongering – has also been a dominant feature of *Henry V* on the stage, particularly during the twentieth century. The burden of these opposing interpretations tends to coalesce around a few key scenes and speeches in the play: the Archbishop's speeches about the young Prince's reformation on taking up the throne in 1.1, the reporting of the death of Falstaff in 2.3 and the King's implication in this in 2.1, the treatment of the conspirators in 2.2, Henry's threats before the Governor of Harfleur in 3.4, the execution of Bardolph in 3.7, and Henry's attitude to Williams during and after their meeting before Agincourt in 4.1 and 4.7. More recently, Henry's instruction that the French prisoners be executed (4.7.7) before the discovery of the butchered English boys has

---

8 Norman Rabkin, 'Either/Or: Responding to *Henry V*' in *Shakespeare and the Problem of Meaning* (Chicago and London: University of Chicago Press: 1981), p. 34; p. 49; Ralph Berry, *On Directing Shakespeare: Interviews with Contemporary Directors* (London: Hamish Hamilton, 1989), p. 62.

been a focus of interest provoking one essay with the title, 'Henry V, War Criminal?'.[9] The Prologue, Epilogue and Choruses have also served to locate distinct and often mutually exclusive attitudes to the play, as realist or stylised, as *actualité* or pageant. As the Commentary to this edition demonstrates, these loci of particular interpretive conflict highlight different approaches and assumptions about the play's tone and its characterisation of its central protagonist.

Two brief examples, discussed in detail later in the Introduction, can serve as the rabbit and the duck to sketch out these poles. The first is Laurence Olivier's 1944 film version of the play; the second is Michael Bogdanov's touring production of the 1980s. Olivier's Henry, thanks to the comic undermining of the episcopal conspiracy of 1.1 and extensive cuts to 2.2, 3.4, 3.7 and 4.7, is presented as an unproblematically heroic military leader. He avoids appearing inappropriately gung-ho and cuts a romantic dash in Act 5. The miraculous victory at Agincourt over effete and two-dimensional French enemies is notably bloodless and therefore sanctified. Olivier presents a Henry for a war-weary generation with victory in its sights and with its ethics of heroism fundamentally unchallenged. By contrast, Bogdanov's production sought to undermine the last vestiges of patriotic chivalry for his late twentieth-century audiences. His Henry had an unnerving and unpredictable capacity for brutality, foregrounded in his behaviour in 2.2, 3.4 and 3.7, and his soldiers were rampaging, xenophobic yobs whose cause it was impossible for audience members to espouse without considerable discomfort. The French, by contrast, were dignified and civilised, with outdated weaponry and obsolete forms of courtesy. The war was dirty, both literally and metaphorically; the production unflinching in its iconoclasm.

At one level, these interpretive differences are attributable to historical moment – the difference between attitudes in 1944 and in the mid-1980s – but it is also important to recognise that the movement of productions of *Henry V* has not been a straightforward switch from heroic to cynical. To illustrate this, we might put the fulcrum of the rabbit–duck polarity at another recent production, Kenneth Branagh's film of 1989. Branagh keeps much of the problematic textual material which would seem to cloud the presentation of Henry and the English cause, yet manages to maintain his ultimately sympathetic rendition of the eponymous hero, reinventing a modern version of masculine heroism deriving in part

---

9 See Taylor, *Henry V*, pp. 32–4; John Sutherland and Cedric Watts, *Henry V, War Criminal? And Other Shakespeare Puzzles* (Oxford: Oxford World's Classics, 2000).

from contemporary action films. In a suggestive reversal of the terms of the interpretive debate and a counterpoint to Trevor Nunn's description of the 1964 production, James Loehlin judges that Branagh's film is more conventional than it first appears, offering 'the official version of the play disguised as the secret one'.[10] The play's deployment as part of these 'official' and 'secret' discourses is a recurrent theme of its history on the stage.

1599–1642: EARLY PERFORMANCES

Most critics agree that *Henry V* offers unusually specific internal evidence about the date and circumstances of its first performances. Firstly, the Prologue's reference to 'this wooden O' (1.0.13) and the choric stress on the inadequacy of theatrical representation, have been widely accepted as allusions either to the shortcomings of the old Curtain Theatre, which was about to be superseded by the new Globe, or as an emphatic mock-modest description of this new playhouse itself. Either interpretation fixes the date for the play some time in 1599, as the lease on the site of the Globe was signed by the Lord Chamberlain's Men in February 1599 and the new venue is known to have been operative by September of the same year. Secondly, the parenthetic comparison between the victorious Henry and 'the general of our gracious empress' 'from Ireland coming,/ Bringing rebellion broachèd on his sword' (5.0.30–2) seems to fix the date of the play to spring or summer 1599, before the ignominious conclusion of the Earl of Essex's much-vaunted expedition to Ireland to quell the rebellion against English rule was well known.

Both these pieces of evidence are, however, rendered problematic by the existence of the earliest text of *Henry V*, published in 1600 under the title *The Cronicle History of Henry the fift, With his battell fought at Agin Court in France. Togither with Auntient Pistoll.* This text of the play differs in several crucial respects from the text published in the First Folio of 1623 as *The Life of King Henry the Fift*, the text on which this edition, like all other modern editions, is based. *The Cronicle History of Henry the fift* is, at a little over 1,600 lines, only half the length of the Folio text; it does not include the Folio's opening scene between Canterbury and Ely (1.1), nor the Scots and Irish captains (3.3), nor Henry's famous exhortation 'Once more unto the breach' (3.1), nor the second of the scenes featuring the French lords before the Battle of Agincourt (4.2). Most significantly, it does not include any of the

10 James N. Loehlin, *Shakespeare in Performance: Henry V* (Manchester: Manchester University Press, 1996), p. 145.

Chorus speeches nor the Prologue and Epilogue. Thus, the text as it was published in 1600 does not provide any of the evidence, detailed above, for dating the play to 1599.

Most accounts of the Quarto text have been concerned to demonstrate its limitations by contrast to the Folio, and, indeed, it has been used as a prime example of what the editors of the First Folio denigrated as those previously printed texts, 'stolen and surreptitious copies, maimed and deformed'.[11] It has also been argued, however, that it represents a version of the play derived, in some way, from performance: cut for touring or for presentation by a reduced cast, or to make it more politically orthodox and therefore more acceptable.[12] Andrew Gurr suggests that the 'Chorus was fitted to the play fairly early on, to strengthen a celebratory and patriotic reading, providing a means of coercing the audience into an emotionally undivided response':[13] by contrast, Annabel Patterson's view is that the Quarto is the more politically orthodox text. More recently, Gurr has argued that it is the Quarto text, not the Folio, which uniquely represents the play as it was performed in 1599, suggesting that the Quarto moderates potentially hostile comments on Henry, cutting the dialogue in 2.1 about the King being to blame for Falstaff's death.[14] In their self-consciously revisionist edition of *The Cronicle*, Graham Holderness and Bryan Loughrey distinguish between the two texts of the play on generic grounds, finding the Folio 'epic and heroic, realistic and historical', and the tone of the Quarto 'deflect[ed] . . . to the comic mode', in which 'the new historical style . . . interacted with older modes, with the conventions of romance and the manners of comedy'.[15] Even at this early point in the play's stage and textual history, therefore, the questions of genre, of realism and historical immediacy, and epic and comedy which were to engage, and sometimes vex, generations of directors and actors – the rabbit and duck, in fact – are apparently already in their

11 T.W. Craik (ed.), *The Arden Shakespeare: King Henry V* (London and New York: Routledge, 1995), pp. 11–19.

12 On these possibilities, see Gary Taylor, 'We Happy Few: the 1600 Abridgement' in Stanley Wells and Gary Taylor, *Modernising Shakespeare's Spelling, with Three Studies in the Text of 'Henry V'* (Oxford: Clarendon Press, 1979); Taylor, *Henry V*, pp. 12–20; Annabel Patterson, *Shakespeare and the Popular Voice* (Oxford: Oxford University Press, 1989).

13 Andrew Gurr (ed.), *King Henry V* (Cambridge: Cambridge University Press, 1992), p. 7.

14 Andrew Gurr (ed.), *The First Quarto of Henry V* (Cambridge: Cambridge University Press, 2000), pp. 2–12.

15 Graham Holderness and Bryan Loughrey, *The Cronicle History of Henry the fift* (Hemel Hempstead: Harvester Wheatsheaf, 1993), pp. 24–6.

frictive place. So too is that other constant in the play's varied history on the stage: its persistent topicality.

London in 1599 was certainly in need of a feel-good play, and the famous English victory at Agincourt, already familiar to Elizabethan play-goers from earlier plays on the subject, was the perfect scenario. Fears of foreign invasion, high food prices, the repeated musters for soldiers for campaigns in the Low Countries and in Ireland, the requisitioning of horses, food supplies and other commodities needed for the military, all took their toll on Londoners. The long military campaign in Ireland, memorably dubbed by one historian 'England's Vietnam',[16] was a particularly insistent part of English metropolitan consciousness at the time of the play's first performances, and the play's reference to 'kern of Ireland' (3.8.49), Pistol's 'Colin o custure me' on hearing the French soldier speak (4.4.3), Henry's promise to Katherine 'England is thine, Ireland is thine, France is thine' (5.2.217), and Macmorris, Shakespeare's only Irish character, all register this preoccupation. It has been convincingly argued that for contemporaries Shakespeare's French represented a version – and an idealised, conquerable version – of the intractable Irish.[17] Seen in this light, the play offers a highly topical fantasy: a vicarious stage-victory against overwhelming odds, achievable in the theatre and, as the Chorus to Act 5 makes clear, much longed-for, but elusive, outside it.

When it was performed in 1599, the play also featured as part of a serial dramatic *Bildungsroman* on the maturation of Prince Hal, already presented in *1 Henry IV* (performed in the early months of 1597) and *2 Henry IV* (performed in 1598). Audiences had had their appetite misleadingly whetted at the end of *2 Henry IV*, after the coronation of Hal as Henry V and his banishment of his erstwhile companion Falstaff, where the Epilogue promises a further play where 'our humble author will continue the story with Sir John in it, and make you merry with fair Katherine of France, where, for anything I know, Falstaff shall die of a sweat' (Epilogue, 21–3).[18] Strikingly, this establishes the essentially comic material – Falstaff and Katherine – of the proposed *Henry V* as its major attraction, and this hint of the play's generic instability is highlighted in eighteenth-century adaptations discussed below.

16 C.G. Cruikshank, *Elizabeth's Army* (Oxford: Clarendon Press, 2nd edn, 1966), p. 16; R.B. Outhwaite, 'Dearth, the English Crown and the "Crisis of the 1590s" ' in *The European Crisis of the 1590s: Essays in Comparative History*, ed. Peter Clark (London: George Allen and Unwin, 1985), pp. 22–43, p. 32.

17 Joel B. Altman, ' "Vile Participation": The Amplification of Violence in the Theater of *Henry V*', *Shakespeare Quarterly* 42 (1991), p. 19.

18 Giorgio Melchiori (ed.), *The Second Part of King Henry IV* (Cambridge: Cambridge University Press, 1989).

The sense, for contemporaries, of the play in an extended dialogue with previous plays was lost from virtually all performances up until the middle of the twentieth century, when the fashion for playing the history plays in sequence was invented.

Whichever theatre the play was written for, it requires relatively few props. One recent editor argues that 'in other of Shakespeare's plays battles have their exits and their entrances . . . but *Henry V* alone wholly dedicates itself to dramatizing this brutal, exhilarating, and depressingly persistent human activity'.[19] While this may be true, it is worth stressing that this most martial of plays does not include any onstage fighting other than the dishonourable and often-cut scene between Pistol and the French soldier Le Fer (4.4). While it may indeed be impossible for 'this cockpit [to] hold / The vasty fields of France' (1.0.11–12), it is striking that the play does not make use of the short scenes of hand-to-hand combat, the established stage synecdoche to represent battles, as in the depiction of the Battle of Shrewsbury at the end of *1 Henry IV*. Thus, chief among the props required are some items of armour and armaments including a cannon (3.0.33), and the 'four or five . . . ragged foils' (4.0.50) mentioned by the Chorus would probably suffice. A single throne would be needed to serve for both the English and French courts thus stressing the visual parallels between 1.2 and 2.4, and some 'scaling ladders' (folio stage direction at 3.1) are called for at the siege of Harfleur, at which the *frons scenae* must have served for the city walls. The gallery over the stage would provide the platform for the Governor of the town to parley with Henry (3.4.43). Costumes would have been, as was the Elizabethan theatre norm, contemporary rather than historical. It is likely that the chief tragedian of the Lord Chamberlain's Men, Richard Burbage, would have taken the part of Henry. The number of actors required to perform the play has been the subject of much debate, but doubling may have enabled a cast of fifteen or so players to put it on.[20] Both Quarto and Folio versions of the play are dominated by Henry's character (549 or 34 per cent of 1,600 lines in the Quarto, and 1,056 or 31 per cent of 3,380 lines in the Folio[21]), with Llewellyn the next most vocal character in both versions.

19 Taylor, *Henry V*, p. 1.
20 See Thomas L. Berger, 'Casting *Henry V*', *Shakespeare Studies* 20 (1988), pp. 89–104; T.J. King, *Casting Shakespeare's Plays: London Actors and their Roles 1590–1642* (Cambridge: Cambridge University Press, 1992), pp. 86–7; and also Pauline Kiernan, *Staging Shakespeare at the New Globe* (Basingstoke and London: Macmillan, 1999), on the 1997 New Globe production of *Henry V* with a cast of fifteen.
21 For comparative figures for principal characters in other plays, see King, *Casting Shakespeare's Plays.*

Perhaps because of its very immediate topicality, the play does not seem to have been a runaway theatrical success. The only evidence for the play's production history in the seventeenth century suggests that it was revived for a single performance at court in January 1605, and then sank into obscurity. It is not known whether the text for this performance was closer to the Folio or Quarto: although 'we have to hope that the company was sensitive enough to their new patron's accent and ancestry'[22] to cut the significantly named Scottish character Jamy when they performed before King James. While other of Shakespeare's plays continued to be reprinted and, occasionally performed, up to the 1630s, *Henry V* was largely neglected. The Quarto text was reprinted in 1602 and in 1619 (the title page of this third edition bears the false date '1608'): perhaps the play's apparent inscription in the political narrative of the summer of 1599 meant that it was quickly, and seemingly irrevocably, out of fashion.

ADAPTATIONS 1642–1738

Theatrical Shakespeare was restored to England along with the monarchy, as plays from the pre-Civil War theatre were adapted to the new theatrical and social climate. *Henry V* was not, however, one of the earliest rehabilitations. When Samuel Pepys records attending two performances of *Henry V* in 1664 and again in 1668 with Thomas Betterton in the central role, it seems likely that this was not Shakespeare's play, but the rhymed verse drama by Robert Boyle, Earl of Orrery. Boyle's play seems only to confirm the contemporary insignificance of Shakespeare's, in that it shows no discernable trace of the earlier dramatic account of Henry's reign. It begins almost where Shakespeare leaves off: the Battle of Agincourt is concluded, offstage, between Boyle's first and third scenes, leaving the rest of the play for a representation of Henry not as military leader but as victorious lover. A secondary love plot, between Anne of Burgundy and Henry's brother the Duke of Bedford, highlights the significance of the romance plot to this exercise in the Restoration heroic genre. It is not until the eighteenth century that Shakespeare's play begins its – literally – piecemeal return to the stage.

In 1700, Betterton's *The Sequel of Henry the Fourth* comprised most of Shakespeare's *2 Henry IV* with the addition, in its final act, of material from Acts 1 and 2 of *Henry V*, ending with Henry's 'No king of England if not king of France!' (2.2.188). In the same year, Colley Cibber also took some

---

22 Andrew Gurr, *The Shakespearian Playing Companies* (Oxford, Clarendon Press: 1996), p. 288.

lines from the play, largely from the Chorus to Act 5, for his *The Tragical History of King Richard III*, first performed at the Theatre Royal in July 1700. The early eighteenth century thus saw the play as having some meritorious speeches, rather than as a performable script in its entirety. It seems that its generic hybridity as both comic and epic was troubling: two more thoroughgoing reworkings of the play by Charles Molloy and Aaron Hill each choose and highlight one genre in their retelling. Charles Molloy's *The Half-Pay Officers: A Comedy* of 1720 tells its readers that 'The Character of *Fluellin* has been esteem'd, (next to that of Sir *John Falstaff*) the best and most humorous, that *Shakspear* ever wrote; there are many other Things in this, that have been reckon'd good Comedy',[23] and proceeds to embroil 'Fluellin' and Macmorris in a comedy of manners among various non-Shakespearean characters. Some comic set pieces from *Henry V* are imported, and there is a scene in which a character named Culverin takes Pistol's place in the enforced consumption of a leek. There is, however, hidden in this comedy a definite anti-French sentiment: the Prologue decries debased English tastes:

> In vain Old Shakespear's Virtue treads the Stage,
> On empty Benches doom'd to spend his Rage;
> When we would entertain, we're forc'd to Ship ye
> Tumblers from France, mock Kings from Mississippi!

Molloy's selective use of *Henry V* is significantly connected to this implicit manifesto for native theatricals, as a salvo in the struggle between Britain and France for global cultural and political hegemony.

If Molloy chooses to extract the comic characters from *Henry V*, a later adaptation by Aaron Hill plumps for tragedy. His *King Henry the Fifth: Or, the Conquest of France, By the English. A Tragedy* includes much more material from Shakespeare than does Molloy, and he also makes use of Orrery's earlier play.[24] In Hill's story, Henry has been followed to France by his spurned mistress, Harriet, a niece of the conspirator Scroop. In true comic Shakespearean fashion, she has dressed in men's clothes for the escapade, and, indeed, *Twelfth Night* plays a significant supporting role in the play's construction. Harriet's fury against her erstwhile lover prompts her to join the conspiracy of Scroop, Grey and Cambridge against the King, but she is discovered and brought to Henry. She explains how her anger drove her to seek revenge, but Henry disarms her by arguing that 'Kings must have no

---

23 Charles Molloy, *The Half-Pay Officers: A Comedy* (London, 1720), p. v.
24 See Landon Burns, 'Three Views of King Henry V', *Drama Survey* 1.3 (1962), pp. 278–300.

Wishes for Themselves! / We are our People's Properties'. Assuring her that 'Were I now what I was, when Harriet bless'd me / Still were I Hers – My Love can never die!',[25] Henry persuades her to betray the conspiracy. She then kills herself 'Since, without it, you can ne'er be happy',[26] leaving Henry free to marry Catherine. In the meantime, Catherine has been forced into marriage with a Henry she has never met, while she is nursing a love for a mysterious Englishman, Owen Tudor, who wooed her the year before. Her brother the Dauphin tries to stop the marriage, and so the Battle of Agincourt is explicitly figured as a fight for Catherine. The battle itself is not represented, but substituted by a scene in which 'The Genius of England rises, and sings' a paean to 'Albion' and an exclamatory commentary on the course of the combat:

> They bend, they break! the fainting Gauls give way!
> And yield, reluctant, to their Victor's Sway.
> Happy Albion! – strong to gain!
> Let Union teach Thee, not to win, in vain.[27]

Catherine and Henry are united, whereupon the Princess realises that the conquering King is none other than her own Owen Tudor ('Tis He! – 'Tis Tudor! – O! amazing Chance!'[28]).

Hill's 'Preface to the Reader' describes the play as a *'new Fabrick*, yet I built on *His* Foundation',[29] and expresses the disingenuous hope that it will not be popular given the debased and lightweight tastes of the age. Like Molloy, Hill identifies his work as engaged in a commercial and dramatic Agincourt with other, implicitly Frenchified, entertainments: a struggle which is both aesthetic and nationalistic:

> No *French Tricks*, however, in the Days of *my* Hero, were able to stand before him: Fortune favour'd him, *then*, against incredible Odds! and who knows, (if the Ladies will forgive me the Presumption of comparing *small* Things with *Great*,) but he may, *now*, become a Match, even for *Eunuchs*, and *Merry-Andrews!*
>
> Yet the Victory, at *Agencourt*, was an Action, not more wonderful! And it is, I fear, become impossible, since I have, imprudently, neglected to list those Squadrons of *light-arm'd* Forces, which have, so often, won the Day, for Our *Leaders*, in modern Poetry.[30]

25 Aaron Hill, *King Henry the Fifth: Or, the Conquest of France, By the English. A Tragedy* (London: 1723), p. 41.

26 *Ibid.*, p. 43.   27 *Ibid.*, p. 57.   28 *Ibid.*, p. 127.

29 *Ibid.*, sig. A3–v⁰.   30 *Ibid.*, sig. A4–v⁰.

A new Prologue addresses a theme which was to be of considerable importance to subsequent eighteenth- and nineteenth-century productions of Shakespeare's play: the paucity of its roles for women. 'Hid,' we are told, 'In the Cloud of Battle, Shakespear's Care, / Blind, with the Dust of War, o'erlook'd the Fair', and this lack is to be made good in Hill's version. Here 'Love softens War, – and War invigo'rates Love'. The Prologue also draws attention to the play's 'Example', arguing that the differences between the Dauphin and Henry demonstrate 'the diffe'rent Genius of the Realms disclos'd'. The French are 'vain', 'boastful', 'proud' as opposed to the English 'calmly resolv'd'. It is internal politics, however, which dominate, and the rebellion of Grey, Scroop and Cambridge is not a prefatory incident as it is in Shakespeare, but the main business of Hill's play. The overriding message of civil harmony is affirmed in Henry's concluding lines:

> O! that the bright Example might inspire!
> And teach my Country not to waste her Fire!
> But, shunning Faction, and Domestic Hate,
> Bend All her Vigour, to advance her State.[31]

Ultimately, the Epilogue confirms that these aims for civic harmony are thwarted under the reign of his weak son. Whereas Shakespeare identifies the young Henry VI's responsibility for losing France, Hill stresses how 'Division, Faction, and Debate / And that rank Weed, Rebellion, choak'd the state'.[32]

Hill's claim in his preface to be out of step with prevailing fashions is disingenuous: his *Henry V* is an index to the tastes of his age. Out go the indecorous battle and tavern scenes and the disreputable prose of Henry's erstwhile companions; in comes the melodramatic spurned-mistress plot to give a prominent breeches role and the opportunity for pathos at her death. In place of Shakespeare's Chorus who moves the action back and forth across the Channel, Hill adheres more closely to classical unities, by confining the action to France and opening the play at Harfleur. Where Shakespeare includes comic characters and scenes, Hill purges them to fix his play as a tragedy. The play becomes an account of the King's loves, not his wars: Princess Catherine and Harriet vie for the emotional heart of the play, as other actions are subordinated to this intrigue. Henry appears relatively little in his own play, as the stage is dominated by the two women. Henry is revealed, 'despite Hill's attempts to launder his indiscretions . . . as a

31 *Ibid.*, p. 61.   32 *Ibid.*, p. 62.

singularly untrustworthy potential husband, his conquest of France an extension of his conquest of Catherine, rather than vice versa'.[33]

Aaron Hill's version of the play was printed in 1723, the year of its first performances at Drury Lane. Its main theatrical innovation was the introduction of a practicable bridge on stage to enable Act 3 scene 1 to begin: 'SCENE changes to a Barrier, on a Bridge, Trumpets from Both Sides: Enter, on one Part, the French King, on the Bridge, attended by the Dukes of Orleans, and Bourbon, &c. below: – On the other Side of the Bridge, King Henry, with the Dukes of Exeter, and York, Scroop, Cambridge, and Gray, below.' The play was revived for seven performances in 1735 and a further two in 1736 at Goodman Fields, and then adapted for performance in August 1746 at Drury Lane as a one-act play *The Conspiracy Discovered*, with the pointed subtitle 'French Policy Defeated'. The play promised an unmissable combination of history and contemporary politics, with a newspaper reporting 'rich antique Habits of the times' and a playbill describing 'a Representation of the Trials of the Lords for High-Treason in the Reign of King Henry V'.[34] The contemporaneous trial of noblemen indicted after the Jacobite Rebellion of 1745 supplied the necessary topicality. In 1746 Shakespeare's play was performed in the same season as Hill's version, but even as performances of the original *Henry V* became more common, Hill's play was not quickly forgotten. Forty years later, a review of John Kemble's performance of Shakespeare's Henry began with a survey of adaptations of the play, and noted that Hill's play was 'not contemptible, but then we still see Shakespeare's jewels in the shrine he has made for them'. The reviewer goes on to recall that 'we cannot but admire Mr Hill's idea of introducing Lord Scroop's niece Harriet'.[35] The issue of roles for women, so ingeniously addressed by Hill's adaptation, was to continue to resurface in the history of Shakespeare's play in performance.

THE MID-EIGHTEENTH CENTURY

Since the play's inhospitality to female performers and audience members had been seen as an obstacle to its successful reception, it is striking that *Henry V* owes its return to the stage to the Shakespeare Ladies'

---

33 Michael Dobson, *The Making of the National Poet: Shakespeare, Adaptation and Authorship 1660–1769* (Oxford: Clarendon Press, 1992), p. 96.

34 A.H. Scouten, *The London Stage 1660–1800, part 3 1729–47* (Carbondale: South Illinois Press, 1960–8), p. 1244; Charles Beecher Hogan, *Shakespeare in the Theatre 1701–1800* (Oxford: Clarendon Press, 1952), vol. I, p. 199.

35 *The Prompter*, 27 October 1789, p. 14.

Club. This was a circle of aristocratic women who petitioned theatre managements, including Covent Garden's John Rich, to revive more Shakespeare plays in place of the commercially favoured Restoration comedies and Italianate operas. Garrick later acknowledged their important role in prompting theatres to perform the plays: '*It was you Ladies* that restor'd Shakespeare to the Stage.'[36] When, at Covent Garden in February 1738, Shakespeare's *Henry V* was performed on four successive nights, marking its return to the stage after an absence of over 120 years, the playbill described the revival as 'at the Desire of Several Ladies of Quality'.[37] There were a further five performances that year, with a full cast including Dennis Delane as Henry. Thereafter the play was revived at Covent Garden and becomes a regular, although not frequent, part of the London repertoire, with one or two performances in most years between 1739 and 1782.

The play's popularity in the eighteenth-century theatre thus lagged well behind the tragedies of *Hamlet*, *Macbeth*, *Othello* and *King Lear*, and also well behind a more popular history play such as *1 Henry IV*. At the same time, however, the play's hero was closely associated with its author and his growing reputation during the eighteenth century. In 1741 the monument to Shakespeare unveiled in Westminster Abbey incorporated a bust of Henry V, with Richard III and Elizabeth I, alongside the full-length marble statue of the playwright. Royal associations accrued through performance, too. In January 1739, *Henry V* was performed 'By his Majesty's command' in front of the 'King, Duke, Princesses Amelia, Caroline, Maria and Louisa', and performances in the 1750-1 season were advertised 'by command of their Royal Highnesses the Prince and Princess of Wales'.[38] At some points, particularly during the Seven Years War against France (1756–63), the play was performed every year, with playbills bearing the emphatic subtitle 'With the Conquest of the French at Agincourt'. If the listing order of actors on playbills is any testimony, the comic roles of Llewellyn (particularly in performances by John Hippisley from 1738 to 1746, 'fam'd in *Fluellin, Pistol's* Hector' as the *Bath Journal* put it at his death in 1748[39]) and a swaggering Pistol (established by Theophilus Cibber's performances in the 1740s) were also popular elements. In November and December 1761, with William Smith in the title role, the play was given an unprecedented twenty-three

---

36 Quoted by Dobson, *The Making of the National Poet*, p. 148.
37 Scouten, *The London Stage*, p. 704.
38 G.W. Stone, *The London Stage 1660–1800, part 4 1747–76* (Carbondale: South Illinois Press, 1960–8), p. 223.
39 Quoted by Cecil Price, *Theatre in the Age of Garrick* (Oxford: Basil Blackwell, 1973), p. 184.

successive performances. This popular production also appears to have begun a practice that was to dominate nineteenth-century stagings by introducing 'the Procession from the Abbey at the Coronation': the coronation scene from *2 Henry IV*. This was initially included to celebrate the coronation of George III, but was apparently retained and supplemented with further pageantry. In 1767, Covent Garden was again advertising Smith as Henry, 'to which will be added the Procession from the Abbey at the Coronation, with the Representation of Westminster Hall and the Ceremony of the Champion',[40] and it may have been that a real horse was brought on to the stage for this final tableau. Spectacle and pageantry were increasingly becoming key to theatrical success.

Apart from these obvious scenic interpolations, it is hard to trace the precise variations of these different performances. Playbills up to 1759 make it clear that the Chorus was a part of these performances, sometimes doubled by the actor playing the Archbishop of Canterbury. Perhaps to pre-empt criticism of this non-naturalistic intrusion, playbills of the 1740s often include the parenthetical classical justification '(after the manner of the Ancients)'[41] before the actor's name. In 1744 'a New Prologue' was promised, along with the stirring musical inclusions 'Songs *To Arms* and *Britons Strike Home*'.[42] The performance of 25 April 1754 was concluded with an Epilogue by Theophilus Cibber, who also played Pistol, 'in the character of Nobody'.[43] In 1747 and 1748, Garrick played the Chorus, dressed in eighteenth-century costume including a powdered wig. In a letter of March 1748, he defended, with characteristic pedantry, his delivery of the Prologue to the Shakespearean Peter Whalley, author of *An Enquiry into the Learning of Shakespeare*: 'I cannot but think you have mistook me in the Prologue to Henry the 5th – surely the little pause was made at *Fire!* and I connected the subsequent Relative, Verb and Accusative Case (*that would ascend the brightest Heav'n &c.*) in one Breath? I know in the general I speak it so, but may have fail'd the Night you heard me.'[44] In performances from 1760 to April 1767, however, despite the fact that many of the other actors remain constant, there is no mention of the Chorus role, until playbills for performances in September 1767 promise that the Chorus will be 'restored'.[45] It

---

40 George C.D. Odell, *Shakespeare: From Betterton to Irving* (London: Constable, 1963), vol. I, p. 428.
41 Scouten, *The London Stage*, p. 1102.
42 *Ibid.*, p. 1103.
43 *Ibid.*, p. 1170.
44 David M. Little and George M. Kahrl (eds.), *The Letters of David Garrick* (London: Oxford University Press, 1963), vol. I, p. 93.
45 Hogan, *Shakespeare in the Theatre*, vol. II, p. 285.

may well be that this role was a casualty of new inclusions such as the coronation procession and Ceremony of the Champion. The increasingly illusionistic and spectacular productions of the play could not sustain the demystificatory tones of the non-naturalistic choric voice: the scenic efforts made to represent such pageants as the coronation were not to be under-mined by the Chorus' continual mock-modesty. If the Chorus was restored in late 1767, it seems to have been dropped again for subsequent perfor-mances, although productions in 1778 and 1779 advertise the 'original Chorus'.[46]

Some idea of other omissions from the play in performances can be gleaned from Bell's acting edition of Shakespeare, published in 1774, with editorial comment by Francis Gentleman. Bell's *Henry V* is described 'As Performed at the Theatre-Royal, Covent-Garden. Regulated by Mr Younger, Prompter of that Theatre', and its text is informative about the kinds of cuts made for eighteenth-century performances. The 'Advertisement' sets out the method:

> as the Theatres, especially of late, have been generally right in their
> omissions, of this author particularly, we have printed our text after
> their regulations; and from this part of our design, an evident use will
> arise; that those who take books to the Theatre, will not be so puzzled
> themselves to accompany the speaker; nor so apt to condemn
> performers of being imperfect, when they pass over what is designedly
> omitted.[47]

The edition, however, is not only descriptive but sometimes prescriptive: 'it has been our peculiar endeavour to render what we call the essence of Shakespeare, more instructive and intelligible; especially to the ladies and to youth; glaring indecencies being removed, and intricate passages explained'.[48] Such indecencies included the language lesson of 3.5, and speeches which might blur the lines of Henry's heroic characterisation such as his anger at the traitors in 2.2 and his threats before Harfleur in 3.4. Bell's edition, following Molloy and Hill in their adaptations, acknowledges that the play is generically mixed: 'the plot is irregular and tainted with some low quibbling comedy'.[49] The annotations to the text give a clear indication of

---

46 Stone, *The London Stage*, p. 171.
47 *Bell's Edition of Shakespeare's Plays, As they are now performed at the Theatres Royal in London; Regulated from the Prompt Books of each House By Permission; with Notes Critical and Illustrative; By the Authors of the Dramatic Censor* (London and York, 1774), vol. I, pp. 6–7.
48 *Ibid.*, p. 10.
49 *Ibid.*, p. 3.

which parts of the play were valued and which disparaged. Shakespeare's 'prolixity' is often remarked upon, the comic scenes are thought unworthy and dramatic unity is often thought wanting. Bell's edition is thus explicitly evaluative in both moral and aesthetic terms – and not merely, or reliably, the representation of the play as performed in the theatre.

KEMBLE

In 1755 theatrical and cultural Francophobia was at its height. David Garrick's Drury Lane theatre was attacked by a mob angered by the engagement of a French troupe, and a salvo from the Anti-Gallican faction resurrected Shakespeare's ghost to advise him:

> 'To give you Pardon, I encline,
> If you'll revive a Work of mine;
> You need not fear it will miscarry,'
> 'What Play d'ye mean, Sir' – 'My *fifth Harry*'.[50]

As if in delayed answer to this summons, John Kemble played the role of Henry on sixteen occasions between October 1789 and 1792 in a landmark production as London theatregoers shuddered at bloodthirsty reports of events in revolutionary France. Kemble's version of the play was clearly designed to clarify Henry's heroism within this context of contemporary popular anti-French opinion, and his adaptation of Bell's Covent Garden acting edition made more extensive cuts and scene switches to produce a theatrical script which was to dominate the play in performance for the next half-century. It is striking how, apparently independently, Kemble's acting text closely resembles the first published version of *Henry V*, the Quarto text of 1600, and it may be that this coincidental similarity adds a retrospective endorsement to the dramatic qualities of this often-disparaged early text. In November 1803, after the failure of the Peace of Amiens permanently to end the Napoleonic Wars between Britain and France, a benefit performance of the play in aid of the 'Patriotic Fund' was concluded with an 'Occasional Address to the Volunteers'.[51] The *Times'* review felt that the production worked 'to convince our Gallic neighbours that in the midst of all their triumphs they are but mere mortals'.[52] In the same year, invasion fears prompted the *Gentleman's Magazine* to reproduce a

---

50 Quoted in Dobson, *The Making of the National Poet*, p. 203.
51 See Jonathan Bate, *Shakespearean Constitutions: Politics, Theatre, Criticism 1730–1830* (Oxford: Clarendon Press, 1989), p. 63.
52 *The Times*, 2 October 1789.

broadside called 'Shakspeare's Ghost', in which 'Shakspeare now speaks in the character of a true Englishman and a sturdy John Bull, indignant that a French Army should wage war in our Isle'. Patriotic passages, largely from *King John* and *Henry V*, were tweaked for the occasion, so that the last line of Henry's speech at the siege of Harfleur became 'Cry God for us! for England! and King George!'.

Kemble's biographer James Boaden, writing in 1825, gives his own reasons for the relative unpopularity of the play before Kemble's revival, although he overstates the case in stating that it had been unperformed for twenty years. Again, the main objection to the play seems to be on gender terms: 'it may be presumed that the mob always like to be told, that Englishmen, extenuated by disease and in numbers as one compared with ten, are yet sure to become the conquerors of France'. However, while the play may have masculine appeal, it suffers from 'so little female interest in the drama, that we cannot wonder at the coldness of our fair country-women to these fighting plays'.[53] Even the charms of Miss De Camp, playing Katherine, could not compensate: even if she did speak 'the few broken sentences . . . incomparably',[54] eighteenth-century decorum demanded the excision of one of her two scenes and some swingeing cuts to the remaining one. Of Kemble's own performance, the reviews were variable. *The Prompter* found much to praise, including Henry's address 'to the divinity' (4.1.263ff.), his treatment of the three traitors and his conversation with Williams. Their only advice to the leading actor was 'to sacrifice a very little of his declamation, in some passages of this beautiful play, to easy expression', although his delivery of the lines following 'And Crispin Crispian shall ne'er go by' (4.3.57) was described as 'supremely conceived and uttered'.[55] Elsewhere, however, these same lines are highlighted to mock Kemble's habitual slow delivery and stiff posture. A satirical squib entitled *How to Tear a Speech to Tatters* pictured an unbendingly formal Kemble reciting 'From – this – day – to – the – end – ing – of – the – world – – Ti – tum – tum – ti – ti – tum – ti –'.[56] However, Kemble's appeal to patriotic anti-French sentiment was undeniable: he 'had a way of placing emphasis on the nobility of dying in the King's company while at war with France, and for this he was rewarded with much applause'.[57] *The Prompter*, however, would have liked more clarity about the play's disparagement of the French enemies,

53 James Boaden, *Memoirs of the Life of John Philip Kemble, Esq.* (London, 1825), vol. II, p. 8.
54 *The Monthly Mirror*, December 1801, p. 422.
55 *The Prompter*, 27 October 1789, p. 15.
56 Quoted by Bate, *Shakespearean Constitutions*, p. 35.
57 *Ibid.*, p. 63.

criticising Mr Barrymore as the Dauphin for his failure to show sufficient insolent disdain.

Kemble's production was designed to be spectacular. Character lists in the promptbook seem to work on the principle of amplification wherever possible: where a stage direction reads 'Herald' or 'Lord', a careful hand has inserted 'Two' or sometimes 'Four'. 1.2, for example, includes not one but two heralds and four supernumerary lords in addition to those with speaking parts. Diagrams of the blocking of different scenes suggests that the stage was almost always full of actors. Its nineteen scenes were played in some fourteen or fifteen impressive sets, including 'Audience Chamber', 'French Court at Troyes' and extensive landscapes for the battle scenes, one including a view of the eponymous Castle of Agincourt, for Henry to gesture towards at 4.7.78. Some elaborate sets are described, such as one at Harfleur, which may owe something to Aaron Hill's innovations some sixty years previously: 'When the Gates are opened, a Bridge is discovered. The 12 French soldiers and their Captain, drawn up on it, salute as the King crosses it.'[58] At the end of Act 3, there are repeated handwritten admonitions in the promptbook. After the stage direction 'A March' the annotation reads 'very long', and there is a reminder 'Beg them to take time in this scene', presumably in order that King Henry's tent for Act 4 could be shifted into position.

The elaborate staging this implies was not, however, to the taste of 'A.A', writing in *The Monthly Mirror* in December 1801. A.A demolished the production for its systematic anachronism in properties and furnishings, and for the paucity of its decoration. Reminding readers that the play is set in 1415, A.A. is scornful at 'the Audience chamber' with its mishmash of architectural details, and, 'as for Henry's throne, if a few steps, a modern arm chair, can make it so, why it is well'. Southampton is represented by 'a wretched daub . . . of modern ships, a light-house &c.', Henry's clothing is part Caroline, part Elizabethan, part modern, and his tent lamentably under-furnished with 'one table, two candelabras and two stools'. There are woefully few banners – only one for Henry and none at all for France, and the difference between tastes at the turn of the nineteenth century and those of two centuries earlier is demonstrated in the exclamation: 'some half dozen blanket coverings hung on trees or tied to poles. This for the warlike state of France'. Perhaps it would have been better for Kemble had he pre-empted such criticisms by retaining the Chorus' apologia: instead, his adaptation pushed the play towards the patriotism and historical spectacle which were to dominate nineteenth-century stage interpretations.

58 Kemble promptbook, p. 29.

VICTORIAN SPECTACLE: MACREADY, PHELPS, KEAN AND CALVERT

Kemble's success was shortlived. After a few undistinguished revivals of his production, including his own last performance in 1811, and disappointing performances by a declining Edmund Kean at Drury Lane in 1806 and 1815, there was little theatrical interest in *Henry V* for a couple of decades. The early years of the nineteenth century were lean ones for the play in performance and in the study. In his *Characters of Shakespear's Plays* (1817), Hazlitt described it as 'but one of [his] second rate plays', with a central protagonist with 'no idea of any rule of right or wrong, but brute force, glossed over with a little religious hypocrisy and archiepiscopal advice'.[59] Leigh Hunt, writing after seeing the play in 1830, confirmed 'it is not a good acting play – at least not for these times', finding the military events inadequately represented by 'a little huddle of soldiers'.[60] Hunt's comments echo A.A's disparaging remarks about the staging of Kemble's production: increasingly, the only way the play could hope for theatrical success was as a convincing spectacle. 'Public observation', as one contemporary commentator wrote, 'is now keenly turned to any instance in which classical, historical, or even tasteful authority is violated.'[61] Whereas eighteenth-century editions and playbills had tended to call the play a tragedy, the nineteenth century stressed it as history. The stage was thus set for William Macready's lavish archaeological revival of 1839.

Macready had already played Henry some five times in the two decades before this major production. Indeed, it was an earlier performance of his which so disappointed Leigh Hunt, and another review in 1825 contrasted his style with his predecessor, Kemble:

> Kemble's King Henry was conceived in the very spirit of chivalry: the
> character well accorded with the animated tone and manly ardour of that
> superb actor. It had all the fire and daring of perfect heroism, with the
> highest polish of intellectual grace. Mr Macready dashed through the part
> with considerable energy: he gave it no repose, even when something
> more is required than mere declamation. He wanted the hilarity and
> buoyancy that distinguished Kemble's performance. He was fierce – but

59 William Hazlitt, *Characters of Shakespear's Plays* in *The Selected Writings of William Hazlitt* ed. Duncan Wu, vol. I, p. 198; p. 194.
60 Leigh Hunt, *Dramatic Essays Selected and Edited with Notes and an Introduction*, ed. William Archer and Robert Lowe (London, Walter Scott: 1894), pp. 179–80.
61 John Ambrose Williams, *Memoirs of John Philip Kemble Esq. With an Original Critique on his Performance* (London, J.B. Wood: 1817), p. 73.

his fierceness was tempered with neither grandeur nor majesty: still, in the present state of the drama, the effort was praiseworthy.[62]

After these undistinguished attempts at the role, the revival of 1839 was Macready's most ambitious Shakespearean production, and a significant *Henry V* in setting the tone for Victorian Agincourts. Although Macready's text was taken from Kemble, its greatest *coup de théâtre* was highlighted in the playbill, where the management of Covent Garden offered 'a few words in explanation or apology for what may seem an innovation':

> The play of *King Henry V* is a *dramatic history*, and the poet, to preserve the continuity of the action, and connect what would otherwise be detached scenes, has adopted from the Greek Drama the expedient of a Chorus to narrate and describe intervening incidents and events. To impress more strongly on the auditor, and render more palpable those portions of the story which have not the advantage of action, and are still requisite to the drama's completeness, the narrative and descriptive poetry spoken by the Chorus is accompanied by pictorial illustrations from the pencil of Mr Stanfield.[63]

The reinstating of the Chorus, with the added visual spectacle of Royal Academician Clarkson Stanfield's diorama staging, was the great highlight of the performance. In his journal, Macready himself took credit for developing this idea, which was realised by John Vandenhoff as Chorus, representing the figure of Time complete with scythe and hourglass. At the opening of the play, a richly embossed curtain featuring the French and English coats of arms was removed to reveal Chorus standing on a pedestal against a vast framework of clouds. These parted to reveal various illustrative devices, such as an allegorical picture of Henry with 'famine, sword and fire' at his heels in the first Chorus, and pictures of the conspirators taking bribes from the French in the second. The interplay between painted and live sequences was much remarked upon, as a review in the *Oddfellow* of June 15 reported: 'The melting away of the pictorial into the real siege was truly wonderful; and the transition was managed with such consummate skill, that it was utterly impossible for any one to detect the precise moment at which either the one ended, or the other commenced.'[64] *The Spectator* considered the scenery paintings as 'an exhibition in themselves' and 'better historical pictures than any we see at the Royal Academy', remarking that the effect of moonlight on

62 D.G., *King Henry the Fifth: An Historical Play* (London, John Cumberland: 1825), p. 7.

63 *The Diaries of William Charles Macready 1833–51*, ed. William Toynbee (London: Chapman and Hall Ltd., 1912), pp. 6–7.

64 Odell, *Shakespeare*, vol. II, p. 221.

the water 'is the nearest approach to reality the stage has ever given'.[65] This strenuous attempt at painted realism, so far from the self-reflexive theatricality of Shakespeare's Chorus, developed Kemble's stagecraft to become characteristic of nineteenth-century staging.

Not all Macready's reviews were positive, however, and attempts at impressive realist spectacle could be a stick with which to beat the production. One reviewer chastised him for 'over-embellishing his author',[66] and a long review in *The Spectator*, while praising the 'historical spectacle', was of the opinion that: 'The scenic effects, instead of being kept subordinate to the dialogue and action, as the accessories of a picture, are made principal, and divert the attention too much from the poetry and the personation: and moreover the attempt physically to realize what can only be suggested to the mind, sometimes defeats itself.'[67] Harfleur besieged with a single 'uncouth piece of ordinance which, once being fired, once and no more, had made a most abortive explosion'; Agincourt represented with a 'handful of soldiers' – as with Kemble's production, reviews turned the terms of Shakespeare's Chorus into disparagements of theatrical inadequacy. Anticipating such derision, Macready gathered a large cast for his 1839 production, with over seventy actors named on the playbill, including as supernumeraries ten English nobles, ten French nobles, four English heralds, three French heralds, and, presumably to pre-empt the perennial criticism that the play has no female interest, 'Mesdames Mathews, Payne, Reed, Valanduke, Hunt, Corder, Morgan, Mew, Solway, Deither, Byers, E. Byers, Collet, Francis, Guischard, R. Morgan' as attendants to the French Queen and Princess. Macready also favoured armour for Henry in 1839, after the newspaper reviews of the 1837 production were quick to point out the incongruity of the Battle of Agincourt fought in velvet doublet and silken hose. One illustration (fig. 1) from the earlier performances shows him in Roman-style tunic, sporting a hat with enormous ostrich feathers, a costume described in *Dolby's British Theatre* (1825) as 'white satin shirt and black velvet cloak, trimmed with gold spangles and ermine; white hose; black velvet hat with a coronet around it, and white feathers; russet shoes'.[68] By contrast, his journal for the days before the opening of his 1839 revival reports how Macready practised wearing his armour at home: 'Tried on my armour, which I wore through the afternoon, and was obliged at the last to put it off for its weight.'[69] Most

65 *The Spectator*, 15 June 1839, p. 558.
66 Odell, *Shakespeare*, vol. II, p. 222.
67 *The Spectator*, 15 June 1839, p. 558.
68 *Dolby's British Theatre* (London: 1825), vol. XI, p. v.
69 *The Journal of William Charles Macready 1832–1851*, ed. J.C. Trewin (London: Longmans: 1967), p. 138.

1   Macready as Henry V, pre-1839.

reviewers remarked on the lavishness of costuming in the 1839 production, with *The Spectator* commenting on Macready's own 'preeminently superb' appearance in his 'polished steel armour'.[70]

Macready's production was staged twenty-one times, and pronounced a great success for its star. In 1852 the play was revived by his theatrical heir, Samuel Phelps. Phelps had already played Exeter and the Constable of France in previous Macready stagings, and he produced his own *Henry V* very much on the Macready model, with the Chorus as 'Time' and a bevy of attendants and extras. Blocking sketches in the promptbook indicate large numbers of supernumeraries with, for example, twenty-four extra nobles on each side framing the encounter between the French and English Kings in Act 5, despite the fact that Phelps' Sadler's Wells management was more financially constrained than those of Covent Garden or Drury Lane. John Coleman's explanation that Madame Tussaud's had helped swell Phelps' meagre troupe by providing dummy soldiers attached to the forty real actors as they 'defiled behind a setpiece which rose breast high' to give the impression 'they were marching three abreast'[71] is engaging, but quite possibly, like much else in his rather egotistic *Memoirs of Samuel Phelps*, spurious. Phelps' production was able, due to circumstance, to avoid the scenic excesses attributed to Macready. He included the Chorus but without the added dioramic illustration, which the *Morning Advertiser* review found 'so far from being tedious . . . it was felt, as it was doubtless intended to be, a relief from the din, roar, and conflict of the war-like scenes'. In a production transported to Windsor on 10 November 1853 for a performance before Queen Victoria, Phelps apparently succeeded in capturing the self-confident mood of the early 1850s: the same review praised the St Crispin's Day speech: 'It is not the mere bloodthirsty instincts of our nature that are appealed to, but the latent and indomitable daring and energies that make us the monarchs of the billows, and inventors and guides of the fiery steam-engine.'[72]

Some twenty-five years later, Phelps' own farewell to the stage was also in a production of *Henry V*, that mounted by John Coleman at his newly acquired Queen's Theatre, Long Acre, in 1876. Coleman spent a huge budget of over £6,000 on the production, making use of drawings and research undertaken for Kean's Princess's Theatre production and adding to the elaborate spectacle already accreted around the play in the theatre. Coleman's set for Westminster Abbey, used for the coronation scene

---

70 *The Spectator*, 15 June 1839, p. 558.
71 John Coleman, *Memoirs of Samuel Phelps* (London, 1886), p. 217.
72 Quoted in W. May Phelps and John Forbes-Robertson, *The Life and Life-Work of Samuel Phelps* (London: 1886), pp. 125–6.

extrapolated from *2 Henry IV*, was modelled from photographs 'by the special grace of Dean Stanley', and 'Permission was obtained from the Horse Guards for the pick of the British Army to assist in the Coronation, the Siege of Harfleur, the Battle of Agincourt, the Royal Nuptials, and the Triumphant entry of Harry and Katherine de Valois into London.' Not surprisingly, these intricacies required a backstage crew of eighty-eight men to manage the scene changes, and the playbill begged 'public indulgence . . . for such delays between the acts as may be found necessary' to prepare the set pieces 'of great magnitude'.[73] Coleman himself played Henry, there was a female Chorus played by Mrs Herman Vezin, and Coleman's predecessor, Phelps, took the role of Henry IV, in a prologue including the King's soliloquy of sleep, the episode of the crown and the dying father, and the son's reconciliation with the Chief Justice taken from *2 Henry IV*.

In 1859, Henry's – and Macready's – mantle passed to Charles Kean, whose Princess's Theatre production elaborated on the pageantry of twenty years before. During its eighty-four performances between March and July 1859, the production set a new standard for historical pageantry and spectacle on the Victorian stage. Prefaced to the printed edition of Kean's version is a playbill catalogue of its 'Scenery and Incidents' (fig. 2). This exciting register is followed in the printed text by an account of each actor's costume or costumes, from Henry's own 'crimson robe, with very long sleeves, trimmed with ermine, crown, collar of SS, a girdle of gilt balls hanging from the waist' to Canterbury's 'episcopal dress of the 15th century' and Mistress Quickly's 'brown stuff gown, white apron, black caul cap, with white cap under',[74] all stressing the dual functions of lavish spectacle and historical accuracy. '*Accuracy*, not *show*, has been my object', Kean wrote, 'and where the two coalesce it is because the one is inseparable from the other', but notwithstanding this justification, a peculiarly Victorian historicist spectacle was the keynote of the production.[75] Even the printed playtext was amply supplied with historical notes, offering extra commentary from historical sources about Henry's French campaign.

This antiquarianism, however, was not at the expense of topicality in these years immediately following the Crimean War. One critic compared the active politics of the stageplay with the legislative stagnation of the contemporary parliament: '[W]hat a Prime Minister dare not utter in Parliament

---

73 John Coleman, *Fifty Years of an Actor's Life* (London, 1904), vol. II, pp. 652–3; p. 325.
74 *Ibid.*, pp. 7–8.
75 Kean, *Shakespeare's play of King Henry the fifth, arranged for representation at the Princess's theatre, with historical and explanatory notes by C. Kean* (London: 1859), p. vii.

2 Playbill from the Princess's Theatre for Charles Kean's 1859 production.

... the actor seemed to embody on the stage ... It was not, therefore, without political significance, that the nightly prayer was so exquisitely breathed by our tragedian ... "O God of battles! Steel my soldiers' hearts".[76] Kean's biographer, writing in the same year, also drew attention to the play's seemingly prophetic relevance:

> The records of that warlike age, the campaigns in France, make the hearts of Englishmen swell; and are well recalled at a time when a restless neighbour, armed to the teeth, is evidently in search of an antagonist, anywhere, in any pretext; and when constant alarms warn us to be on our guard, and prepared in case of unprovoked attack.[77]

It may be, however, that the play's relatively short run meant that audiences were wary of its martial tone. As John Cole remarked in his memoirs of Kean, the siege of Harfleur 'vividly embodied the carrying of the

76 Quoted by Richard W. Schoch, *Shakespeare's Victorian Stage: Performing History in the Theatre of Charles Kean* (Cambridge: Cambridge University Press, 1998), p. 137.
77 John William Cole, *The Life and Theatrical Times of Charles Kean, FSA* (London: Richard Bentley, 1859), vol. II, p. 342.

Malakoff',[78] the Russian fortress on a hill over Sevastopol taken, significantly *by* rather than *from* the French in September 1855: topicality may have
come too close for comfort.

Of Kean's staging of the siege of Harfleur, *The Saturday Review* enthused
that it was 'the first genuine battle ever seen on theatrical boards – a noisy,
blazing, crowding, smoking reality that appeals to all the senses at once'.
Gone were the common complaints about handfuls of soldiers; here 'his
army may be a hundred thousand strong, for all the spectators know to the
contrary, as he never allows its head or tail to be seen', although the reviewer
was later relieved to see that the lines about the theatrical representation
disgracing 'the name of Agincourt' (4.0.49–52) had been cut.[79] The second
sensational sequence in the staging was the interpolated episode of Henry's
triumphant return to London before Act 5. For this historical episode there
was widespread admiration, although there was some unease that the poetic
beauty had been sacrificed to the 'trumpery satisfaction of gazing at a group
of supernumeraries'.[80] Some sense of the numbers involved in the production can be gleaned from the promptbook's reminder of those to be involved
in Act 3, in the siege of Harfleur. In addition to the fifteen speaking characters, almost two hundred extras in the form of standard-bearers, axemen,
double axemen, archers, cannoneers, French knights, trumpeters, body
guards, boys, lancemen, harpooners and spearmen were required. The historical episode employed a chorus of twenty-four dancers, twelve each of
kings and prophets and twenty boys, as well as a substantial civic procession
of aldermen and their attendants and the King's own procession with seven
standard-bearers, eight cannoneers and twenty-four archers.

Kean's own address to theatregoers printed on the *Henry V* playbills
registers another innovation. Kean solved two frequently voiced difficulties with the play – its Chorus and its limited roles for actresses – at a
single stroke: including his wife as the Chorus in the character of Clio,
the Muse of History so that 'thus, without violating consistency, an opportunity is afforded to Mrs Charles Kean which the play does not otherwise
supply, of participating in this, the concluding revival of her husband's
management'.[81] A note at the end of the souvenir promptbook of Kean's
production gives a running time of just over four hours. Kean's own textual
reshaping added to that of Kemble to produce a play that was not
only shorter than the Folio text (cutting some 1,550 lines), but with a substantially different running order. Thus the cost of this increasingly scenic
and lavish staging was Shakespeare's text: by the mid-nineteenth century, the

---

78 *Ibid.*, p. 344.   79 *The Saturday Review*, 2 April 1859, pp. 401–2.
80 Schoch, *Shakespeare's Victorian Stage*, p. 53.   81 *Ibid.*, p. 11.

3 Mrs Kean as Chorus as the Muse of History, Act 1.

standard stage version of the play was only about two-thirds of the length of the Folio.

It may seem so far that the play's only stage history is a London one. There were, however, a few provincial revivals. Macready took a three-act version of *Henry V* to Bath and Bristol in 1834, and in 1853, George Vandenhoff, son of John Vandenhoff who played the Chorus in Macready's 1839 production, played 'the gallant Henry' in Liverpool. Despite good houses, the twenty-three-night run did not recoup the management's costs: the expectation of London scenery and extras was crippling outside the capital's theatrical economy. As Vandenhoff glumly remarked, 'Shakespearean revivals, when got up with new and appropriate scenery and appointments, never remunerate the management', and this economic argument may have influenced his apparently aesthetic feeling that spectacular staging was 'very serious and prejudicial to the moral and intellectual effect of the Drama itself'.[82] During the 1870s, however, Charles Calvert's important and lavish production was performed in his native Manchester to great acclaim in 1872, from whence, after a run of over seventy performances, it travelled to New York in 1875 at the start of an American tour, and then

82 George Vandenhoff, *Leaves from an Actor's Note-book; with Reminiscences and Chit-Chat of the Green-Room and the Stage in England and America* (New York: D. Appleton and Co., 1860), pp. 251–3.

reached Drury Lane in 1879, as the star turn in the ambitious reopening of the theatre under the management of Augustus Harris.

Like his theatrical precursors, Calvert also used a shortened text, cutting 1,200 of the Folio's 3,380 lines. Although Phelps was his acknowledged mentor, Calvert's production also borrowed extensively from Kean's, as the text of the play 'as produced at Booth's Theatre, New York' makes clear in its echoing of the costumes and scenery of the earlier staging. In citing, however, some fourteen printed authorities consulted for historical details on costumes, heraldry and arms, Calvert attempts, on aesthetic and antiquarian grounds, to trump Kean's pageant. Rivalry with Kean's production was evident in other quarters, too. Mrs Charles Calvert, like Mrs Charles Kean, took the role of Chorus, and, in her memoirs some years later, could not resist a dig at her predecessor:

> My husband was very undecided about the part of Chorus. He had seen,
> many years before, Charles Kean's fine production at the Princess's Theatre,
> London, but the Chorus of Mrs Charles Kean, clad in vivid blue and scarlet,
> and with her hair done in the Victorian style (from which she never deviated,
> no matter what part she was playing) had remained in his recollections as
> unpoetic, and slightly wearisome.[83]

Instead Mrs Calvert favoured pale-grey silk robes, and soft pale-blue lighting for her Chorus who, in the guise of Rumour borrowed from *2 Henry IV*, stood under a clump of rocks, adopting different accessories as the story progressed.

Mrs Calvert's account of the play in her memoirs claims that it was 'acknowledged to eclipse all its predecessors in splendour, as well as in archaeological accuracy of detail'.[84] Part of this additional splendour was to inflate the already numerous extras: the printed text names and casts more than a score of noblemen who, according to the chronicles, were also present during Henry's campaign although not mentioned by Shakespeare, and one reviewer noted that the Drury Lane playbill mentions four hundred auxiliaries, though 'I cannot believe that there are quite so many.'[85] Elaborate staging was described in the printed text: clouds, as in Macready's and Kean's versions, parted to reveal various tableaux described by the Chorus, the walls of Harfleur were built on an elevation and masked with 'rock and earth pieces', gothic arches and a stained glass window through which

83 Mrs Charles Calvert [Adelaide Helen], *Sixty-Eight Years on the Stage* (London: Mills and Boon, 1911), pp. 137–8.

84 *Ibid.*, p. 134.

85 Dutton Cook, *Nights at the Play: A View of the English Stage* (London: Chatto and Windus, 1883), vol. II, p. 231.

sunlight was pouring were provided for the final scene in Troyes Cathedral, a scene so elaborate that Pistol's leek-eating had to be repositioned and drawn out to give the stagehands time to prepare the scenery.[86]

Calvert's production combined spectacular and emotional impact, favouring a stylised representation of battle over the attempts at verisimilitude, and using tableaux to halt the action at heightened dramatic moments: 'There is no swaggering attempt to represent the dealing of actual blows, which often converts a bloody tragedy into an amusing burlesque: but a picture in still life is presented on a crowded stage of the very death grapple of two hostile armies – a picture so telling and effective, that the audience demanded its representation twice.' A combination of actors and painted figures gave the illusion of many soldiers, and Harfleur was given three different locations: 'The English Entrenchments. Within a bowshot of Harfleur', 'The neighbourhood of the mines. The Duke of Gloucester's quarters', and 'The siege of Harfleur. At the breach. Signs of a severe conflict'. Despite this visual display, at least one review confessed 'to have liked Mr Calvert best in the night scene before the battle of Agincourt',[87] preferring emotional proximity to spectacular stage effects. Calvert's production may have been the first to uncover something of what the director Trevor Nunn was to describe, a century later, as a hidden, anti-war play within the popular heroics. Despite cutting around a third of the Folio text, episodes potentially embarrassing to Henry's reputation, such as the execution of the conspirators, the hanging of Bardolph and the order to kill the French prisoners, were retained. Additionally, Richard Foulkes, arguing against the common belief that Victorian stage historicism was incompatible with contemporary topicality, points out that 'not even the most blinkered antiquarian could have been unaware of the parallels between recent events [in the Franco-Prussian War] and King Harry's expedition to France'.[88] These insistent parallels turned the French into victims rather than arrogant enemies, and, along with Calvert's own connections with the Manchester Quaker community, made his production more conscious of the costs, as well as the glories, of war. One review noted that this was 'a spectacle in which the glories and horrors of war are a little too faithfully represented'; Calvert's associate Alfred Darbyshire described how the production's 'stage tableaux,

86 Calvert, promptbook, p. 4; *Henry the Fifth: A Historical Play in Five Acts by William Shakspeare. As Produced at Booth's Theatre, New York, February 8 1875*, ed. Charles E. Newton (New York, Robert de Witt: 1875), pp. 3–6.

87 Review of the Manchester production in 1872 from the *Examiner and Times*, quoted by Richard Foulkes in 'Charles Calvert's *Henry V*', *Shakespeare Survey* 41 (1989), pp. 23–34, p. 30.

88 *Ibid.*, p. 28.

4 Historical episode in Act 5 of Charles Calvert's 1879 production.

or living pictures [represented] the horrors of war, the sufferings entailed, and the blessings of peace'.[89]

It appears from comparing reviews of the production in Manchester and then in New York, that Calvert's own performance of Henry was more suited to this reflective commentary on the play's martial narrative than was George Rignold's, who cut a more unequivocally heroic dash. Under Calvert's direction, the historical episode inherited from Kean was 'no indulgent, thoughtless escape into jingoism, but a judicious blend of rejoicing and sorrow', although it was still spectacularly staged (fig. 4). Darbyshire recalled in his memoirs a quarter-century later:

> the distant hum of voices, and how the volume of sound swelled as the little army approached on its march from Blackheath; how the sound burst into a mighty shout as the hero of Agincourt rode through the triumphal archway, the 'Deo gratias Anglia redde pro Victoria' and other hymns of praise filled

89 Press comment included in *Shakespere's Historical Play of Henry the Fifth As Produced by Mr George Rignold at Drury Lane Theatre November 1st 1879* (London, 1880); Alfred Darbyshire, *The Art of the Victorian Stage: Notes and Recollections* (London and Manchester, Sherratt and Hughes: 1907), p. 50.

the air, showers of gold dust fell from the turrets, red roses of Lancaster covered the rude pavements, the bells clashed out, and a great thanksgiving went up to heaven for the preservation of the gallant King and his little army of heroes. The curtain descended on a perfect picture of medieval England.[90]

Another feature of the pageant caught the eye of the *Weekly Times* reviewer: 'A tragic interest of a most touching nature is given to the scene by the introduction of groups of anxious women who scan the faces of the returned warriors to distinguish, if possible, a husband, son or brother.'[91] This particularly gendered crowd was noticed elsewhere: another press notice described the scene as 'an apparently enormous body of warriors, who file through a central gateway amidst the cheers of a populace very feminine and very picturesque'.[92] One illustration of the production showed a group gathered round a woman prostrate with grief on hearing of the death of her loved one, and this poignant touch was also included in the subsequent New York production by Richard Mansfield. Calvert allowed further scope for women in the play by reintroducing a shortened version of the language-lesson scene between Katherine and Alice into the beginning of Act 5, which cut any hint of dishonour by ending, quite properly, at '*de elbow*' (3.5.43).

Many reviewers commented on Master Harry Grattan's performance as the Boy ('The Boy is – for the first time within our recollection – played by a real boy, and a delightful boy too'). Pistol, Nym and Bardolph were pronounced overdone,[93] but otherwise reviewers were preoccupied by the presentation of Henry himself. Despite Calvert's own view that the leading role should be rendered 'harmonious in its relations to the other characters, graceful, temperate and natural',[94] Henry dominated the play. The play on the stage had become, firstly, a star vehicle for actor/directors, and secondly, a showcase of theatrical spectacle. Rignold, who took the part in America and in London, was much praised for his performance. Dutton Cook's memorable description deserves quoting:

> He is most heroically pugnacious of aspect; he looks a born leader of
> fighting men; he exhibits indefatigable vigour alike as swordsman and
> orator; he overwhelms his foes both by force of arms and strength of lungs.

90 Darbyshire, *The Art of the Victorian Stage*, p. 45.

91 *Ibid.*, p. 32.

92 Press comment included in *Shakespere's Historical Play*.

93 *The Referee*, 2 November 1879; press comment in *Shakespere's Historical Play*.

94 Richard Foulkes, *The Calverts: Actors of Some Importance* (London: Society for Theatre Research, 1992), p. 57.

As, falchion in hand, clothed in complete steel, with a richly emblazoned tabard, he stands in that spot so prized by the histrionic mind, the exact centre of the stage, the limelight pouring upon him from the flies its most dazzling rays, and declaims speech after speech to his devoted followers, he presents as striking a stage figure as I think I ever saw.[95]

Elsewhere Rignold's physical stature was stressed. *The Referee* praised him for his 'fine presence and capacious chest'. Here, it seems, was a martial Henry in whom audiences could believe, at least until he spoke: Cook's recollection of a 'gabbling effect [which] mars certain of his best speeches' was echoed elsewhere.[96] Henry James, who saw the production in New York, found that despite the fact that the play 'offers but the slenderest opportunities for acting' and being rather suited to presentation as an 'animated panorama', Rignold made 'a charming impression': 'He plays the part in the most natural fashion, looks it and wears it to perfection, and declaims its swelling harangues with admirable vigour and taste. He is worth looking at and listening to.'[97]

James criticised the production, however, for its crucial misapprehension that verisimilitude was the mode of the play – a debate which was to feature widely in twentieth-century stagings – revealing the 'grotesqueness of the hobby-horses on the field of Agincourt and . . . the uncovered rear of King Henry's troops, when they have occasion to retire under range of your opera-glass'.[98] This elaborately illusionistic staging might come perilously close to farce. Rignold's performance toured the east coast of America and included a performance in cramped conditions in Colorado Springs in 1878, as reported by a contemporary reviewer:

When Crispin appeared on the scene, his tail touched the back of the stage and his forefeet were firmly planted among the footlights. The climax was reached when King Henry, animating his dispirited troops with hot, impassioned words, waved above his head the royal standard. The spear head on the staff became implanted in the low ceiling, and could not be disentangled. Rignold stopped, completely overcome, saying: 'This is really too ridiculous, ladies and gentlemen. You must be content simply with the beautiful words of Shakespeare for I've nothing more to offer you.'[99]

95 Cook, *Nights at the Play*, p. 230.
96 *Ibid.*, p. 231.
97 Henry James, *The Scenic Art*, ed. Allan Wade (London: R. Hart-Davis, 1949), p. 26.
98 *Ibid.*, pp. 26–7.
99 Quoted by Levette J. Davidson, 'Shakespeare in the Rockies', *Shakespeare Quarterly* 4 (1953), pp. 39–50, p. 45.

The debate about the relative importance of poetry and spectacle which rumbled through the reception of nineteenth-century stagings of *Henry V* here reached its bathetic apogee.

THREE TURN OF THE CENTURY HENRYS: WALLER, BENSON AND MANSFIELD

Despite Calvert's careful interpretation of the play, the late nineteenth century saw the solidifying of Henry's reputation as the quintessential English soldier-king and the increasing use of the play as the cultural auxiliary of English imperialism. George Bernard Shaw's dislike of Shakespeare's 'thrust[ing] such a Jingo hero as his Harry V down our throats' had its echoes, in, for example, Max Beerbohm's dismissive commentary that the play was 'the mere hack-work of genius, and had far better be neglected'.[100] These jibes did not seem to stick, however, as, by the end of the nineteenth century, *Henry V* had become firmly established as the favourite Shakespeare play for study in school, as a dramatic amplification of the spirit of Henry Newbolt's oft-quoted paean to public-school Englishness in his poem 'Vitai Lampada': 'the regiment blind with dust and smoke. / The river of death has brimmed his banks, / And England's far, and Honour a name, / But the voice of a schoolboy rallies the ranks: / "Play up! play up! and play the game!".' Three heroic productions, influenced by the martial mood of the Boer War, decked stages on both sides of the Atlantic during the 1900–1 theatrical season.

Frank Benson had directed the play at the Shakespeare Memorial Theatre in Stratford in 1897, in a production that was revived there in fifteen of the following thirty years, often as part of the celebrations for St George's Day and Shakespeare's birthday. In February 1900, despite the loss of their props in a theatre fire in Newcastle, Benson's touring company made use of the Lyceum Theatre in London during Henry Irving's tour of America to put on a spectacular production with Benson himself in the lead. Dancing girls in the French camp before Agincourt attempted a suitably exotic and degenerate touch, although Isadora Duncan's first appearance on the London stage was not a great success. Benson's wife, who played Katherine, recalled that Duncan 'was never quite at home in the Bacchanalian dances, and lacked abandon in the French camp scene', and

---

100 George Bernard Shaw, *Our Theatres in the Nineties* (London: John Constable & Co., 1931), vol. II, p. 134; Max Beerbohm in *The Saturday Review*, 24 March 1900, p. 359.

Oscar Asche, who played Pistol, was unsparing in his account of her as 'plain and dowdy'.[101]

Benson's production was characterised by vigour and athleticism (fig. 5), exemplified in his own pole-vault in full armour on to the walls of Harfleur during the siege, and mercilessly guyed by Max Beerbohm in a snootily metropolitan review of the touring company's London season:

> Alertness, agility, grace, physical strength – all these good attributes are obvious in the mimes who were, last week, playing 'Henry the Fifth' at the Lyceum. Every member of the cast seemed in tip-top condition – thoroughly 'fit'. Subordinates and principals all worked well together. The fielding was excellent and so was the batting. Speech after speech was sent spinning across the boundary, and one was constantly inclined to shout 'Well *played*, sir! Well played *indeed*!'[102]

Whereas Newbolt's stirring verses equated sporting and military honour, here Beerbohm diminishes the production by likening it to a cricket match. To point up the vigour of the English, Alfred Brydone represented the French King as insane, attended by a jester with whom he played cards or cup and ball, a reference to Holinshed's description of Charles' 'old disease of frensie' and inaugurating a tradition which was to recur during the century.[103] The Choruses were cut. In general, commentators felt that *Henry V* was just the play for what *The Illustrated London News* called 'this hour of national excitement and patriotic fervour', although the same review was unsparing in its criticism of the 'mechanical' and uninspired reading of Henry by Benson himself: 'admirable distinctness, vigorous declamation, and keen intelligence hardly atone for ill treatment of the blank-verse line, hard monotony of voice and absence of passion'.[104] Other reviews found more to praise. *The Times* found Benson 'a grave and thoughtful king', and that the production understated the typically 'swashbuckler, bragging monarch' with 'very little swagger'.[105]

Lewis Waller's production of 1900–1, which opened at Christmas at the Lyceum, was generally pronounced the more spectacular. Gordon Crosse, in his often acidic review of sixty years of playgoing between 1890 and 1952,

101 Lady [Constance] Benson, *Mainly Players: Bensonian Memories* (London: Thornton Butterworth, 1926), p. 174; Oscar Asche, *Oscar Asche: His Life, by Himself* (London: Hurst and Blackett, 1921), p. 88.

102 *The Saturday Review*, 24 February 1900, pp. 233–4.

103 Raphael Holinshed, *Holinshed's Chronicles of England, Scotland and Ireland*, vol. III (London, 1808), p. 68.

104 *The Illustrated London News*, 24 February 1900, p. 249.

105 *The Times*, 14 September 1900.

5   Frank Benson as a heroic Henry (1897).

described 'the scene in Picardy with a view of the flooded Somme [as] about the most beautiful I have ever seen [the programme advised theatregoers that there would be a two-minute hiatus with the tableau curtain lowered before this wonderful scene could be revealed], and that at Southampton with the gorgeously decked ships and all the bustle of embarkation was not far behind it'. Waller retained a female Chorus, played by Lily Hanbury in flowing red robes and a crown of flowers, and in his souvenir pamphlet to accompany the production, Shakespearean Sidney Lee proposed a topical emendation to that most topical of lines in the play, the Chorus' speech before Act 5, at line 31: 'We feel instinctively that the change of a simple word ("Afric" for "Ireland") would carry a step further Shakespeare's method of vivifying the past by associating it with the present, and would give this sentence an application even more immediate to our own contemporary history.'[106] Whereas spectacle had been the major element in the reception of nineteenth-century *Henry V*s, Lee stresses the play's patriotism as a fitting expression of British imperialism. Audiences at Waller's production would feel, like their Elizabethan ancestors three hundred years previously, the same emotions the play 'still rouses in every man, woman and child of English birth and breeding, who is endowed in normal measure with the healthy instinct of patriotism', and Henry himself was a character who might justly prompt 'a sense of pride among Englishmen that a man of his mettle is of English race'.[107]

Waller's Henry was thus the masculine conqueror for the new century, what W.B. Yeats described as 'the sailor or soldier hero of a romance in some boys' paper'.[108] He always commanded the stage, characteristically entering with some propulsion apparently gained by pushing himself away from the backstage wall with one foot, and favoured entering from upstage centre so as to dominate the composition immediately. One account of the production crackles with the evident *frisson* of his stage presence:

> The breach at Harfleur, when Waller staged it, was a grim, sweaty place reeking of death, slippery with blood and beginning to be filled with a sense of fear, panic and defeat . . . [the King] climbed upon a great mass of fallen masonry and stood there, quivering, virile, sword in hand, a thing of force and strength, panting to regain his breath. He radiated power.[109]

106 Sidney Lee, *Shakespeare's King Henry the Fifth: An Account and an Estimate* (London: Smith, Elder & Co., 1900), p. 11.

107 *Ibid.*, p. 4; p. 16.

108 W.B. Yeats, 'At Stratford-upon-Avon' in *Essays and Introductions* (London: Macmillan, 1961), p. 104.

109 W. Macqueen-Pope, *Ghosts and Greasepaint: A Story of the Days that Were* (London: Robert Hale & Co., 1951), pp. 101–2.

The climax of Waller's production was said to be the St Crispin's Day speech, which was delivered by Henry standing front of stage with his back to the audience, addressing a half-circle of his kneeling followers, which, Crosse remarks, 'swept the audience into an enthusiasm such as I have seldom known in the theatre'. Waller's magnetic stage personality and his 'complete masculinity'[110] were a success with both sexes: Lady Benson was kissed ardently after the end of one of her occasional performances by a woman playgoer claiming that kissing Katherine, just kissed by her Henry, was the nearest she would ever come to kissing Lewis Waller himself! In his memoirs Ben Iden Payne writes, tongue in cheek, of women wearing button with the initials KOW – Keen Order of Wallerites. [111] So thoroughly nineteenth century in feel was Waller's production that that most nineteenth-century of objections to the play, its poverty of 'feminine interest', was a feature of some reviews – the language-lesson scene was extensively cut by Waller as, as one reviewer noted, 'unsuited to modern tastes', although Miss Sarah Brooke won praise for her Katherine. Waller's domination of the play was substantial, but a few other words for the rest of the cast were spared in the reviews: William Mollison made a 'comic and dilapidated rascal' of Pistol, and Kate Phillips was 'an excellent Hostess', although one critic advised, 'she might, however, look a little more disreputable since otherwise she is no conceivable mate for Pistol'.[112]

The third of these turn–of–the–century Henrys was Richard Mansfield's American production. One New York reviewer of Calvert's production had voiced doubts about the play's relevance to American theatregoers: 'As the play may be regarded as a series of tableaux, eulogistic of the martial glory of England, it may not possibly interest Americans so keenly as it may the inhabitants of Great Britain.'[113] This intrinsic Britishness, however, was a challenge to Mansfield, whose acting edition of the play begins with a defence of his choice. The 'healthy and virile tone' of the play has induced him to produce it, along with 'the lesson it teaches of godliness, honour, loyalty, courage, cheerfulness, and perseverance', but he also admits to the spur of 'the desire to prove that the American stage is, even under difficulties, quite able to hold its own artistically with the European'. Mansfield's reputation was as a character actor specialising in villains, but his performance against type seems to have been a considerable

---

110 *Ibid.*, p. 105.

111 Ben Iden Payne, *Life in a Wooden O* (New Haven and London: Yale University Press, 1977), p. 38.

112 *The Athenaeum*, 29 December 1900, p. 867.

113 Unattributed press cutting in Folger Shakespeare Library edition, PR 2812 A35 c. 1 Shakespeare. Col., Folger Shakespeare Library, Washington D.C.

success. The elaborate staging at the Garden Theatre, New York, included some 250 actors, choristers and dancers in nineteen stage settings. Mansfield included many elements of Calvert's, and through him, Kean's, productions, including the female Chorus, the white horse, the triumphant romantic ending with the marriage of Henry and Katherine, and the historical episode of Act 4, in which the returning soldiers were 'ragged and stained by the hardships of the campaign, but their grizzled faces grinned the joy of home-coming. The ranks were broken and their files depleted in sad evidence of the price of the victory.'[114] Mansfield embraced what previous reviewers may have intended as a slight, declaring that the play was a straightforward matter of declamation and display. He stated confidently in his preface to the play that the St Crispin's Day speech was the most popular, needing 'only a breezy, wholesome and wholehearted delivery', but felt that the speech before Agincourt, in its specific musings on the condition of kingship, 'is almost beyond the comprehension of the average man'.

COUNTER-CLAIMS: POEL AND HIS FOLLOWERS

Nineteenth-century stagings, such as those by Macready and Kean, seemed to have established lavish historical pageantry as the only way to present the play. Indeed, by the turn of the century, it was commonplace for reviewers and critics to suggest that the play had only spectacle to commend it to playgoers. Costumes, armour, martial stage business and supernumeraries were all augmented to maximise visual impact, as productions vied with their predecessors for the greatest display. Inevitably, however, a backlash against this traditional form of staging began to be felt, and *Henry V*, with its explicit articulation of the essential limitations of the Elizabethan stage in the chorus speeches, was a key text in the debate.

The challenge to traditional illusionistic staging in the early years of the twentieth century is usually identified with the establishment in 1895 of the Elizabethan Stage Society under its maverick founder William Poel. Poel had seen Waller's production at the Lyceum Theatre, and gave his approval to it as entertainment but not as 'Shakespearian representation': 'Mr Waller has got it wrong with his play because he wanted to get stage-pictures out of it when Shakespeare never dreamt of such a thing . . . he goes out of his way to put in a chorus into the play especially to enable the spectators to do

---

114 Paul Wilstach, *Richard Mansfield: The Man and the Actor* (London: Chapman and Hall, 1908), pp. 353–4.

without stage-pictures.'[115] Poel had produced a version of the play for the Shakespeare Reading Society in 1887, intended as a recital, though an intensively rehearsed recital, rather than a performance. In collaboration with Ben Greet he produced *Henry V* in the open air at Stratford in October 1901 and the next month at Burlington Gardens in London, according to his revisionist theatrical manifesto of returning the plays to their original playing conditions. In the case of *Henry V*, however, this did not involve the sacrifice of all the visual effects audiences had come to expect: an open campfire made Henry's armour dazzlingly bright, and the twenty-six-year-old Robert Loraine was allowed a dramatic entrance to deliver the St Crispin's Day speech on the now inevitable white horse. Nor did Poel's quest for 'authenticity' extend to the use of the Quarto text of the play. Ben Greet, writing of the provincial tour of their *Henry V* during 1902, noted that it was not well received, but, albeit slowly, the tide was turning their way in more mainstream dramatic opinion. Whereas mid-nineteenth-century reviewers had been merciless in their scorn for productions without extensive casts and costumes, now some critics were starting to wonder whether all this visual spectacle was in fact necessary. As *The Times* wrote of Benson's production in 1900, 'it is useless to try and make the drama realistic. It is essentially poetic and unreal. It must "on our imaginary forces work". Yet this view seems to have escaped Mr Benson', and some years later *The Athenaeum* commented on the Stratford season, 'we believe it is a mistake to assume that the public insists on realistic scenery'.[116]

Henry V was cited by both sides in the traditional versus 'Elizabethan' theatrical debate of the early twentieth century. For Herbert Beerbohm Tree, among the last of the great Victorian actor-managers, the Chorus speeches represented Shakespeare's realisation of the limitations of his stage, but, 'with the prophetic eye of his genius, he foresaw the time when a later stage would achieve for him, in the way of scenery, costume and effects, what the playhouse of his own day was powerless to accomplish'. Sidney Lee, on the other hand, interpreted the Choruses differently, as a recognition of the intrinsic and inescapable unreality of theatre, both in the Elizabethan and, implicitly, the Edwardian periods:

> the words have no concern with the contention that modern upholstery and spectacular machinery render Shakespeare's play a justice which was denied them in his lifetime. As reasonably one might affirm that the modern theatre

115 Alan Gomme, 'William Poel: A Bibliography', unpublished typescript in the
     Theatre Museum, London, Z 8699.4, vol. II, p. 279.
116 *The Times*, 16 February 1900; *The Athenaeum*, 30 April 1920.

has now conquered the ordinary conditions of time and space; that a modern playhouse can, if the manager so will it, actually hold within its walls the 'vasty fields of France'.[117]

While it took some time to set in, however, the eventual break away from spectacular staging was assured. The twentieth century was largely to favour anti-illusionistic, continuous staging in place of the lavish but disjointed set pieces of the nineteenth.

Alongside continued revivals of Benson's quintessentially Edwardian production were two productions, directed by John Martin-Harvey and by William Bridges-Adams, both influenced, in some measure, by research into the original staging of Shakespeare's plays. John Martin-Harvey's 1916 production, 'in the Elizabethan manner', as the playbill announced, was performed at His Majesty's Theatre in London. In his autobiography, Martin-Harvey credits Darrell Figgis' 1911 book *Shakespeare* for the concept behind his production. The stage at His Majesty's was arranged to resemble the thrust stage of the Elizabethan playhouse, without sacrificing any seats to this design. Hence the effect was achieved by

> erecting a false proscenium – i.e. we set up deep wings, each having an entrance, joined together by a border about half-way up and over the stage proper. This structure was permanent. Behind this false proscenium we hung a variety of curtains – decorative, neutral, of homely material, of gold tissue. When these curtains were closed the front area of the stage suggested either an exterior or an interior.

Action could take place in front of the closed curtains while stagehands noiselessly prepared scenery behind them. The curtains could then be drawn to reveal a small inset scene, 'and immediately the entire area of the stage becomes part of this locality – suggested by the small set at the back'. This innovation in staging allowed the play to bowl along much more quickly than was customary as there was no need for lengthy scene-changing breaks, although, in deference to audience expectations there were still two intervals. Just as Poel had not entirely banished all spectacle from his production, nor did his dramatic successor Martin-Harvey. While claiming the inner and outer stages as an Elizabethan reconstruction, Martin-Harvey was able to exploit the theatricality of revelation in a manner akin to Macready's use of the diorama. The use of the curtain to reveal spectacular images such as the King's fleet bedecked in red and gold at harbour in Southampton, or the

117 Herbert Beerbohm Tree, *Thoughts and Afterthoughts* (London: Cassell, 1915), p. 305; Sidney Lee, *Shakespeare and the Modern Stage* (London: John Murray, 1906), p. 21.

great portcullis of Harfleur crashing down to the accompaniment of trumpet peals and booming cannon, led Martin-Harvey's biographer to describe the production as 'Christmas pantomime', adding, perhaps rather surprisingly, that 'Shakespeare had never thought of it. If he turned in his grave it would have been to wish he had.'[118]

Wartime productions were bound to have a particular flavour. Benson had some success with his wartime revivals of *Henry V*, especially at a performance on Boxing Day 1914 for which he incorporated, in deference to the prevailing national mood, a stirring Chorus. *The Times* noted that 'his performance throughout was marked by an unwonted fervour. Evidently he felt himself not merely playing the stage part, but delivering a solemn message.' One member of the audience of a performance in Nottingham in 1916 recalled 'the whole of the Theatre Royal filled with men in hospital blue'.[119] In 1915 Eric Williams produced a film entitled *England's Warrior King,* featuring men from the Royal Scots Greys regiment who were stationed at York, to be accompanied by a text derived from the play read by a narrator in the cinema: a cinematic wartime Henry which anticipates Olivier's famous film of 1944. During the First World War, two female companies are known to have performed the play. In 1919, a fifteen-year-old girl, Fabia Drake, played Henry in 'the war scenes and the wooing scene of the last act' in a programme including extracts from *The Merchant of Venice* and *The Merry Wives of Windsor*. The show, held at the YMCA Shakespeare Hut near the British Museum and directed by Edith Craig, had an audience of four hundred ANZAC soldiers waiting to be repatriated (Drake was to direct the play herself in similar circumstances in 1945).[120] Given the play's much-vaunted patriotism during the nineteenth century and the Boer War, however, it did not receive much attention during the First World War. Lena Ashwell's account of concert parties and troop entertainment, *Modern Troubadours*, does not mention the play except to quote a Canadian colonel who burst spontaneously into 'Once more into [*sic*] the breach, dear friends', and when troops fighting in France asked for Shakespeare productions to supplement the diet of light one-act Edwardian dramas, the Lena Ashwell Concert Party supplied scenes from *Macbeth* rather than *Henry V.*[121] Perhaps, as Shaw

118 Maurice Willson Disher, *The Last Romantic: The Authorised Biography of Sir John Martin-Harvey* (London: Hutchinson & Co., 1948), p. 230.

119 J.C. Trewin, *Benson and the Bensonians* (London: Barrie and Rockliff, 1960), p. 211; p. 214.

120 Fabia Drake, *Blind Fortune* (London: Kimber, 1978), pp. 36–7. Drake's memoirs also include a fine photograph of her diminutive Harry in baggy chain mail.

121 Lena Ashwell, *Modern Troubadours: A Record of Concerts at the Front* (London: Gyldendal, 1922), pp. 141–2.

suggested in a letter to Robert Loraine, who had played Poel's Henry, about Loraine's wish to produce it again, 'people are sick of jingoism and fed-up with Agincourt speeches'.[122] French battlefields, particularly the Somme, which the nineteenth-century theatre had specifically named as the backdrop for the play's account of noble victory, took on different and terrible associations with carnage rather than triumph. The First World War's devastating demolition of complacent ideas about war's chivalry and glory meant that its iconography was to be invoked in numerous late twentieth-century stagings of *Henry V* as the ultimate reproach on the play's apparent warmongers. David Jones' meditation on his wartime experiences, *In Parenthesis*, first published in 1937, drew explicit parallels between war in the trenches and the theatre of *Henry V*: 'no one, I suppose, however much not given to association, could see infantry in tin-hats, with ground-sheets over their shoulders, with sharpened pine-stakes in their hands, and not recall ". . . or may we cram,/Within this wooden O. . ."'. This ability to empathise with the events of the play – 'we are in no doubt at all but what Bardolph's marching kiss for Pistol's "quondam Quickly" is an experience substantially the same as you and I suffered on Victoria platform'[123] – shifted the play's realism from the antiquarian search for correct heraldic devices or Elizabethan staging methods into an emotional realm of wartime experiences, of separation, fear, bereavement, comradeship. A play which had been considered psychologically unnuanced, 'a declaiming much more than an acting play', as *The Times* put it in February 1900, was beginning to emerge as complexly and expressively shaded.

One such complication was described in a definitive post-Armistice article on the play. Although there had been critical attacks on Henry before, notably by Hazlitt, Yeats and Shaw, these had tended to suggest that Henry was a hero for Shakespeare's time, but not for the moderns. Similarly, cuts to the play in performance to eliminate any potentially damaging references or actions had often been justified by a similar historicizing. Richard Mansfield, for example, assumed that all of Henry's actions would have been endorsed by contemporaries, so that the apparent bargain with God before the battle 'was all then the custom of those times', and 'we must remember that when Shakespeare wrote, affairs were managed rather differently'. All such cuts were doing, therefore, was reinstating an original or intended reading of the character for modern audiences. Gerald Gould's essay in *The English Review* of 1919, 'A New Reading of *Henry V*',

---

122 Winifred Loraine, *Robert Loraine: Soldier, Actor, Airman* (London: Collins, 1938), p. 268.
123 David Jones, *In Parenthesis* (London: Faber, 1963), pp. xi, xv.

thoroughly undermined this assumption. Gould struck a chord with post-war sensibilities, introducing a radical and extremely influential interpretation of the play. His essay opened:

> None of Shakespeare's plays is so persistently and thoroughly misunderstood as *Henry V*, and one is tempted to think that there is no play which it is more important to understand. Irony is an awkward weapon. No doubt the irony of *Henry V* was meant to 'take in' the groundlings when it was first produced: had it failed to take them in, it would have invited bitter and immediate unpopularity. But Shakespeare can scarcely have intended that the force of preconception should, hundreds of years after his death, still be preventing the careful, the learned, and the sympathetic from seeing what he so definitely put down. *The play is ironic.*[124]

His argument that the play was ironic, a satire, rather than an endorsement, of 'imperialism, on the baser kinds of "patriotism", and on war', suggested that, for the more discerning spectators, there was an anti-patriotic play hidden beneath an ostensibly patriotic one. Looked at one way, the play undermines and critiques the attitudes which, from another perspective, it might have seemed to praise – anticipating Norman Rabkin's rabbit-duck illustration.[125] Gould focused his argument on three now-familiar elements, all of which had already been problematic for celebratory productions of the play and all of which had tended to be cut in performance: the prelates' plotting in 1.1 and the confusions of the Salic law in 1.2; Henry's 'unscrupulous brutality', particularly in the threats before Harfleur which Gould quotes at length and asks 'is it seriously maintained that Shakespeare means us to admire Henry *here*?';[126] and the play's repeated reminders of the rejection of Falstaff. It had taken a devastating war for the explicit discovery in this most martial of plays of a coded, ironic warning against warfare. While it would be some years before the full consequences of Gould's reading would be realised on the stage, the play was never quite the same again.

The second of the Poel-inspired productions of the period was William Bridges-Adams' production which played at Stratford in 1920, and for a short season at London's Strand Theatre. Like his mentor, Bridges-Adams favoured uncut texts – Ben Greet referred to him as 'Una-bridges-Adams' – although *Henry V* was not, as the publicity had led reviewers to expect,

---

124 Gerald Gould, 'A New Reading of *Henry V*', *The English Review* 128 (1919), pp. 42–55, p. 42.

125 Rabkin, *Shakespeare and the Problem of Meaning*.

126 Gould, 'A New Reading of *Henry V*', pp. 52–3.

performed in its entirety. The major distinction of this production was its speed and fluency, with nineteen scenes and only one short interval, and a total running time of less than three hours. Bridges-Adams, one of a coming breed of producer/directors and thus one of the first directors of the play not to star in it, made use of a few full-stage sets, but most of the play was performed in panel form between sliding curtains. A female Chorus, Ethel Warwick, was a predictable although not now an entirely popular choice (the *Athenaeum* reviewer complained that the Chorus should be 'nothing but the Spirit of War; his speeches require all the weight and virility that an actor of powerful physique can give them'[127]), and in many other details, Bridges-Adams was indebted to earlier productions and earlier styles: his desire to reinvigorate the Stratford company was hampered by his short rehearsal times and the consequent need to use experienced Shakespearean actors who had their own inheritance of gestures and inflection, described by Harley Granville-Barker in a letter to Bridges-Adams as 'this rubbish heap' of performance tradition.[128] Murray Carrington played a 'manly and lovable Henry' who 'did not indulge in point-making'.[129] The *Athenaeum* review sympathised with the production's desire 'to make this fearful cockerel [Henry] as human and unaffected as possible', but noted, in an echo of Shaw, that this was difficult for modern audiences 'who do not admire conquerors [or. . .] who have been taught by Napoleon and modern imperialists to prefer cynical to pious ones', and, in a reference designed to raise hackles, described the 'Bismarckian brutalities' of the wooing scene. Following Gould, attitudes to Henry were obviously changing. The same review dwelt, for the first time ever in theatrical notices, on the absent Falstaff, as 'the real dominating figure of the play', an ideological counterpoint to the unremitting militarism of Henry and his followers: 'Not all the banners and the shouting and the speeches and the state prayers avail to dupe us when we think of that smile and shrug. Sir John had weighed up all these things and condemned them.' Falstaff, the reviewer maintained, 'could not have delivered Henry's false prayer at Agincourt to save his soul. Ah! If Shakespeare really wanted his pageant to go down he ought not to have brought even the corpse of Falstaff into it.'[130] It was a way of reading *Henry V* against the grain that was to gain popularity over the century.

127 *The Athenaeum*, 22 October 1920.
128 Sally Beauman, *The Royal Shakespeare Company: A History of Ten Decades* (Oxford: Oxford University Press, 1982), p. 78.
129 Archibald Haddon, *Green Room Gossip* (London: Stanley Paul and Co., 1922), p. 63.
130 *The Athenaeum*, 22 October 1920, pp. 561–2.

WARTIME AGAIN

Apart from a production by Nigel Playfair at the Lyric, Hammersmith in 1927, with Lewis Casson as Henry and Sybil Thorndike doubling the Chorus and Katherine, *Henry V* was not a popular part of the repertoire of the 1920s and 1930s. It was not chosen as part of the opening season of the new Memorial Theatre in Stratford in 1932, where the only history play was *1 Henry IV*, although Robert Atkins directed a production at Stratford in 1934. As the storm clouds of European war gathered by the end of the 1930s the play's place in the theatre again looked uncertain, as its ostensible militarism sat awkwardly alongside the politics of appeasement.

Experiments with 'Elizabethan' staging continued, however. Robert Atkins' production on a thrust stage at the Ring in Blackfriars in November 1936 drew on Poel's techniques and pushed the actors right into the audience in a venue that had formerly been a boxing stadium. The audience sat on three sides of a platform, almost bare of props, with a curtained structure representing an Elizabethan tiring house at the back of the stage. Leslie French was particularly noted as the Chorus. Ben Iden Payne's 1937 production at Stratford was another Poel-inspired project. Payne had built a reproduction Elizabethan theatre on the stage at the Memorial Theatre, by erecting a penthouse roof supported by two wooden pillars within the proscenium arch. Under the jutting roof was a two-tiered stage, with the upper stage as a balcony and the lower as a discovery space or small inner set. The half-timbered interior was often commented on by reviewers.

Like his mentor Poel, Payne's Elizabethanism was not, however, unadulterated, and he made use of painted scenic backdrops and sets, including striking use of formal white, blue and gold for the French court, and a prominent finale where the red and blue of the two countries were united. Reviews of the production praised the look of the theatre, describing it as 'a fine piece of pageantry'. W. A. Darlington in the *Daily Telegraph* saw 'a representation as exact as it may be of the settings and clothes of the period when men were at their most picturesque', although he allowed himself to ponder 'what all these glittering fighters looked like when they had to fight in bad weather'. Clement McCallin, a 'tall, athletic figure [with] an air of authority',[131] played Henry, and an eloquent Donald Wolfit, who had previously played Llewellyn in repertory in the 1920s, was the Chorus. In this production Andrew Leigh was criticised for that old shortcoming of failing even to attempt a Welsh accent for the part of Llewellyn, and overall 'the comic war of Thistle and

131 *Daily Telegraph*, 2 April 1937.

Leek was less amusing than it might – nay should – have been'.[132] There may be a whisper of the tense European politics of the late 1930s in the *Birmingham Mail*'s expressed preference for the 'half-witted senility of previous renderings' of the French King, notably in productions by Benson and Waller, over the 'present exponent's diplomatic urbanity',[133] and other reviews also made veiled references to contemporary events. 'At the moment an excuse for a whole-hearted revival of "King Henry the Fifth" is not far to seek: in fact, the play almost demands to be put on this year,' noted the *Birmingham Post*, applauding the production for giving a much-needed occasion 'to give ourselves a collective pat on the national back, so to speak'; and the *News Chronicle* identified the speech on ceremony (4.1.205–57) as among the most effective, suggesting 'there are other aspects where parallels with today ought not to be closely pursued'.[134]

Laurence Olivier performed the role of Henry in 1937 – in the Old Vic production by Tyrone Guthrie. Olivier was uncomfortable with the declamatory style that had accrued around the part, but his attempts to perform 'gravely and quietly at rehearsals' infuriated his director, who told him: 'It's too disappointing for your audience, you're taking all the thrill out of the play, and for heaven's sake that's all it's got!'.[135] Olivier recollected later that the mood of the 1930s was 'against heroics', but that his performance managed to carry off the heroic interpretation urged by Guthrie and influenced by Lewis Waller.[136] One reviewer noted that this was done with 'a minimum of heroic gestures and a clear avoidance of rant', still contriving 'to impress the mind with the image of a heroic character'.[137] Despite this, however, there was an attempt to intellectualise Henry and to present him as a character riven with self-questioning: more of a Hamlet than a Hal. Gordon Crosse was not impressed by the production he listed in his chapter on 'Oddities', recalling its 'attempt to present *Henry V* as a pacifist tract. The Archbishop became an unprincipled cleric driving a well-meaning young man into a course which his conscience disapproved.' Crosse recalled Henry 'prowling about the stage trying to make up his mind about the war, and all along thoughtfulness kept breaking in, whereas what the play calls for is straightforward, dashing rhetoric and no nonsense about the ethics of

---

132 *Yorkshire Post*, 2 April 1937.
133 *Birmingham Mail*, 2 April 1937.
134 *Birmingham Post*, 2 April 1937; *News Chronicle*, 2 April 1937.
135 Laurence Olivier, *Confessions of an Actor* (London: Weidenfeld and Nicolson, 1982), p. 110.
136 Laurence Olivier, *On Acting* (London: Weidenfeld and Nicolson, 1986), p. 58.
137 *The Times*, 7 April 1937.

war'.[138] This clarity was perhaps more easily attained by Olivier's warwork, doing a one-man show in military camps 'geared to whip up patriotism' and reaching a climax in his delivery of Henry's speech before Agincourt: 'By the time I got to "God for Harry . . ." I think they would have followed me anywhere. Looking back, I don't think we could have won the war without "Once more unto the breach . . ." somewhere in our soldiers' hearts.'[139] *The Times* described the Old Vic production's scenery and costumes, designed by Motley, and praised the richly coloured shields, hangings and banners 'which fall forward and fold themselves into tents for the camp scenes'. Contrasting the production with the Iden Payne version running at Stratford, the reviewer found the Old Vic's use of curtains as a backdrop rather than 'realistically painted vistas' as an 'appeal to a more adult aestheticism',[140] thus registering the shift away from spectacle in the play's stage history. The Chorus demonstrated 'the pride and excitement of the civilian in national events', an observer rather than participant. Henry's speech on ceremony was pronounced 'the moving centre-piece of the whole performance'.[141]

In 1938 Lewis Casson produced, at Drury Lane, 'a form of spectacular Shakespeare appear[ing] like a revenant',[142] with matinée idol Ivor Novello in the central role and Miss Gwen Ffrangcon-Davies as a declamatory boy-Chorus. With much pageantry and use of cannon fire, this was not the play for the politics of the Munich period, and the production closed after a three-week run. During the wartime summer of 1941, Robert Atkins produced the play, with a cast of twenty-one, in Regent's Park. Wartime had brought a special poignancy to the play, and it is striking that reviews highlighted not the set-piece speeches nor the central characters, noting instead that 'the eternal ways of the common soldier, on active service, perhaps the best of the play, are well set out'. One reviewer movingly observed that 'some war plays, and this may be one of them, seem to go better in the piping times of peace'.[143] Shortages meant that the original conditions of staging the play referred to in the Chorus were necessarily rediscovered for 'these makeshift days',[144] and when the play was performed at Stratford for a rather depleted Birthday celebration in April 1943, costumes from Ben Iden Payne's 1937

138 Gordon Crosse, *Shakespearean Playgoing 1890–1952* (London: A.R. Mowbray & Co., 1953), p. 105.

139 Olivier, *On Acting*, p. 66.

140 *The Times*, 7 April 1937.

141 Audrey Williamson, *Old Vic Drama* 1 (London: Rockcliff, 1948), pp. 90–1.

142 J.C. Trewin, *Shakespeare on the English Stage 1900–1964* (London: Barrie and Rockliff, 1964), p. 177.

143 *The Times*, 20 August 1941.   144 *Ibid.*

production were revived. One review noted the 'austerity' of the production, whereas another found Payne's bright pageant costumes and drapes jarring: 'in these days when camouflage has distorted our vision, the British camp in one scene looks very like a row of brand new bathing tents'.[145] Other than this, there was relatively little reference to the war in reviews, and only the *Birmingham Post* was ungallant enough to mention that Baliol Holloway, a Bensonian who had cut his *Henry V* teeth as Pistol in 1912 and was now sixty years old, played 'a somewhat mature king'.[146] Charles Reading played the Chorus as Shakespeare himself. Other productions of the play are recorded during the war – most notably, for its echo of all-women troupes in the First World War, Nancy Hewins' all-female Osiris Repertory Company, which toured the country putting on Shakespeare and modern plays in church and school halls.

OLIVIER'S FILM

The 1944 film of *Henry V* stands as the most remembered and probably the most influential single production of the play, as a milestone in its performance history and in the history of Shakespeare on film. It is striking, therefore, to register its fine balance between the spectacle of the nineteenth century and the psychological realism of the twentieth, as a production on the cusp of two distinct approaches to the play. Many elements can be traced to previous productions. Olivier's own stage performance, directed by Tyrone Guthrie, was inevitably a considerable influence. Guthrie had, for example, introduced comedy to the explanation of the Salic law, and some actors were part of both productions, including Harcourt Williams, who played the French King in Guthrie's production and in Olivier's film and Leo Genn, who had played Burgundy at the Old Vic and took on the role of the Constable in the film. Olivier's own performance was, of course, at the centre of both productions. But Olivier's film also revived and alluded to numerous other stage performances. The white horse had been an essential conveyance for stage Henrys since Calvert, some seventy years previously; bright heraldic decoration and medieval costumes also had their roots in the antiquarianism of Victorian revivals; the use of the Elizabethan theatre owed something to Poel and the debates about 'original' staging during the first decades of the century, as well as to Robert Atkins' recent production on a thrust stage at the Ring in Blackfriars in 1936. Harcourt Williams linked the film to the traditions established by F. R. Benson, as he had first played the French King in the company in 1914; Olivier acknowledged his own debt to

145 *The Stage*, 29 April 1943.   146 *Birmingham Post*, 27 April 1943.

Lewis Waller. George Robey, who played Falstaff in the interpolated scene, was best known as a music-hall performer, thus giving the presentation of Falstaff an added nostalgic poignancy. The prominence of William Walton's score for the film recalled the importance of music in previous theatre productions, especially those of Kean and Calvert. Walton's music was itself performed at the Proms in 1945.[147]

As well as these theatrical influences, Olivier's film nods to certain explicitly cinematic antecedents too: the scenes at night before the battle, and the combat on horseback can be identified with the narrative and visual codes of the western, and the film's use of Technicolor also linked it to American Hollywood pictures. Olivier noted his debt to Sergei Eistenstein's *Alexander Nevsky* (1938), evident particularly in the montage sequence of the battle; the wooing of Katherine drew on Olivier's Hollywood romantic hero persona gained through films such as *Wuthering Heights* (dir. William Wyler, 1939) and *Pride and Prejudice* (dir. Robert Leonard, 1940); the sequence at Agincourt in which English archers drop from the trees to topple French riders from their horses derived some of its swashbuckling wit in quoting directly from Michael Curtiz' *The Adventures of Robin Hood* (1938). In drawing together these diverse influences, Olivier's film combined the play's well-tested amenability to spectacle with more recent attempts to present an anti-illusionistic drama. His mission was 'to bring Shakespeare to the screen, to bring caviare to the general audience; not in a snobbish sense but because I love caviare'.[148]

From the outset, Olivier – a reluctant and first-time director after William Wyler, Carol Reed and Terence Young all declined the project – was conscious of the need to adapt to the new medium. The film opens with bells ringing, then cuts to the monumental lettering of the dedicatory inscription '[t]o the Commandos and Airborne Troops of Great Britain, the spirit of whose ancestors it has been humbly attempted to recapture in some ensuing scenes', the film's only explicit reference to contemporary events. Then the camera gives us an aerial view of London, gradually zooming on a polygonal structure by the river outside, which is revealed to be an Elizabethan theatre. The film opens as the play is about to begin – in a theatre. A playbill is blown towards the camera, and gives the title as 'The Chronicle History of King Henry the Fift with his Battell fought at Agincourt in France. By Will Shakespeare' – the title *Henry V* never appears in the film. The date is given as 1 May 1600. Oliver wrote later of his intentions in this opening sequence:

---

147 John Huntley, *British Film Music* (London: Skelton Robinson [1947]), p. 74.
148 Olivier, *On Acting*, p. 190.

> The goddam play was telling me the style of the film. Dress the Chorus as an
> Elizabethan actor (which he was), get him – with broad gestures – to
> challenge the imaginations of the unruly audience in the cockpit. Maybe
> that way the film audience would be challenged. Play the first few scenes on
> the Globe stage in a highly, absolutely deliberate, theatrical style; get the film
> audience used to the language, and let them laugh its excesses out of their
> systems before the story really begins.[149]

This knowing manipulation of the conventions of theatre, the possibilities of film, and the expectations of audiences is characteristic of Olivier's
direction. Leslie Banks is a grandiloquent Chorus in the fashionable garb of
an Elizabethan fop for the Prologue, but later Choruses use him as a voice-
over rather than introducing him physically into the action. It is striking that,
by dividing some of the Chorus speeches, Olivier extends the play's six into
ten, making more use of this essentially theatrical device in the scenes that
leave the initial Globe setting behind. In this way the Chorus's commentary
may work 'as subtle flattery, suggesting that *we* are actually creating all these
splendid images in our heads'.[150] While Olivier did not cut 1.1, the scene
with the prelates, he did nevertheless minimise its importance, setting it in
the artificial and restricted arena of the Globe stage and characterising its
protagonists as bumbling and inept, and its on-screen theatre audience as
impatient and contemptuous. By using comic stage business to shift attention away from the politics of the opening scene, he was able to introduce
his essentially patriotic, heroic interpretation of Henry to cinema audiences.
Perhaps tellingly, however, the film's first view of Henry is as he waits backstage for his cue, clearing his throat in anticipation. This is an actor, and
a King, ready to give the most important performance of his life, and the
self-consciousness of the moment is carried through the film.

Henry is often presented as personally vulnerable, in removing his helmet
to deliver the 'Once more unto the breach' speech bare-headed, in shrugging
on a light chain mail shirt – made, Olivier revealed in contemporary interviews, with an eye to the communal make-do ingenuity of wartime austerity,
from silver-painted string – an image immediately juxtaposed with the heavy
and unwieldy image of the armoured Dauphin being winched on to his
horse, in the reflective voice-over mode and a close-up of his sad-eyed
expression in the soliloquy on ceremony. He grows in personal stature
through the film, from underdog to victor, although the film allowed little
contradiction or difficulty in the central characterisation, partly through the

149 *Ibid.*, p. 187.
150 Harry M. Geduld, *Filmguide to Henry V* (Bloomington: Indiana University Press,
     [1973]), p. 37.

cuts to the text of the play. The film Henry, unlike Olivier in Guthrie's stage production, did not have to deal with the conspirators – one review suggested that this was cut because it 'could have been interpreted as an allusion to the existence of a well-organised fifth column'[151] – and the Governor of Harfleur needed no threats to make him surrender since the whole of Henry's speech at 3.4 was cut. The film did, however, include a cameo role for George Robey, the music-hall comedian known as the 'Prime Minister of Mirth', in poignant mood as the dying Falstaff. Olivier included lines from *2 Henry IV* as Falstaff, lying sick in bed at the Boar's Head Inn, starts up with memories, and hears King Henry's rejection of him 'distantly, as if out of the past': 'I know thee not, old man' (*2 Henry IV* 5.5.43).[152] Olivier 'wanted the audience . . . to have a concrete image of the dear old man', and the interpolation adds poignancy to the Hostess' speech on his death which might otherwise be delivered comically, but one effect of this sombre added scene is to present Henry, if only momentarily, in a harsher light.[153]

While more recent critics of the film have been able to read ways in which its layering of illusion and 'reality' serve to deconstruct its own ostensibly patriotic message, it is clear that for viewers of the film at the time – it was extremely popular in Britain in 1944–5 where, for example, many schools hired cinemas to show it to their pupils *en masse*, and later in the United States in 1946 – that the patriotic, Churchillian qualities of the film were totally dominant. A clever advance publicity campaign, with posters showing simply the red cross of St George on a white background, or a gold fleur-de-lys on a blue background, aroused public interest. Reviewers were clear about its message. The critic James Agee commented: 'I am not a Tory, a monarchist, a Catholic, a medievalist, an Englishman, or, despite all the good that it engenders, a lover of war: but the beauty and power of this traditional exercise was such that, watching it, I wished I was, thought I was, and was proud of it.'[154] The recollections of people who saw it at the time confirm this lasting impression. Room for contrary interpretations was almost non-existent, although one viewer recalled how seeing the film on a school-arranged excursion prompted her classmates to the expression of specifically anti-French, rather than anti-German or pro-British, sentiments, suggesting that the general critical assumption that audiences seamlessly replaced Hitler's Germany for the Dauphin's France in the play's figuration of the

151 *Hollywood Quarterly*, 11 October 1946.
152 Olivier, Shooting Script, Folger Shakespeare Library, Washington D.C.
153 Olivier, *On Acting*, p. 187.
154 Quoted in Charles W. Eckert (ed.), *Focus on Shakespearean Films* (Englewood Cliffs, NJ: Prentice-Hall, 1972), p. 56.

national enemy may be over-simplistic: Raymond Durgnat's explanation that 'the English are the English but Agincourt is D-Day where the French are the Germans until Henry courts Katherine when the French are probably the French' allows for the right amount of confusion.[155] The film's influence on the fragile post-war relationship between Britain and France is interestingly revealed in a memo dating from 1947 in the French Ministry of Foreign Affairs questioning whether the authorities should intervene in its distribution. In the memo, *Henry V* is acknowledged as a great artistic and commercial success, but 'it is the case nonetheless that, for the French, the spectacle which it offers is, in certain of its scenes, extremely painful and almost intolerable':

> It is not that the French monarchy is vanquished at Agincourt . . . but the depiction made with Shakespearian violence and crudity, yet also with consummate artistry, of the moral faults and weaknesses of the French. Such scenes which show the French knights before the battle, their lack of restraint, their heedlessness, their inability to bother themselves with what matters, that is to say, the victory of the next day, these scenes risk being considered not as the representation of the faults and errors of a past age, but . . . as the permanent traits of our character. It is very serious furthermore that comparisons could be made in the military field with a recent event.[156]

If the characterisation and mood of the film were relatively simple, its own diegetic mode was not. Throughout it continued to experiment with different levels of self-conscious illusion, most notably in its use of two-dimensional painted backdrops reminiscent of medieval illustrations from the Duc de Berri's hour book *Les Très Riches Heures* to represent the French court. Much of the film was shot at Denham studios, but it goes on location for the Battle of Agincourt (fig. 6). Whereas the comic and romantic scenes of the film are shot in self-evidently pantomimic or storybook style, the battle sequence itself shows a panoramic scope. Even here, however, there was a glaze of unreality. Olivier evokes violence through suggestion, and there is, notably, no blood at the Battle of Agincourt, which is aestheticised through montage techniques into a beautiful 'panorama of chivalrous action'.[157] The

155 I am grateful to the readers of Oxford's *North Oxford Association News* for supplying me with their reminiscences of the film; Raymond Durgnat, *Film and Feelings* (Cambridge, MA: MIT Press, 1967), p. 262.

156 For the text of the memo, see John W. Young, 'Henry V, the Quai D'Orsay, and the Well-being of the Franco-British Alliance, 1947', *Historical Journal of Film, Radio and Television* 7 (1987), pp. 319–21.

157 Geduld, *Filmguide*, p. 45.

6 The Battle of Agincourt in Laurence Olivier's film (1944).

only bloodied casualty is the dead Boy who has been killed (off-screen), by the French. Ace Pilkington discusses how this bloodless effect was developed through an analysis of differences between the shooting and release scripts, all of which work to make the film less explicitly violent.[158] There was, one might assume, enough real bloodshed around for audiences in 1944. Whereas the techniques of film might have been employed for the greater realism that had been demanded by reviewers of the play on stage, it was in fact used to underline this *Henry V*'s unreal, mythic, self-reflexive mode. Olivier's aesthetics of stylisation was a bold fusion of the techniques of cinema and of theatre, and a sophisticated response to the play's own discourse on the possibilities of representation.

The Agincourt sequence was the film's major expense and, arguably, its major exploitation of the resources uniquely available to film. Generations

158 Ace Pilkington, *Screening Shakespeare from Richard II to Henry V* (Newark and London: University of Delaware Press, 1991), pp. 104–5.

of directors had tried to present the scope of the battle on the stage, and had been variously applauded and derided for their attempts. Olivier's Agincourt accounted for £80,000 of a total initial budget fixed at £300,000, but which eventually swelled to just over £475,000, making it the most expensive British film ever then made. There is no evidence of government sponsorship for the film, but it is clear that it enjoyed official support, and that, at the behest of the Ministry of Information, Olivier was released from his war service in the Fleet Air Arm to make it. It was shot in Eire where, because of Irish neutrality, there were no blackout regulations or shortage of extras, and there is apparently no irony in the weekly magazine *Illustrated*'s headline for an article on the location shooting of the film: 'The Battle of Agincourt is being refought in neutral Eire'.[159] If, when the play was first performed in 1599, its figuring of France stood in for Ireland in the imagination of its audiences, three hundred and fifty years later the reverse was true, as Powerscourt Park in Co. Wicklow stood for the field of the decisive battle with France. The bright colours of the Agincourt sequence were set off by the film's clever juxtaposition of gaudy and sombre scenes, and garish colours were used to characterise the French soldiers as vain and dandyish compared with the honest frieze of the English bowmen. The film's conclusion with the long wooing scene 'is a reminder that the war will soon be over and that it will be necessary to come to terms with the vanquished foe' and also a reversion to Olivier's romantic screen persona.[160] The apparent popularity of this scene, and of Renée Asherson as Katherine, for wartime audiences may give an indication of its original wish-fulfilment and escapist function during its first performances in the war-weary London of 1599. Renée Asherson reprised her role in a performance otherwise entirely cast from American service personnel directed by Fabia Drake in the summer of 1945. Drake also used some of the film's costumes, and sent her actors 'to see Larry's film to get the "feel"'.[161] It was the first of a long line of post-Olivier productions which were to use the film as background research, as the film provided the visual imagery and emotive power which were to be associated

159 *Illustrated*, 17 July 1943. Not all commentary was as oblivious to the ironies of the republic's hosting of this hymn to monarchy: the *New Statesman* (5 June 1943) contained a parody by its satirical poet 'Sagittarius': 'Advance, you stout Sinn Feiners, brawny supers / Whose limbs were made in Eire, show us here / That you are worth your wages: which I doubt not / Are ten times more than those of Harry's bowmen! / And he that doth enact this scene with me, / Let him be never so Republican / He is this day King Harry's follower!'.
160 James Chapman, *The British at War: Cinema, State and Propaganda, 1939–45* (London and New York: I.B. Tauris, 1998), p. 247.
161 Drake, *Blind Fortune*, p. 130.

with the play for the rest of the century, even for those directors who sought to undermine such interpretive certainties.

Dorothy Green's production at Stratford was the first post-war *Henry V*, and the first to be explicitly compared with Olivier's film. The *Birmingham Mail*'s review suggests that the impression created by the film itself had settled into the long haul of 'winning the peace':

> The ringing patriotism of *Henry V* was as well-suited to the mood of the Elizabethans . . . as it is to English minds today as they grope after the slow fruits of a greater, but less swift, victory. There is in it, as the wider circle of cinema patrons have found, much profound thought on the evil nature of war and the quality of national unity; it is no mere matter of heady heroics.[162]

Heady heroics were not much in evidence in this production 'for a war-scorched generation'. Paul Scofield, then twenty-four years old, played Henry with an eye to emotional verity rather than high oratory. *The Stage* wrote that he 'humanises Henry for modern sympathies and is at his best in the camp and the wooing scenes, playing a convincing fighting man rather than a legendary monarch', and a local paper added, somewhat equivocally, that 'Scofield's humorous humanity gives the king a coat of whitewash much needed for modern taste'. This was a performance more thoughtful than swashbuckling, and perhaps a performance that shared Olivier's initial doubts about the role a decade previously. For some reviewers this was not so much restraint as underperformance. *The Times* judged the actors 'lifeless' as 'they declaim rather than interpret their parts'.[163] Green had herself played the Chorus in the handful of Benson's performances that had included the role, but she chose not to continue the tradition of casting a woman. Robert Harris played the Chorus, emerging from the scenes of the action to speak his lines rather than entering, as was customary, from the wings.

Dorothy Green was the first woman to direct a professional production of *Henry V*, a play long associated with a masculine world and judged to have little appeal to women. Thus far, she has had few female heirs in the job. When Di Trevis, who later directed comedies at Stratford, was interviewed for the post of assistant to Terry Hands, who was himself to direct *Henry V*, she 'said that the play that interested me was *Henry V* and they just went "Oh!!!"', and this seems to have been a general reaction to the idea of a

---

162 *Birmingham Mail*, 11 May 1946.
163 *The Stage*, 16 May 1946; *Stratford-upon-Avon Herald*, 17 May 1946; *The Times*, 13 May 1946.

woman director for the play.[164] One review in 1946 concluded that Green had 'done a man's job with this stirring, sweeping chronicle play', but others suggested that, for better or worse, a more domestic-scale play had emerged from the spectacle. The production 'lack[ed] the purple patches of excitement, but [was] very strong in the smaller detail'; the scene between Katherine and Alice was characterised as 'first-rate', the wooing scene 'set against a background of cypresses and cedars limned on the evening sky' was 'lovely'.[165]

STRATFORD AND THE FESTIVAL OF BRITAIN

Scholarly criticism of Shakespeare's histories during the early part of the century had tended to stress their distinctness and discontinuities, but the work of critics such as E.M.W. Tillyard in the 1940s began to suggest that the plays should be viewed as a sequence.[166] This was a concept not entirely alien to theatrical history: W. B. Yeats recorded his favourable impressions of a partial sequence as presented by F. R. Benson at Stratford at the turn of the century:

> I have seen this week *King John*, *Richard II*, the second part of *Henry IV*, *Henry V*, the second part of *Henry VI*, and *Richard III* played in their right order, with all the links that bind play to play unbroken; and partly because of a spirit in the place, and partly because of the way play supports play, the theatre has moved me as it has never done before.[167]

By the 1950s, the idea that *Henry V* made sense in the context of the earlier history plays was gaining ground, and this change of emphasis allowed a less positive image of Henry to emerge.

Richard David's review of Glen Byam Shaw's Old Vic production of 1951 felt that Alec Clunes' gallant Henry carried his family history at his back, especially in moments which explicitly refer to events before the play begins, such as his response to the news of Bardolph's execution or his prayer before Agincourt.[168] Byam Shaw's production also picked up on the retreat from pageantry, with indicative, rather than fully naturalistic, scenery and

---

164 Di Trevis, interviewed in Elizabeth Schafer, *MsDirecting Shakespeare: Women Direct Shakespeare* (London: The Women's Press, 1998), p. 169.

165 *Birmingham Gazette*, 11 May 1946; *Birmingham Evening Despatch*, 11 May 1946; *Birmingham Mail*, 11 May 1946.

166 E. M. W. Tillyard, *Shakespeare's History Plays* (London: Chatto & Windus, 1944).

167 W. B. Yeats, 'At Stratford-upon-Avon', pp. 96–7.

168 Richard David, 'Shakespeare in the Waterloo Road', *Shakespeare Survey* 5 (1952), pp. 121–8.

costumes designed for movement rather than show. The utilitarian style of the English soldiers was contrasted with the jewel-encrusted encumbrances given to the French, 'as though each man had provided himself with a Maginot line of defence'.[169] Byam Shaw's production was praised particularly for its fellowly Henry who combined 'authority and familiarity', and for its representation of the Chorus, played by Roger Livesey, dubbed 'Our Public Relations Officer' in the programme, 'a friendly and inspiring' presence whose attempts to get the audience's co-operation in the theatrical enterprise won 'our complete sympathy and loyalty'. Significant detail was the hallmark of the production, from the dirty bandages on the soldiers after the battle, to the lights on the masts of Henry's fleet at Southampton. The French, led by their mad King, were presented in an exaggeratedly unattractive light and their uniforms suggested 'the colours of a more recent and deadly enemy of England, and their foppery, like Goering's medals and flash uniforms, covered not so much cowardly feebleness as real viciousness and degeneracy'.[170] The Dauphin's personal and unchivalric brutality was stressed in such added touches as his drunken pursuit of a young woman fleeing from his tent. Byam Shaw's production was compared favourably with the production, directed by Anthony Quayle, in Stratford in 1951. Quayle's production was the first real trial by theatre of the Tillyardian view of the plays as primarily a sequence. The same set was used and the same actors were cast in *Richard II*, *1 and 2 Henry IV* and *Henry V* to underline what the programmes called 'a cycle of the historical plays'.

Richard Burton had played Prince Hal in the *Henry IV* plays and here took on the part of Henry, with Michael Redgrave reprising his role of Chorus from Guthrie's pre-war production (Quayle had taken on this part himself later in the Old Vic run). The set and costumes were designed by Tanya Moiseiwitsch on an eclectically Elizabethan or anti-illusionistic theme, with a wooden platform raised on scaffolding, with centre doors which could be closed or left open to reveal metal scaffold poles. This uncompromising design allowed the plays to run unhindered by elaborate staging, and provided a strong utilitarian aesthetic to unify the sequence. The fact of the play's position in the cycle was important. T. C. Worsley, in the account of the cycle published in 1952, admitted that 'the production of *Henry V* is not essentially different when it is played in the cycle than what it would be at any other time. But the attitude of the audience towards the king undergoes a

---

169 Programme note quoted by Audrey Williamson, *Old Vic Drama 2* (London: Rockcliff, 1957), p. 58.

170 *Ibid.*; *The Sketch*, 14 February 1951; David, 'Shakespeare in the Waterloo Road', p. 125; p. 127.

considerable modification', and this qualification is a significant one. Worsley believed that audience responses were sharply divided between those who had seen all four plays and those who came 'hoping to see, as Mr Ivor Brown puts it, the Lewis Waller of the 1950s. The second party were, on the whole, disappointed', although some reviewers enjoyed its 'record of a time when war was personal and brief and relatively simple in its issues as a tonic draught for minds that have been reared on the inglorious preliminaries and complex horrors of modern war'.[171] The interpretation of the sequence had been to lead up to the glory of Henry's reign, so that those elements from the previous plays which might have compromised Henry's characterisation in *Henry V* were downplayed. Quayle himself had played a thoroughly dis-likeable Falstaff, for example, so as to undermine any sense in which Falstaff's treatment might reflect badly on the King. Burton's own perfor-mance was, however, the major concern of reviewers and, as ever, opinions were sharply divided. His height was repeatedly mentioned, as a 'bantam surrounded by full-sized cockerels', but one with 'the moral if not the physi-cal stature for the part'.[172] He was more effective in the low-key moments than in the high rhetoric, and some reviewers found this latter quality more, perhaps too much, in evidence in the performance of Redgrave as Chorus. The Welshness of the King (4.1.50) was interestingly conveyed by Burton, and there were strong performances by Hugh Griffith as a wily Archbishop of Canterbury, Alan Badel as a suavely menacing Dauphin and Robert Hardy as a suitably vociferous Llewellyn. Burton played Henry again in 1955 at the Old Vic under the direction of Michael Benthall, when the theatre critic Kenneth Tynan described his stern performance as 'true and watchful and ruthless': Burton's Henry was 'a cunning warrior, stocky and astute, unafraid of harshness or of curling the royal lip. The gallery gets no smiles from him and the soldiery none but the scantest commiseration.'[173]

Quayle's innovation in presenting the play as part of a sequence was an influential one. It was repeated by Peter Hall and John Barton for their pro-duction of a complete cycle of history plays from *Richard II* to *Richard III* as part of the 1964 Shakespeare Quartercentenary celebrations, with Ian Holm as another Henry 'at his best in quiet moments'. Holm's Henry was one of the soldiery, 'no heraldic Henry moving in spotless armor across a blood-soaked battlefield, but a man discovering his kingship within himself and

171 J. Dover Wilson and T.C. Worsley, *Shakespeare's Histories at Stratford, 1951* (London: Max Reinhardt, 1952), p. 52; p. 79; *Coventry Evening Telegraph*, 1 August 1951.
172 *News Chronicle*, 1 August 1951.
173 Kenneth Tynan, *A View of the English Stage 1944–63* (London: Davis-Poynter, 1971), pp. 164–5.

7   Ian Holm as Henry in John Barton and Peter Hall's 1964 production.

through his comradeship with other men' (fig. 7). One reviewer remarked that on seeing Henry again after seeing the previous three plays the audience greets him 'as an old friend, and feel[s] an almost proprietary interest in his success as King, as soldier, and, finally, as unorthodox lover'.[174] The production, designed by John Bury, took its visual and intellectual cue from Polish director Jan Kott's influential interpretation of the history plays as the working of a 'Grand Mechanism', using metallic imagery for the whole sequence, with polished steel for England and a golden backdrop to the French scenes in *Henry V*.[175] The play used a thrust stage with monochrome, emblematic sets.

The Barton–Hall production has been identified in retrospect as the first truly anti-war production of the play, although this was not always registered by contemporary reviewers. Ralph Berry has astutely described it as a production which 'managed to be pro-Henry – this side of idolatry – anti-war

174   *Guardian*, 4 June 1964; Robert Speaight, 'Shakespeare in Britain', *Shakespeare Quarterly* 15 (1964), p. 387; *Daily Telegraph*, 4 June 1964.

175   Jan Kott, *Shakespeare our Contemporary* (London: Methuen and Co, 2nd edn, 1967), pp. 3–46.

and anti-romantic', and another commentator argued that the production was less anti-heroic than newly, differently heroic: a play about 'sheer, dogged pugnaciousness . . . the heroism of the First World War trenches . . . it is, in short, democratic twentieth-century heroism'.[176] Trevor Nunn identified the contemporary ' "make love not war" movement and the horror of the Vietnamese situation' as the catalyst to the production's discovery of what the radical playwright John Arden described in a letter to the *New Statesman* as this 'secret play inside the official one'.[177] The Chorus' speeches were deliberately at odds with bloody events on stage. W. A. Darlington, writing in the *Daily Telegraph* rather missed this in saying that 'he seems to be ordering the audience about rather than appealing to it': the production traced the tension between the 'exciting myths and fictions' of the Chorus and the 'more real, harder, cooler, more ambiguous' tenor of events.[178] The interpretations of Gerald Gould and of other Henry-sceptics had found their expression on stage in this *Henry V* for a cynical and anti-authoritarian generation.

HENRYS OUTSIDE BRITAIN

The stage history of *Henry V* has already been identified as a particularly British phenomenon, with only a handful of notable productions in other countries. While British productions of the play, including those of Macready, Calvert, Benson and Benthall had toured or transferred to North America, Richard Mansfield's New York *Henry V* at the turn of the century was the first that could be identified as an American production. It was not until the second half of the twentieth century that others followed.

In 1956 Michael Langham directed the play at the fledgling Shakespeare Festival in Stratford, Ontario, with Christopher Plummer in the title role. The presentation of Henry offered the then traditional combination of heroism and reflection, with Plummer an attractive and rounded character especially in the wooing scene. The production was most noticeable for its casting of French Canadian actors from the Théâtre du Nouveau Monde in Montreal to play the French. Reviews were interestingly positive about the characterisation of the French, whose costuming suggested their national 'flair and theatricality' rather than the usual effete dandyism, 'impressing the

---

176 Ralph Berry, *Changing Styles in Shakespeare* (London: Allen and Unwin, 1981), p. 77; Gareth Lloyd Evans, 'Shakespeare, the Twentieth Century and "Behaviourism" ', *Shakespeare Survey* 20 (1967), p. 139.
177 Berry, *On Directing Shakespeare*, p. 62; *New Statesman*, 19 June 1964.
178 *Daily Telegraph*, 4 June 1964; Berry, *On Directing Shakespeare*, p. 62.

audience with their concern for the higher things of life compared with the stolid Puritan shopkeepers' values which the English are concerned about'. There were specific resonances for contemporary Canadian politics in the last act's slow establishment of 'a compromise between the beaten French and the victorious English'.[179]

Ralph Berry has argued that a more general shift in attitudes to the play can be read into the differences between Langham's 1956 production and his second version a decade later, this time with Douglas Rain as Henry. Again, French Canadian actors played the French roles, and this time the ambivalent contrast between their jaunty grace and the English phlegm was emphasised by the hardening of the 1966 production's attitude to warfare. The programme quoted from the First World War poet Wilfred Owen and showed a photograph from the Vietnam war, and Rain played an anti-heroic Henry, 'more like a commoner than a king'. The French prisoners and the English boys were killed on stage, the battles were brutal and bloody, and after Agincourt Henry's disaffected troops looted French corpses.[180] A sardonic Chorus, played by William Hutt, emphasised the gap between the lofty commentary and the grim events on stage. Langham looked back on his previous version as sentimental and unrealistic, particularly in its vision of Anglo-French harmony, and questioned the traditional interpretation of the play, and its relevance for the Canadian context, in his programme notes: 'What has this jingoistic national anthem of a play to do with our age? It glorifies war, exploits the inanities of nationalism, is offensively class-conscious, and – as if to encourage philistine thinking in Canada – is patently and exultantly anti-French.'[181] The production was filmed for Canadian television under the direction of Langham and Lorne Freed (1966).

Despite Langham's change of direction, however, heroic *Henry V*s continued to flourish. Douglas Seale, who had played Bardolph in Dorothy Green's 1946 production of the play in Stratford, England, directed it in Stratford, Connecticut in 1963. James Ray was Henry amid a striking set comprising a series of high poles in a 'semi-circle behind a playing area which included a sizeable forestage. At the outset these surrounded a throne, later they were hung with ship's rigging, and in the grand finale they supported a great tent.'[182] The French were dressed in blue and white, the English in

179 Arnold Edinborough, 'Consolidation in Stratford, Ontario', *Shakespeare Quarterly* 7 (1956), pp. 403–6.
180 Samuel L. Leiter (ed.), *Shakespeare Around the Globe: A Guide to Notable Postwar Revivals* (New York: Greenwood Press, 1986), p. 215.
181 Berry, *Changing Styles in Shakespeare*, p. 72.
182 Roberta Krensky Cooper, *The American Shakespeare Theatre: Stratford 1955–85* (Washington D.C.: Folger, 1986), p. 96.

reds and browns, and the overall interpretation was heroic and positive. Joseph Papp's New York productions of 1960, 1965 and 1976 attracted large audiences with a combination of epic pageantry on the thrust stage of the Delacorte Theater, a cast of almost sixty actors, and swashbuckling, Olivier-inspired staging such as the shooting of scores of arrows into the air during the battles. In 1965 an African American, Robert Hooks, played Henry before an enthusiastic and largely black Harlem audience. Christopher Plummer, who had played Henry in 1956, returned to it in 1981 at Stratford, Connecticut, this time doubling the role with that of Chorus. Under Peter Coe's direction the self-consciously artificial qualities of the play were stressed by tableau staging, with the French on the central balcony, the comic characters on the left and right balconies, and the English centre stage. The French were unindividuated, all dressed in blue-black costumes and given a sinister force. In 1984 Kevin Kline played Henry in Central Park directed by Wilfred Leach, in a production which used aspects of the play which might be thought to compromise Henry to establish him as a positive hero, including having him kill one of the French prisoners himself. The *New York Times* headed its review 'Finally, This Henry Becomes a Living, Breathing Hero.'[183]

The most important American production was not a heroic inter-pretation, but Michael Kahn's controversial version for the American Shakespeare Festival at Stratford, Connecticut, in 1969. Amid growing protests about the ongoing war in Vietnam, Kahn saw little to admire in the play's depiction of warfare. Kahn used the metaphor of a game for the pro-duction, beginning with an improvisational opening scene in which the company, dressed in jeans and T-shirts, played ball on the forestage as the audience took their seats. 'Finally they lay on their backs, kicking their feet in the air and hissing. And the Prologue is delivered by several individuals, the group periodically interjecting its first phrase "O for a Muse of Fire" as a refrain.' The set was designed to recall a children's adventure playground, with a large swing on which Henry (Len Cariou) was crowned. Battles were fought with the juvenile play-weapons of sticks and oil-drums, as a Harfleur patently constructed of cardboard and brown paper was pelted with small balls. The French wore heavily padded sports clothing and cricket batsmen's shinpads, and their scenes were translated into French and retranslated by interpreters on the side of the stage. Kahn was concerned to show the contra-dictions in Henry, as a man

> who loves his men and yet is always willing to sacrifice them; a man who at
> one moment can weep over the death of one of his lords and upon the next

183 *New York Times*, 15 July 1984.

> instant order the throats cut of prisoners taken in war . . . a man who can
> woo willingly and humbly at one moment and strike a hard bargain on his
> defeated future in-laws in the next

but the overall impression from reviewers was that the production was
explicitly negative about Henry rather than ambiguous or balanced. The
New York Times review was headed 'Betrayal of the Bard': its author railed
against a production in which 'what Mr Kahn has most wanted is to demonstrate his superiority to Shakespeare's play'.[184] The use of Brechtian alien-
ation techniques to preface each scene with an oral announcement of its title
gave a clear steer about audience interpretation. For example, the scene of
the conspirators' discovery (2.2), was headed 'Ruses. The First Victims. The
Emergence of the Warrior King', and the St Crispin's Day speech before
Agincourt 'The Machine Creates the Believable Lie. Point of No Return'.
The dead of Agincourt remained on stage as masked spectres throughout the
wooing scene, resuming the children's games that had begun the play.

In addition to these North American productions a couple of continental
European Henrys are notable, as much for their rarity as for their specific
interpretation of the play. *Henry V* is the only one of Shakespeare's histories
to have been virtually ignored in Europe and the Slavic world.[185] Two significant exceptions, from Germany and France, should be cited. German director Peter Zadek's *Held Henry* (Henry the Hero), which opened in Bremen in
1964, is described by Wilhelm Hortman as 'a pacifist collage, an ahistorical
multimedia show against heroism and militarism. The text was not greatly
changed, but many means were employed to reinforce the message that patriotism is *made* and that the hero is a *product* of cult and of manipulation.' Thus
film projection showed Hitler's troops marching into Paris and Henry taking
their salute. Kings and queens pictured on a backdrop were shown to be
interchangeable with contemporary celebrities and politicians, as some of
them were changing into images of Hitler, Stalin, Billy Graham, Nazi rocket
scientist Wernher von Braun, football stars and so on. Zadek's Henry was
a particularly television-conscious public figure for a modern age.[186] Zadek
thus made *Henry V* speak to post-war Germany's uneasy fascination with
and terror of military heroes.

---

184 Cooper, *The American Shakespeare Theatre*, pp. 148–9; *New York Times*, 15 June
1969.
185 Thomas Healy, 'Remembering with Advantages: Nation and Ideology in *Henry V*'
in *Shakespeare in the New Europe*, eds. Michael Hattaway, Boika Sokolova and Derek
Roper (Sheffield: Sheffield Academic Press, 1994), pp. 174–93, p. 175.
186 Wilhelm Hortman, *Shakespeare on the German Stage: The Twentieth Century*
(Cambridge: Cambridge University Press, 1995), p. 222.

In France the play's history of Francophobic associations ensured that it was not performed in French until the Avignon Festival in 1999, when it was directed by Jean-Louis Benoit. The production was greeted with chauvinistic disdain. Thomas Healy imagines that a production of the play in modern France would be 'a perverse beast':[187] perversity seems to have been the main feature of this production. Benoit's decision to play up Shakespeare's negative representation of the French as braggarts, 'jerky feathered puppets, stupefied simpletons, escaped lunatics' as one onlooker described, was particularly reviled, with one reviewer feeling that the production had aspired to the absurdist condition of *Monty Python* but reached only the level of *Astérix*. Philippe Torreton, who played a ferocious, quick-tempered Henry, was widely quoted as fanning the flames: 'Shakespeare really does portray the French as a bunch of pretentious cretins. Yet I'm afraid my compatriots [are] pretty much the same today – which is to say rather more arrogant than effective on the field of battle.'[188] Both play and production were generally condemned: *Libération* damned it as 'one of the least exciting of Shakespeare's plays done as burlesque'.[189] Pasteboard castles and self-evidently wooden sabres made sense of the Chorus' protestations about theatrical inadequacy, and did not attempt to hide the artificiality of the production, but there were few positive words for the enterprise in the French press. The translator, Jean-Michel Déprats, agreed that the play posed particular difficulties for French audiences, who had little reason to identify with its account of a patriotic English triumph.[190] The stage history of the play – the films by Olivier and Branagh, as well as the recent production at the Globe Theatre in London and the apparently anti-French reactions of its audiences, were all mentioned in French newspaper coverage of the production: it seems from this single French example that the juggernaut of the play's associations in the English-speaking theatre could not be halted.

RSC – BBC

Like Quayle in the Festival of Britain year, and Barton and Hall for the Shakespeare Quartercentenary and the Royal Shakespeare Company during

187 Healy, 'Remembering with Advantages', p. 177.
188 *Daily Telegraph*, 14 July 1999; *Guardian*, 11 July 1999. Of course, there is a certain chauvinistic relish in these British newspaper reports.
189 *Libération*, 12 July 1999: 'là où il rêvait peut-être de retrouver l'esprit des Monty Python, il se hisse péniblement au niveau d'*Astérix*'; 'L'une des pièces les moins palpitantes de Shakespeare en version burlesque'.
190 *Le Monde*, 11–12 July 1999: '*Henry V* est une pièce portée par le lyrisme d'un triomphe patriotique anglais auquel il y a peu de raisons que les Français s'identifient.'

the Millennium year, Terry Hands also chose the play, and a cycle, for another celebration – this time the centenary of the Stratford Shakespeare Theatre in 1975. Hands' cycle stressed not the epic of guilt and expiation traced through a sequence from *Richard II* to *Henry V* and often called the Henriad, but 'a rather muted national epic, a *Bildungsroman* structured around a three-cornered Oedipal contest between Prince Hal, Bolingbroke and Falstaff': *Henry IV Parts I and II*, *The Merry Wives of Windsor* and *Henry V*.[191] The production made use of some interesting cross-casting, so that the Boy was played by Peter Bourke, who had played Francis in *Henry IV*, and the Chorus, played by Emrys James, registered the uncanny presence of Henry's father. Many of these connections, however, were occluded by the structure of the sequence: *Henry V* opened a month before *Henry IV Part I* and *Part II* opened two months after that, and because *Henry V* was the most financially successful, it remained as a stand-alone in the RSC repertoire in Stratford, London and on tour until 1978, long after the other plays of the sequence had been dropped.

Most strikingly, financial constraints made a spectacular production impossible, and necessitated a minimalist style more in keeping with the Chorus. A cast of twenty-five carried the play, with an English army numbering seven. Farrah's designs stripped out all the cladding from the Royal Shakespeare Theatre, revealing the bare brick of the proscenium arch and the pipes, bridges, lamps and wiring of the stage machinery. The stage had a fierce one-in-twelve rake and bare boards, 'designed to launch the actors into the audience' and 'to give the audience a sense of danger' in the storming of Harfleur. The visual austerity of the production was softened by the use of a large canopy, initially brightly decorated with heraldic designs and hung over the heads of the actors to suggest a richly adorned ceiling. This later collapsed on to the ground, revealing a muddy underside to represent the field of Agincourt, and making a strong visual connection between the chivalric pageantry and the slaughter. The production began, like Michael Kahn's, with the cast in their rehearsal clothes, stressing the formal artificiality of the robed French Ambassador with his gift of tennis balls (fig. 8), and gradually as the play continued their costumes developed into medieval garb. The Chorus, however, remained in a casual open-necked shirt throughout, emphasising his separation from the action and his focus as a theatrical device. Role-playing was the key interpretive insight of the production: through role-playing Alan Howard's Henry found the inner strength to lead his men and to discover himself in his

191 Robert Shaughnessy, *Representing Shakespeare: England, History and the RSC* (New York and London: Harvester Wheatsheaf, 1994), p. 105.

8 Act 1: Alan Howard and his court in 'rehearsal' clothes in Terry Hands' 1975
production.

kingship in a 'long Odyssey of self-exploration'[192] following on from the
Henry IV plays.

Howard's Henry was a quiet, slightly neurotic figure, whose tears after the
surrender of Harfleur revealed that his threats had been a risky bluff, and
whose agony of grief at the treachery of Scroop showed his vulnerability. For
at least one critic, however, this aspect was overdone: 'in real life Brigadier
Exeter and Regimental Sergeant-Major Gower would have seen to it that
their commander-in-chief was quietly invalided out before his jitters
infected the whole army'.[193] The speech before Agincourt was delivered
almost impromptu as the commander moved among his troops, This was
not, however, a production focused on one-man heroics, but, as Terry Hands
made clear in interviews and the souvenir book of the production, an allegory
for the teamwork of the theatre itself, of the Royal Shakespeare Company
battling with straitened circumstances and, by clever insinuation, of the

192 Sally Beauman, *The Royal Shakespeare Company's Production of Henry V for the
Centenary Season at the Royal Shakespeare Theatre* (Oxford and New York:
Pergamon Press, 1976), p. 31; p. 34; p. 55.

193 Richard David, *Shakespeare in the Theatre* (Cambridge: Cambridge University
Press, 1978), p. 198.

struggles of contemporary Britain: 'a special message of courage to the English in times of gathering darkness, fear, and falling empires'.[194] The backdrop of the ignominious ending of the Vietnam conflict and the escalation of bloodshed in British army-occupied Northern Ireland gave the circumstances of 1975 some striking similarities to those of the play's original performance in 1599. Rather than articulating this, however, the production took what James Loehlin has described as a stance 'typical of the 1970s, frankly apolitical'.[195] Thus the unity the production sought to enlighten was not primarily national or military, but 'that of individuals aware of their responsibilities, both to themselves and to each other, voluntarily accepting some abdication of that individuality in a final non-hierarchic interdependence – a real brotherhood'.[196] This non-hierarchic interdependence did not make the production inappropriate for a Royal Gala performance in front of the Queen, and Prince Philip wrote the foreword to the commemorative volume of the play issued by the RSC. Ultimately, then, the production managed to compromise: one review recognised that Hands 'is not going to heroise Hal and glamorise conquest, nor does he want to slant things the other way, satirising and condemning a bloodthirsty crusade'.[197] Hands' was the ultimate liberal interpretation of the play, which neither glorified nor denigrated the play's heroics, and the ultimate dramatisation of Rabkin's idea of the play's 'inscrutability'.[198] Its popularity at the box office was testament to the contemporary astuteness of his directorial judgement: *Henry V* had boosted the financial viability of the RSC at a difficult time, just as it had established Augustus Harris' management in Drury Lane almost a century previously.

Having seemed innovative in 1951, the decision to place *Henry V* in a sequence of history plays was quickly turned into a convention, as was confirmed by the decision of the producers of the conservative BBC Shakespeare series for television to engage the same actor, David Gwillim, and director, David Giles, through the *Henry IV* and *Henry V* plays. Gwillim's was not the first television Henry. In 1938 Dallas Bower, later to co-write the filmscript for Olivier's *Henry V* with Alan Dent, prepared a version of the play for the BBC, but it was rejected as too ambitious for the new medium. By the 1950s these doubts had been overcome, and there was a rash of BBC TV Henrys, all of which had their origins in stage productions. Clement

---

194 Beauman, *The Royal Shakespeare Company's Production*, p. 6.
195 James N. Loehlin, *Shakespeare in Performance: Henry V* (Manchester: Manchester University Press, 1996).
196 Beauman, *The Royal Shakespeare Company's Production*, p. 15.
197 *New Statesman*, 18 April 1975.
198 Rabkin, *Shakespeare and the Problem of Meaning*, p. 296.

McCallin, who had played the role before the war in Ben Iden Payne's 1937 production at Stratford, was directed for television in 1951 by Leonard Brett and Royston Morley. Colin George was directed by Peter Watts in 1953, in a production by the newly formed Elizabethan Theatre Company of recent Oxbridge graduates, whose motto 'Into a thousand parts divide one man' was taken from the play, and whose brief was essentially Elizabethanist. The television broadcast was a ninety-minute version of a three-hour stage production which toured a number of festivals and venues during the spring and summer of Coronation year. A week later the BBC also broadcast, this time on radio, a production of the play with John Clements as Henry, Valentine Dyall as Shakespeare/Chorus, and, to give added historical authenticity to this play from what was becoming known as the first Eliza-bethan age, the additional role of Raphael Holinshed, the Tudor historian. John Neville, who had played the role at the Old Vic, was directed by Peter Dews for television in 1957, and in 1960 *Henry V* was shown as parts 7, 'Signs of War', and 8, 'The Band of Brothers', of the historical sequence *An Age of Kings: A Pageant of English History*, a version in fifteen hour-long episodes, broadcast fortnightly, of the *Richard II* to *Richard III* cycle. Directed by Michael Hayes, Robert Hardy played Henry in the *Henry IV* plays as well as in *Henry V*. In 1964 a version of the play was broadcast for schools. In the late 1970s, in partnership with TimeLife, the BBC mounted a production of the complete works of Shakespeare, including David Giles' production of *Henry V*, first broadcast in December 1979.

Giles opted, like Olivier, for an anti-illusionistic use of the studio set, arguing that the play was essentially stylised: 'If you do a realistic *Henry V* then you must cut the Chorus, and if you cut the Chorus you don't do *Henry V*.'[199] He chose to place 'realistic facades against a flat white cycloramic background', beginning the action with the Chorus 'in limbo' and then 'slowly advancing towards the camera with a frozen English and French Court in front of a set of medieval castles'.[200] The costumes were, in nineteenth-century manner, carefully researched medieval reconstructions, with assistance from historians and the Royal College of Arms on heraldry and banners, although the set itself was studiedly non-historical, as the set designer, Don Homfray, asserted: '*Henry V* [is] nothing to do with social history, nothing to do with the state of England, it's to do with idealism and

---

199 Harry Fenwick, 'The Production', *The BBC Shakespeare: Henry V* (London: British Broadcasting Corporation, 1979), p. 19.

200 Susan Willis, *The BBC Shakespeare Plays: Making the Televised Canon* (Chapel Hill and London: University of North Carolina Press, 1991), p. 204; Cedric Messina, 'Preface', *The BBC Shakespeare: Henry V*, p. 7.

heroism'.[201] Colour distinctions between the French, in traditional blues, and the English, in beige and brown, were intended to make the story easier to follow for its projected education audience of school and college students as well as general television viewers.

The constraints of studio shooting meant that this was inevitably a small-scale production, favouring domestic-scale angles and medium close-ups, showing, for example, tears in Henry's eyes after he despatches Scroop, Cambridge and Grey. Gwillim was often shot in profile, turning him into the public, static image of a monarch on a coin or medal, and the most naturalistic scenes were, like Olivier's, those at a grassy Agincourt. The idea of a female Chorus was toyed with and rejected, and Alec McCowen played the role as both apart from the action and part of it, entering to give his second speech by catching one of the Dauphin's tennis balls as 1.2 ended in merry sport with the gift. Looking straight to camera, he performed an explicatory, narrative function and drew a kind of authority from televisual association of 'talking heads' for news and other serious programming.

POST-FALKLANDS: NOBLE, BOGDANOV AND BRANAGH

If the BBC hoped that David Gwillim would be 'a Henry for the audience of the 1980s', this was a vain wish.[202] The mood of the decade was identified less with the bland, studio-bound medieval heroism of the television production, and more with the anti-heroic mood of the Thatcherite and post-Falklands era of British politics. Adrian Noble's 1984 production at Stratford took the divergent interpretations of Henry's character as a keynote of the production, with parallel essays in the programme under the headings 'hero-king' and 'scourge of God'. Here was a story of political pragmatism and the muddy, rainy realities of modern warfare, with Bardolph executed on stage as the troops huddled under tarpaulins (fig. 9). As the young Kenneth Branagh, who played Henry, wrote, 'he is a complicated, doubting, dangerous young professional, neither straightforwardly good nor consciously evil'.[203]

Ian McDiarmid played Chorus as a 'wry commentator in timeless costume who remains on stage throughout', a presence who adopts 'a bitchily jocose manner with a swirl of his mephisthophelian black cloak', and Branagh performed a Henry capable of a violence one reviewer dubbed 'psychotic' as

201 Fenwick, 'The Production', p. 20.   202 *Ibid.*, p. 25.
203 Kenneth Branagh, *Beginning* (London: Chatto & Windus, 1989), p. 139.

9   The execution of Bardolph in Adrian Noble's 1984 production.

well as suggesting 'intelligence, gentleness and charm'.[204] In his autobiography, Branagh compared Henry to Hamlet, as a man haunted by his father and
their troubled relationship, and by the ghost of Richard II, and vowed that
'Henry's genuine humility in relation to God would be a cornerstone of my
interpretation'. Branagh consulted Prince Charles in order 'to get my imagination around Henry's royal status, the isolation of his role as spiritual and
military leader', and took from him a sense of the 'delicate balance between
responsibility and compassion'.[205] Bob Crowley's spare designs for the
Royal Shakespeare Theatre stressed concrete, brick and steel. While there
was no actual fighting on stage, artfully choreographed movement with military standards and smoke conveyed the terrible beauty of the battle. As usual,
spectacle was used to characterise the French, who descended before
Agincourt 'godlike, on golden tea-trays', providing 'a scintillating vision of
hubristic splendour' in their shiny armour.[206]

204 *The Times*, 30 March 1984; *Financial Times*, 29 March 1984; *Observer*, 1 April 1984.
205 Branagh, *Beginning*, p. 139; pp. 141–2.
206 *Times Literary Supplement*, 13 April 1984; *Financial Times*, 29 March 1984.

Michael Bogdanov's touring production of the *Richard II* to *Henry V* sequence, later extended to include the *Henry VI* plays and *Richard III*, picked up the mid-twentieth century's taste for the plays as a sequence. Video recordings of the plays are available: *Henry V* is a live performance from the Grand Theatre, Swansea released on commercial video in 1990. Inevitably, over a long run, cast changes, and a huge variety of playing spaces the production changed shape, and James Loehlin has argued that it became less radical over the tour.[207] For Bogdanov, the history plays 'were plays for today, the lessons of history unlearnt', and *Henry V* particularly insistently modern, 'with its war of expedience, ruthless manipulation, bribery and corruption, palpable pacifism, the French superior in numbers but beaten by superior technology'.[208] Bogdanov's interpretive clarity – his *Henry V* was not, as other anti-heroic productions, founded on ambiguity but on a certainty about the play's anti-war message – resulted in some striking images. When Pistol, Bardolph and Nym left Mistress Quickly for the battle at the end of 2.3, the poignancy of the moment was swiftly subverted by their chant, football-supporter style, of 'Here we go', as Union Jacks, bunting, and a banner proclaiming 'Fuck the Frogs' were unfurled on the balcony. The Chorus crossed the stage carrying a placard spelling 'Gotcha' – the infamous headline from the *Sun* newspaper on the sinking of the Argentinian cruiser the *General Belgrano* during the Falklands War – against the patriotic music to 'Jerusalem', thus implicating the play in contemporary discourses of Falklands militarism, 'Last Night of the Proms' flag-waving, tabloid demotic and xenophobic soccer hooliganism. Michael Bogdanov discussed the parallels his production was attempting to draw: 'Imperialism encourages jingoism. So the Falklands. So Agincourt. "Fuck the Frogs". The banner hung out by the send-off crowd at Southampton . . . grew out of the desire to bridge nearly six hundred years of this same bigoted xenophobic patriotism.'

That this had its intended effect is made clear: 'A letter from a member of the public. "The use of the word was offensive and the term 'Frogs' hardly helps promote racial harmony and dispel old prejudices. I was ashamed to be English." Precisely. The case rests.'[209] The reviewer for the *Guardian* commented that the production was 'the first version I've ever seen where you wanted the French to win'.[210] Bogdanov's relentlessly cynical dissection of

---

207 Loehlin, *Shakespeare in Performance*, p. 123.
208 Michael Bogdanov and Michael Pennington, *The English Shakespeare Company: The Story of The Wars of the Roses, 1986–1989* (London: Nick Hern Books, 1990), p. 24; p. 30.
209 *Sun*, 4 May 1982; Bogdanov and Pennington, *The English Shakespeare Company*, p. 48.
210 *Guardian*, 23 March 1987.

the play was a queasy triumph, but an interpretation from which later productions turned away.

In his autobiography, Kenneth Branagh recalled an interview in 1982
with RSC director Ron Daniels, who would direct *Henry V* in 1997, about a
possible production with Branagh in the title role. 'What do you see in the
play?' asked Branagh. 'Mud,' replied Daniels.[211] In the end, Branagh's stage
performance was directed by Adrian Noble, but the association of mud with
the play resurfaced in Branagh's own film of 1989. The film used many of the
details of the stage production, but its overall ideological position was
significantly different. Chris Fitter has argued that in place of Noble's
faith-fully sardonic and poignant interpretation, the film restores 'a fellowly,
idealised Harry', excising some of the theatre production's most telling
moments: 'What Shakespeare has demystified, Branagh persuasively,
affably, immorally, has sanctified.'[212] Part of Branagh's film project was,
inevitably, to take on Olivier's filmic legacy, and in the publicity for the film
he also seemed repeatedly to identify his careerist ambitions with Henry's
own titanic struggle. A baby-faced Branagh – his first appearance in 1.2 is
designed to juxtapose the grandiose imagery of kingship with his own slight,
youthful demeanour among his older advisors – took on the mantle of
Olivier, and also two previous Henrys – Paul Scofield, who had played the
part in 1946 and here played the French King, and Ian Holm, Henry in the
1964 production, here as Llewellyn.

In many ways the two films by Olivier and Branagh are similar, despite
their obvious differences of mood and emphasis. Like Olivier, Branagh constructed flashback sequences to fill in the context of Falstaff's death, movingly related by Judi Dench as Mistress Quickly; Branagh's St Crispin's Day
oration delivered from a cart recalls Olivier's; his reworking of the Prologue
replaces Olivier's Elizabethanism with the demystification of his own art,
as the Chorus of Derek Jacobi moves among the gantries and cameras of a
film set. Although Branagh's cuts to those aspects of the play that have been
problematic for pro-Henry productions were less substantial than those
of Olivier, the screenplay worked similarly to minimise obstacles to a positive interpretation. Henry's threats before Harfleur, shorn of their worst
excesses, are moderated by the close-up of his relief after the town's surrender, as if he had been bluffing; the execution of Bardolph also uses a close-up
of Henry's face suggesting that he does not order this without personal grief;

211 Branagh, *Beginning*, p. 133.
212 Chris Fitter, 'A Tale of Two Branaghs: *Henry V*, Ideology, and the Mekong
     Agincourt' in *Shakespeare Left and Right*, ed. Ivo Kamps (London and New York:
     Routledge, 1991), p. 260; p. 275.

10 After the battle: Kenneth Branagh's 1989 film.

his wooing seems sincere and ingenuous. Branagh's film does not glorify or underestimate the costs of war: the most telling sequence is the extended tracking shot after the battle, as Henry, caked with mud and blood (fig. 10) and carrying the corpse of the murdered Boy, walks through the terrible field of carnage in slow motion against a rising choral soundtrack. Nor does he minimise Henry's individual heroism, and this parable of personal decency and bravery in a brutal situation drew on the modern ethics of warrior masculinity established by intelligent Vietnam films such as *Apocalypse Now* (dir. Francis Ford Coppola, 1979) and *Platoon* (dir. Oliver Stone, 1986), and, to some extent, on their aesthetics of slow-motion, choreographed conflict.

The film's costuming and set were faithfully medieval apart from the anachronistic presence of an overcoated Chorus, both of and outside the action. The associations of muddy boots marching doggedly through the rain evoked more recent conflicts. These echoes of the First World War were picked up more explicitly in the Royal Shakespeare Company's 1994 production at Stratford, directed by Matthew Warchus with Iain Glen as

Henry. Tony Britton, as the Chorus, was dressed in an overcoat and wearing a poppy as for a Remembrance Day service, 'quietly proud but also heavy with experience: he knows . . . that the survivor is a bitter witness as well as a glamorous hero', and the red of the King's robes – which Henry put on to greet the ambassadors in 1.2 – was insistently echoed in poppies strewing the stage. During the Battle of Agincourt, the old soldier helped Henry to his feet. Glen's Henry gave the impression of 'a puritan convert', 'someone painfully trying to square desire with justice, violence with piety', in a performance 'that avoids both Olivier's triumphalism and the post-Falklands ennui of Branagh and Pennington'. His central performance suggested, in Nicholas de Jongh's words, the play as an 'epic of regal neurosis in the face of warfare rather than as complacent royalist propaganda'.[213] Glen stressed Henry's spirituality: he held a cross given to him by the Archbishop as he prayed before the battle, and the list of the Agincourt casualties was read unusually slowly so that each name could sink in. He was also, however, an active military leader, playing a full part in physical activities including hauling the luggage and swinging on a rope on to the parapets during the siege of Harfleur. Warchus made interesting use of some tableau effects in a nod to nineteenth-century stagings of the play: Falstaff's death, for example, was described against an upstage tableau of Henry holding his sword in heroic pose, and the scene between Pistol and Le Fer was played against a frozen tableau of Agincourt (fig. 11). The *Independent* noted the irony that the RSC production in 1994 had opened in the week after the Channel Tunnel: 'since for all the avowals of entente cordiale with which the play ends, it's not the one you'd pick to commemorate the forging of new ties with Europe'.[214]

A number of reviews criticised the laziness of characterising the French as dandified and effete, as they did again for the RSC's next revival only three years later in 1997. Ron Daniels' small-scale touring production with a youthful Michael Sheen as a roguish, sometimes psychotically angry Henry, employed camouflage, smoke and heavy ordnance to give a thoroughly contemporary realism to the battle scenes played against a set covered with engraved names, suggesting the Vietnam Veterans Memorial in Washington D.C. The French, in contrast to the gritty style of the English army, were dazzling in golden armour, and rode golden hobby-horses with visible steel legs under their metallic caparisons. The programme for the production stressed the cost of war and its psychological effects on its par-

213 *Sunday Times*, 15 May 1994; *The Times*, 12 May 1994; *Evening Standard*, 11 May 1994.
214 *Independent*, 12 May 1994.

11 Tableau of the Battle of Agincourt in Matthew Warchus' 1994 production.

ticipants, with extensive quotation from contemporary military leaders and commentators.

THE GLOBE: THE 'WOODEN O' COMES FULL CIRCLE

Daniels, like Hands and Noble and Branagh and Bogdanov and Warchus, chose *Henry V* for its contemporary resonances. Theirs is a strand of the play's stage history which goes back to Kemble's productions against the background of revolution in France, and which includes Kean, Calvert, Waller, Benson and Olivier, all of whose interpretations were in some way shaped by the play's perceived relation to current events. There is, however, another, more recent stage history of the play: that of Poel and Martin-Harvey and Quayle, whose interest in the play has been historical, Elizabethanist. *Henry V*'s inscription of the conditions of its original performance in the speeches of Chorus, and its central role in twentieth-century

12   The audience and the stage in Mark Rylance's 1997 production at
Shakespeare's Globe.

debates about 'authentic' staging, made it an inevitable choice for the
opening season of the ambitious project to rebuild Shakespeare's Globe
Theatre on London's Bankside. Directed by Richard Olivier, son of
Laurence, the production needs to be seen in the light of earlier experiments
with 'Elizabethan staging', as well as Olivier's film and its patriotic
antecedents. The Globe's manifesto was of authenticity in every detail, from
the design of the stage to the design of the actors' underclothes ('No Calvin
Klein here', as the designer, Jenny Tiramani, modishly put it in the souvenir
programme), and thus necessitated an all-male cast for the production. It
also seemed to require what one review called a 'defiantly unfashionable'
reading of the play which de-emphasised the dark elements stressed by
Hands, Noble and Bogdanov, and which chose instead to explore what
Richard Olivier called the 'myth' of the play.

One important element of the Globe's staging was the encouragement
of audience participation. At almost every performance, the French were
roundly booed and hissed in pantomime fashion, and although the production denied orchestrating these responses, such popular expressions of

xenophobia disconcerted many reviewers. Patrick Marmion, writing in the *Evening Standard*, found the audience approval of the slaughter of the French prisoners and the raucous enjoyment of Toby Cockerell's cross-dressed Katherine as appealing to 'lowest common denominator slapstick'.[215] This kind of robust audience response overshadowed the nuances of Mark Rylance's performance as an introspective, rather wistful character, 'only reluctantly bellicose', with 'a strong sense of conscience'. The role of Chorus was split between different actors in the company, to stress the idea of a collaborative story-telling project, and some of the historical background to Henry's kingship was filled in by an introductory ballad. Heavy doubling and, in some cases, trebling of roles enabled the production to run with a cast of fifteen, and often added to the performance by suggesting parallels between characters: the King of France and Erpingham, for example, both veterans of previous wars, or the English traitors and the French lords, or Katherine and the Boy.

The production's major interest was its revival of performance conditions as close to those of the original as theatrical scholarship could ascertain. Despite this, there were calls from reviewers for a more spectacular style. Benedict Nightingale's review in *The Times* could have come from a nineteenth-century notice for Macready or Kean: 'A small English army looks like a slightly expanded version of the Famous Five. Even so, the alarums sounded muffled, the scaling ladders mentioned in the stage direction did not appear, the smoke of war was a cigarette puff, the offstage yells were few and unmartial, and the soldiery seemed unflustered and unenergetic.'[216] Thus the ongoing struggle over the production style for the play, which can be traced throughout its stage history, continues to rumble. The Globe's late twentieth-century brief, to return to the original Elizabethan playing conditions, cannot bypass the questions that have animated the play in production over the intervening four centuries. Is this a play requiring archaeological research or updating? Is this a play about, or against, war? Is this a realist depiction, or a stylised pageant? Is this celebratory or condemnatory? Stage history reminds us answers to these questions can only ever be provisional and historically constituted: in production, *Henry V* continues to offer new possibilities.

215 *Evening Standard*, 9 June 1997.
216 *Observer*, 15 June 1997; *The Times*, 7 June 1997.

KING HENRY V

LIST OF CHARACTERS

CHORUS

CANTERBURY

ELY

KING

GLOUCESTER

BEDFORD

EXETER

WESTMORLAND

CLARENCE

AMBASSADOR

BARDOLPH

NYM

PISTOL

HOSTESS

BOY

SCROOP

CAMBRIDGE

GRAY

FRENCH KING

DAUPHIN

BERRI

BOURBON

CONSTABLE

MESSENGER

LLEWELLYN

GOWER

MACMORRIS

JAMY

GOVERNOR

KATHERINE

ALICE

MONTJOY

RAMBURES

ORLÉANS

ERPINGHAM

BATES

COURT

WILLIAMS

BEAUMONT

GRANDPRÉ

SALISBURY

YORK

FRENCH *Soldier*

WARWICK

English HERALD

QUEEN *Isabel*

BURGUNDY

Attendants, soldiers

THE LIFE OF HENRY THE FIFTH

Prologue *Enter* CHORUS

CHORUS O for a muse of fire, that would ascend
        The brightest heaven of invention,

The Prologue, like the rest of the Chorus speeches, was not included in the Quarto text as published in 1600, and it was also omitted in a number of eighteenth- and nineteenth-century productions. Its purpose, to introduce the play and to raise audience expectation, has been otherwise served by different ways of beginning the play. In 1761 the scene of Henry's coronation interpolated from *2 Henry IV* prefaced the play, in honour of George III's coronation, and this practice was continued through the eighteenth century. Coleman's 1876 production revived and expanded this interpolation, inserting a lengthy prologue from the earlier play, including Henry IV's speech on sleep, Prince Hal's taking of the crown from his father's bed, his accession and reconciliation with the Chief Justice. As in Orson Welles' more thoroughgoing amalgamation of elements and scenes from *Richard II*, *Henry IV* and *Henry V* in the film *Chimes at Midnight* (1966), these prefatory additions serve to situate the play in historical sequence. Other openings have taken up the Chorus' function of establishing the place or mood of the play that follows. Laurence Olivier's film begins with a long aerial shot of a picture postcard Elizabethan London, the camera zooming in on the Globe Theatre as it prepares to start a performance, advertised on a blown playbill, and later by a boy carrying a placard on to the stage, as 'The Chronicle History of King Henry the Fift with his Battell fought at Agincourt in France. By Will Shakspeare'. The camera pans around the filling theatre, on gallants and groundlings and fruit-sellers and young children: 'there is a general bustle of anticipation throughout' (O, Fol). Other pieces of stage business have been introduced to begin the play. Both Michael Kahn and Terry Hands began the play gradually, as the actors wandered on to the stage dressed in their ordinary clothes as theatre patrons were finding their seats: 'it was essential that the actor should be made as aware of *his* function within the collaboration as the audience were to be of theirs' (Beauman, p. 101). The Globe production of 1997 opened with all the cast on stage, dressed simply in white shirts and hose, doing rhythmic African drumming in 'a deliberate anachronism intended to represent the "heartbeat" of the Globe space – an organic building that breathes along with both playgoers and actors during performance' (Kiernan, p. 99). This exciting, warlike sound reached a crescendo before stopping, at the knocking of a heavy stave on the stage, for Mark Rylance, the theatre's artistic director and the actor playing Henry, to step forward to deliver Chorus.

The Chorus' demystificatory remarks on the space and resources of the theatre have been taken as a cue for the staging of other productions. At the RSC, Terry Hands in 1975 and Adrian Noble in 1984 opened on a bare stage stripped back to the brick; the first (and also the last) sight of the stage in Matthew Warchus' 1994 production was 'the king's red robes marooned in a cluster of poppies' (*T* 12 May 1994), roped off like a museum exhibit, immediately calling up the associations of the First World War and Remembrance Day. Adrian Noble's production placed a female cellist on the forestage during the first act to provide 'an ironic counterpart to the rhetorical posturings' (Shaughnessy, p. 117). The Chorus' non-naturalistic function was expressed in this production by having him switch out the houselights, 'taking the audience from his contemporary perspective on the history of war into the play's sense of its own history' (Holland, p. 194).

During the 1740s the role of Chorus was often included, with Garrick taking the part in 1747 and 1748 in eighteenth-century costume. Bell's edition of the play, however, cuts the Choruses, and in his 1789 revival, John Kemble followed this version, as did Macready in his first attempts at the play in the 1820s and early 1830s and, almost a century later, Frank Benson for most of his revivals at Stratford and London. Macready's 1839 production, however, triumphantly reinstated the Chorus, arguing that Shakespeare had adopted 'from the Greek Drama the expedient of a Chorus to narrate and describe intervening incidents and events' (*Diaries*, ed. Toynbee, p. 7): 'On the rising of the green curtain, a handsome drapery is seen with the arms of France and England emblazoned on either side, the initials of the two reigning monarchs, "H" and "C" being introduced on the ornamental bordering.' The drapery parted to reveal Chorus as the figure of Time, standing on a pedestal at the side of an enormous framework of painted clouds and bearing a scythe and hourglass *(The Spectator*, no. 572, 15 June 1839). The innovation of picturing Chorus as Time, perhaps taken from the choric speech in *The Winter's Tale*, was continued in Samuel Phelps' production of 1852, where Mr Marston appeared leaning on a small platform in front of an arrangement of 'circular screens representing a frame with the Armorial bearings of England' and 'curtains with the lion & fleur de Lice emblazoned thereupon' (Phelps pbk).

Another Shakespearean chorus figure was borrowed to give shape to the unidentified Prologue: as Rumour from *2 Henry IV* Mrs Charles Calvert (1872) carried a golden trumpet in a stage landscape of 'grey rocks, [with] soft silk robes of a pale bluey grey, and a pale light upon Chorus, who stood under a clump of the rocks' (Mrs Charles Calvert, *Sixty-Eight Years on the Stage,* London: Mills and Boon, 1911, p. 139). Richard Mansfield's 1900 New York production also employed a woman in this role. From the mid-nineteenth century until the 1930s, Chorus was frequently cast as a woman, to aid the opportunities for actresses in an otherwise inhospitable play. In 1859 Charles Kean cast his wife as Clio, 'the Muse of History, looking like a fine polychrome statue and speaking in accents most musical . . . sanctified in her cloudy dwelling' (*Saturday Review*, 2 April 1859), 'first seen beneath a monopteral Ionic temple, polychromed' (*The Builder*, 2 April 1859). Mrs Kean wore a 'dark blue merino dress with scarlet robe, both trimmed with gold, golden wreath, and sandals' (Kean, p. 8) to identify her with the iconography of Britannia. John Coleman's 1876 production also cast a woman as Chorus in the guise of Clio, with the curtains opening to reveal her on a throne in the Temple of History. The role was played by a woman in Charles Calvert's production – firstly his wife, and later in the run by Mrs Brabrook Henderson – and at the Coronet in 1901, Benson's production cast a 'robed and laurelled' Lily Hanbury. Sybil Thorndike played it as an Elizabethan boy in Nigel Playfair's 1927–8 production at the Lyric, Hammersmith.

The Chorus has often been costumed to stress its detachment from the events of the play. In Matthew Warchus' production, Tony Britton as an upright, dignified, elderly Chorus was dressed in overcoat and campaign ribbons as for a Remembrance Day Service, a witness of past wars such as that remembered at 1.2.105–7. At Stratford, Ontario in 1980 Douglas Rain's casual costume of white crew-neck sweater and dark trousers made him seem 'a commentator on the performance rather than a participant' (*FT* 19 June 1980), and one reviewer found a similar analogy for Ian McCullough in 1987 'like a Prototype Dimbleby' (*I* 16 July 1987). Richard David, writing of Roger Livesey in Byam Shaw's production (1951), saw him as 'an actor in undress, and with the inadequate resources of his stage exposed behind him, come to plead for the audience's co-operation in the reconstruction of history' (*SS* 5 1952, p. 125). For the BBC television version directed by Michael Hayes, William Squire looks directly at the camera from amid the paraphernalia of a stage set; the later BBC version directed by David Giles had Alec McCowen as Chorus, standing still, also looking directly out at the audience from a plain black background. Adrian Noble's production began with the whole cast onstage, remaining there through 1.0. In Ron Daniels' RSC version of 1997, Chorus (Norman Rodway) entered in marching formation with other soldiers and wore the same high-buttoned military tunic. The unit's slow march through the simple box set, which was faced with thousands of names carved in stone in the manner of the Vietnam Veterans Memorial in Washington, D.C., was accompanied by a drum roll. The rest of the soldiers exited, leaving Chorus alone on stage to speak his lines. This Chorus doubled the role with Canterbury (as was common in eighteenth-century productions which included the Chorus) with the simple addition of a cross around his neck. Michael Bogdanov's production drew on a different kind of doubling, this time across the sequence of history plays. His Chorus was played by John Woodvine, who had played Falstaff in the previous plays of the series: 'Before he could open his mouth he was greeted with a spontaneous oration' from an audience 'delighted to find that the whoreson round man had in a sense survived Hal's mortal rejection to return in this trim and reconditioned form' (*Wars*, p. 60).

The tone of the Prologue has been varied. In directing his film Chorus, Derek Jacobi, Kenneth Branagh was 'trying to find a way in which his voice, his whole look, can draw people into this story, by making him a kind of everyman, a kind of, sort of timeless figure' (my transcription, from the ITV documentary 'A Little Touch of Harry: The Making of *Henry V*', National Film and Television Archive, British Film Institute, London, 8009740AA) and

A kingdom for a stage, princes to act,
And monarchs to behold the swelling scene.
Then should the warlike Harry, like himself,   5
Assume the port of Mars, and at his heels
(Leashed in, like hounds) should famine, sword and fire
Crouch for employment. But pardon, gentles all,
The flat unraisèd spirits, that hath dared,
On this unworthy scaffold, to bring forth   10
So great an object. Can this cockpit hold
The vasty fields of France? Or may we cram
Within this wooden O the very casques
That did affright the air at Agincourt?
Oh, pardon: since a crooked figure may   15

when he strikes a match to illuminate the darkness with which the film opens, his face is lit and his manner 'conversational, friendly, intimate. He welcomes us with the clarity and warmth of the great story-teller.' This immediacy contrasts with the description of Michael Redgrave at Stratford in 1951 as 'ceremonial, hieratic even' (David, p. 213), or Emrys James' (Hands, 1975) anonymous, low-key presence, or Roger Livesay (Byam Shaw, 1951) as a confidence-inspiring public relations officer, or Eric Porter's flamboyant 'swaggering elegance' in dandyish Elizabethan costume in Hall's production (*G* 4 June 1964), or Rylance's excited, exhortatory tone at the Globe in 1997.

1.0 To begin the play with the line 'O for a muse of fire' (1.0.1) is to begin with a rhetorical flourish. Olivier's film shows the Elizabethan theatre audience quieting as a flamboyantly-dressed Chorus begins his speech. A number of productions, particularly lavish Victorian spectacles which have included the Chorus have, nonetheless, chosen to cut those lines which stress theatrical inadequacy.

3 Derek Jacobi, in Branagh's film, pulls the switch to illuminate a staircase with electric light, discarding the match he lit at the beginning of his speech, and continues to descend.

7 Macready's dioramic staging made its first revelation here, with the painted cloud backdrop parting to show an allegorical representation of Henry with 'famine, sword and fire' like three Furies at his heels.

8–18 Cut by Calvert and Coleman.

9 Branagh's film makes it clear that Chorus is walking through an empty film set with lamps, scenery, camera towers etc.

11–13 Jacobi in Branagh's film 'speaks to camera like some mysterious MC' (Branagh, p. 16). Kean changed 'within this wooden O' to 'upon this little stage', and Phelps changed 'cockpit' to 'arena' and 'wooden O' (13) to 'little space' in deference to their respective theatres. The question in lines 11–12 was posed directly to the audience of the Globe Theatre in Richard Olivier's production of 1997, getting a number of yeses in return.

Attest in little place a million,
And let us, ciphers to this great account,
On your imaginary forces work.
Suppose within the girdle of these walls
Are now confined two mighty monarchies,   20
Whose high uprearèd and abutting fronts
The perilous narrow ocean parts asunder.
Piece out our imperfections with your thoughts.
Into a thousand parts divide one man,
And make imaginary puissance.   25
Think when we talk of horses that you see them
Printing their proud hooves i'th'receiving earth,
For 'tis your thoughts that now must deck our kings,
Carry them here and there, jumping o'er times,
Turning th'accomplishment of many years   30
Into an hour-glass. For the which supply
Admit me Chorus to this history,
Who, Prologue-like, your humble patience pray,
Gently to hear, kindly to judge our play.   *Exit*

1.1 *Enter the two Bishops of* CANTERBURY *and* ELY

CANTERBURY My lord, I'll tell you, that self bill is urged
            Which in th'eleventh year of the last king's reign

19 At this point in the 1979 BBC/Giles version, the lights come up to reveal a tableau of the French and English courts set out on either side of Chorus. The physical limitations of the 'girdle' are well illustrated by Hayes' BBC production (1960) as the narrow confines of a backstage corridor, against which Chorus braces his arms.

33–4 Cut by Calvert and Coleman.

34 McCowen (BBC/Giles) exits by stepping backwards into pitch black. Jacobi opens huge wooden doors with a dramatic flourish, to reveal only ominous darkness, stressing the bathos of the Chorus' heroic introduction, which leads only to two plotting prelates. Ian McDiarmid (Noble, 1984), gestured with his arms, 'asking us to share responsibility for the show' (*T* 30 March 1984).

1.1 This scene is not part of Q, and it was cut in its entirety by Macready pre-1839, Kean, Calvert, BBC/Hayes and Ron Daniels for the RSC ('destroy[ing] the bathetic contrast between the ostentatious appeal for a "muse of fire" and the spectacle of two princes of

> Was like, and had indeed against us passed
> But that the scambling and unquiet time
> Did push it out of farther question.   5
> ELY But how, my lord, shall we resist it now?
> CANTERBURY It must be thought on. If it pass against us
>   We lose the better half of our possession,
>   For all the temporal lands, which men devout
>   By testament have given to the Church   10
>   Would they strip from us, being valued thus:
>   As much as would maintain to the king's honour
>   Full fifteen earls and fifteen hundred knights,
>   Six thousand and two hundred good esquires,
>   And to relief of lazars and weak age   15
>   Of indigent faint souls, past corporal toil,
>   A hundred alms-houses, right well supplied;
>   And to the coffers of the king beside

the church trying to get out of paying their taxes' (Smallwood, p. 236)). Other directors have made significant cuts to the scene, often because, as Gerald Gould's revisionist article on the play in 1919 identified, the scene's representation of the cynicism of the prelates was a key example in a reading of the play as predominantly ironic. William Poel wrote to William Bridges-Adams about his 1920 production, praising as 'most effective' 'the pause of silence that took place at the end of the first . . . Chorus before the curtains opened over the first scene' (*RSC*, p. 236.). Many productions set the scene in an antechamber in the King's palace, and a shift in the representation of the clerics can be traced. Bell's edition noted that the bishops must have 'the appearance of dignified churchmen and decent solemnity of declamation' (Bell, p. 7), whereas Olivier's film presents Ely and Canterbury as bumbling actors on the stage balcony, unable to hold either the audience's interest or their own papers. In Glen Byam Shaw's 1951 production, Hugh Griffith's Archbishop was 'delightfully malicious and eccentric' (*Punch*, 15 August 1951). A more ominous tone was set by Michael Kahn, whose Brechtian surtitles for his 1969 production here offered 'The Church Becomes Frightened and Makes Plans' – with Canterbury and Ely dressed in padded, cartoonish style. At the Globe in 1997 the clerics, dressed in red habits, talked together at front of stage, the scene quiet, calm after the insistent drumming beat of Chorus. Branagh shot the scene at night-time, when the darkness adds to the sinister feel. The tight shot-reverse shot composition, with close-ups of Ely's and Canterbury's faces lit by candlelight, means that 'the atmosphere is tense and conspiratorial' (Branagh, p. 17)

9–20 Cut by Branagh.
11–20 Cut by Macready and Phelps.

   A thousand pounds by th'year. Thus runs the bill.

ELY This would drink deep.

CANTERBURY   'Twould drink the cup and all.   20

ELY But what prevention?

CANTERBURY The king is full of grace, and fair regard.

ELY And a true lover of the holy Church.

CANTERBURY The courses of his youth promised it not.

   The breath no sooner left his father's body   25

   But that his wildness, mortified in him,

   Seemed to die too. Yea, at that very moment

   Consideration like an angel came,

   And whipped th'offending Adam out of him,

   Leaving his body as a paradise   30

   T'envelop and contain celestial spirits.

   Never was such a sudden scholar made,

   Never came reformation in a flood

   With such a heady currance scouring faults,

   Nor never Hydra-headed wilfulness   35

   So soon did lose his seat, and all at once,

   As in this king.

ELY   We are blessed in the change.

CANTERBURY Hear him but reason in divinity,

   And all-admiring, with an inward wish,

   You would desire the king were made a prelate.   40

   Hear him debate of commonwealth affairs,

   You would say it hath been all in all his study.

   List his discourse of war, and you shall hear

   A fearful battle rendered you in music.

   Turn him to any cause of policy,   45

   The gordian knot of it he will unloose,

   Familiar as his garter, that when he speaks

   The air, a chartered libertine, is still,

24-69 Cut by Kemble, and pruned by Macready who cut 32–6, 52–3, 57–9. Branagh cut 25–54. Presumably the reminder of the King's wild youth, even in a context of his reformation, was considered potentially damaging. For different reasons, Hands cut 24–60 and 63–6: 'Basically only one thing is being said, however long it takes to say: that the wastrel Hal has become saintly. The thought is naive and not born out by the end of 2 *Henry 4*. Furthermore it is belied by what is to follow . . . Furthermore it is not well-written. It is overwritten' (Beauman, p. 103). Noble cut 25–66a, and 39–53.

And the mute wonder lurketh in men's ears
To steal his sweet and honeyed sentences,   50
So that the art and practic part of life
Must be the mistress to this theoric.
Which is a wonder how his grace should glean it,
Since his addiction was to courses vain,
His companies unlettered, rude and shallow,   55
His hours filled up with riots, banquets, sports,
And never noted in him any study,
Any retirement, any sequestration
From open haunts and popularity.

ELY   The strawberry grows underneath the nettle,   60
And wholesome berries thrive and ripen best
Neighboured by fruit of baser quality.
And so the prince obscured his contemplation
Under the veil of wildness, which, no doubt,
Grew like the summer grass fastest by night,   65
Unseen, yet crescive in his faculty.

CANTERBURY   It must be so, for miracles are ceased,
And therefore we must needs admit the means
How things are perfected.

ELY   But my good lord,
How now for mitigation of this bill   70
Urged by the Commons? Doth his majesty
Incline to it or no?

CANTERBURY   He seems indifferent,
Or rather swaying more upon our part
Than cherishing th'exhibiters against us,
For I have made an offer to his majesty   75
Upon our spiritual convocation
And in regard of causes now in hand
Which I have opened to his grace at large,
As touching France, to give a greater sum
Than ever at one time the clergy yet   80
Did to his predecessors part withal.

ELY   How did this offer seem received, my lord?

CANTERBURY   With good acceptance of his majesty,
Save that there was not time enough to hear,

79 In Branagh's film, footsteps outside the door mean the conversation is broken off hurriedly and the rest of scene cut.

As I perceived his grace would fain have done,   85
    The severals and unhidden passages
    Of his true titles to some certain dukedoms,
    And generally to the crown and seat of France
    Derived from Edward, his great-grandfather.
ELY What was th'impediment that broke this off?   90
CANTERBURY The French ambassador upon that instant
    Craved audience, and the hour I think is come
    To give him hearing. Is it four o'clock?
ELY It is.
CANTERBURY Then go we in, to know his embassy,   95
    Which I could with a ready guess declare
    Before the Frenchman speak a word of it.
ELY I'll wait upon you, and I long to hear it.

Exeunt

1.2 *Enter the* KING, GLOUCESTER, BEDFORD, CLARENCE, WESTMORLAND *and* EXETER [*and attendants*]

KING Where is my gracious lord of Canterbury?

90–98 Cut by Noble and by Hands, as 'they slowed up the action unnecessarily' (Beauman, p. 105).

1.2 A number of productions, including Kean, Calvert, BBC/Hayes and Daniels, began the play proper here, having cut 1.1. A splendid regal setting has often been provided. Macready used a canopied throne in the 'Audience Chamber' of the King's palace, with the enthroned Henry in the centre flanked by a herald, two unnamed and five named lords on each side, and the scene heralded by a 'flourish of Drums and trumpets' (Macready pbk). Kean also opened the scene with a trumpet flourish and set it in 'The Painted Chamber in the Royal Palace at Westminster', with Henry discovered on his throne raised on a platform upstage, attended by the lords and a number of extras. Kean's edition of the play alluded to the 'Chronicles' as the authority for this setting, and chose to decorate the throne with a letter S, explaining in a footnote the various historical reasons for this (Kean, p. 11). Calvert's scene was set in 'The Throne Room at the Palace of Westminster'; the King entered on a trumpet flourish and all bowed as he sat on a throne on a richly carpeted dais. In Richard Mansfield's production, the principals entered in ceremonial procession 'preceded by Warwick, bearing the crown of St Edward, the bearers of the swords of State and Justice, a herald, trumpeters, pages and attendants' (Mansfield, p. 6). Noble's production included Scroop, Gray and Cambridge

EXETER Not here in presence.

KING   Send for him, good uncle.

WESTMORLAND Shall we call in th'ambassador, my liege?

KING Not yet, my cousin. We would be resolved,

on stage in this scene (Noble pbk), as did the Globe production of 1997, where Henry and his nobles entered in courtly dress: Henry, wearing his crown, took up his place on a throne centre stage. By contrast, Olivier's film shifts its attention backstage as Canterbury and Ely exit from 1.1, showing the bustle of activity in the theatre wings. Then 'King Henry appears for a moment in large profile shot. Camera pans with Henry right until it centres upon the arch to the stage and then tracks with him as far as the doorway keeping him in close shot' (O, Fol). Branagh's film gives Henry an impressive entrance: initially backlit in an enormous doorway, he looks imposing and we cannot see his face. His nobles all bow as he passes, with the camera tracking behind the cloaked figure and showing the nobles' reaction but not the King himself. 'It's like a meeting of Mafia chiefs with the young king uneasily in charge but betraying little of his nervousness' (Branagh, p. 21), It is only when the King is seated that we finally see his face; he looks very young and small as he sits casually in the great throne, wearing blue robes. There is less ceremony in the BBC/Hayes version, in which Robert Hardy as Henry sits on a bench at a table with his noblemen in the manner of a serious board meeting. Alan Howard, in Terry Hands' 1975 production, wore tracksuit and training shoes as part of the 'rehearsal mode' of the opening scenes, in contrast to the elaborate fleur-de-lys decorated robes of the French Ambassador, and Canterbury too was identified with the illusionistic pretensions of the French, wearing clerical dress. Ron Daniels, having cut 1.1, opened with Henry 'studying a flickering old film of a First World War trench battle, his own shadow cast ominously across the screen as he did so' (Smallwood, p. 236). He, like the other noblemen, was dressed in ceremonial uniform with gold braid. Michael Pennington in Michael Bogdanov's production also wore a red mess-jacket at his first entrance – set against a large drape of the St George Cross – the red of king and nation contrasting with the greys and blacks of the other actors and the setting, and was engaged with a clipboard giving orders to underlings in Victorian morning suits. Michael Sheen, in Ron Daniels' production, was also in uniform. If the King is already in military dress at this point, it gives a good indication that the Archbishop's following justification is for the sake of form only: the decision to go to war with France has already been made. Where he is in 'kingly' dress (as in most Victorian productions) it suggests that the future course of foreign policy does indeed rest on the Archbishop's deposition. It is often difficult to interpret Henry's character in this scene. Branagh's tone is slow and measured, and Rylance's short, laconic delivery gave little away. Noble's production stressed the 'rough, brutal attitudes of Henry's court' (Loehlin, p. 90), thus preparing the ground for later acts of brutality: the execution of the traitors and of Bardolph.

2–6 Cut by Hands to speed up the transition from 1.1 to 1.2, thus opening the scene with Henry greeting the Archbishop.

Before we hear him, of some things of weight   5
That task our thoughts, concerning us and France.

Enter [CANTERBURY *and* ELY]

CANTERBURY God and His angels guard your sacred throne,
And make you long become it.
KING   Sure, we thank you.
My learnèd lord, we pray you to proceed,
And justly and religiously unfold   10
Why the law Salic that they have in France
Or should or should not bar us in our claim.
And God forbid, my dear and faithful lord,
That you should fashion, wrest, or bow your reading,
Or nicely charge your understanding soul   15
With opening titles miscreate, whose right
Suits not in native colours with the truth.
For God doth know how many now in health
Shall drop their blood in approbation
Of what your reverence shall incite us to.   20
Therefore take heed how you impawn our person,
How you awake our sleeping sword of war.

6 Olivier's film makes the clerics into buffoons. A shot of the actors backstage shows that they almost miss their cue, and, as a result, hurry on with their papers in confusion. 'Olivier does not want us to become too aware of the duplicities and complex motivations behind the "justifications" that the Archbishop offers for Henry's invasion of France' (Geduld, p. 28). This attitude to the clergy is in sharp contrast with the Victorian tradition as exemplified by Phelps, where their entrance was marked with '*omnes bow*'. Coleman, whose play began with a prologue sequence from *2 Henry IV*, knitted the two sequences together by giving the Archbishop's part to the Lord Chief Justice from the earlier play.

8–9 At this point the 'first costume element' in Hands' production was revealed, a 'pectoral cross' under the Archbishop's jacket: 'Step by step the play grows towards conventional presentation' (Beauman, p. 106).

13–20 Cut by Branagh.

20 Delivered by Branagh in his film in a slow, measured, threatening tone, sitting in his throne. Discussing his interpretation of the speech in Noble's stage production, Branagh wrote of its 'almost soliloquised quality, a moral *gravitas* which suggest[s] to me genuine emotional weight being given to the thought of the deaths involved' (*Players*, p. 100). Pennington sat behind a desk looking at a paper version of the Archbishop's speech as he spoke to it.

22 In Ron Daniels' 1997 production, Henry watched an old film of the First World War trenches during the scene, and at this point the film is showing troops burying the bodies of the slain.

> We charge you in the name of God take heed,
> For never two such kingdoms did contend
> Without much fall of blood, whose guiltless drops   25
> Are every one a woe, a sore complaint
> 'Gainst him whose wrongs gives edge unto the swords
> That makes such waste in brief mortality.
> Under this conjuration speak, my lord,
> For we will hear, note, and believe in heart   30
> That what you speak is in your conscience washed
> As pure as sin with baptism.
> CANTERBURY Then hear me, gracious sovereign, and you peers
> That owe your selves, your lives and services

24–32 Cut by BBC/Hayes.

33–95 Canterbury's Salic Law speech has often been considered expendable, and heavy cuts have been the norm. Bell and Kemble cut 66–88, with Bell judging the original 'monstrously tedious' (Bell, p. 11); Macready's production cut the speech from sixty-two lines to nineteen although with the prefatory stage direction 'Everyone turned with deep attention to Archb' (Macready pbk). Phelps followed these cuts; Kean cut it to twenty-seven; Calvert left only the first thirteen lines intact. Hands cut 56–64, confessing he was never quite sure whether to play the scene as 'a political ploy with a comic denouement' or 'a real attempt by the Archbishop to explain the problems of succession' (Beauman, p. 110). Hayes has Canterbury hand round copies of a paper detailing the Salic law, which means that the nobles are able to follow his complicated account and thus give it more weight. The impression is of a man genuinely concerned clearly to explain an intricate argument. He still, however, cut thirteen lines. Noble's promptbook indicates that 'the peers start to chat and stop on "and you peers" (33)'. When the speech was delivered in full in Matthew Warchus' 1994 production, however, it added to the characterisation of Iain Glen's Henry: 'it doesn't suggest that the audience needs convincing of the justice of Henry's cause; rather, in his eagerness to hear Canterbury's opinion, Glen shows how badly Henry needs to convince himself that right is on his side' (*I* 12 May 1994). Richard David observed that the unconventional costuming of the Archbishop in Hands' production added to the scene: 'Salic Law was more pungent and intelligible when presented (in full, too) by a dapper salesman in gents' lightweight suiting than by any archbishop in full canonicals' (David, p. 194). Most Henrys have remained expressionless during the speech. Rylance did not look at Canterbury and, positioned downstage right, continued to face the audience rather than the noblemen who were sitting upstage. Kean's Henry remained seated throughout the scene until line 300. By contrast, Iain Glen, directed by Matthew Warchus, was 'a deeply religious man' who knelt before the Archbishop in this scene and carried the crucifix given by him throughout the rest of the play.

To this imperial throne. There is no bar   35
To make against your highness' claim to France
But this which they produce from Pharamond:
In terram Salicam mulieres ne succedant,
– No woman shall succeed in Salic land –
Which Salic land the French unjustly glose   40
To be the realm of France, and Pharamond
The founder of this law and female bar.
Yet their own authors faithfully affirm
That the land Salic is in Germany,
Between the floods of Sala and of Elbe,   45
Where Charles the Great, having subdued the Saxons,
There left behind and settled certain French,
Who, holding in disdain the German women
For some dishonest manners of their life,
Established then this law: to wit, no female   50
Should be inheritrix in Salic land,
Which Salic (as I said) 'twixt Elbe and Sala
Is at this day in Germany called Meissen.
Then doth it well appear the Salic law
Was not devisèd for the realm of France.   55
Nor did the French possess the Salic land
Until four hundred one-and-twenty years
After defunction of King Pharamond,
Idly supposed the founder of this law,
Who died within the year of our redemption,   60
Four hundred twenty-six, and Charles the Great
Subdued the Saxons and did seat the French
Beyond the River Sala in the year
Eight hundred five. Besides, their writers say
King Pepin, which deposèd Childeric,   65
Did as heir general, being descended
Of Blithild, which was daughter to King Clothair,

49 The source of a low chuckle amid the serious business of BBC/Hayes.

67 Olivier's Archbishop forgets the name 'Blithild' and goes through some elaborate stage
business with Ely's proffered papers before alighting on the answer. 'He walks left out of
shot. Camera centres on Ely who exasperated throws the remaining papers over his head'
(O, Fol). Henry makes some attempts to stem the Archbishop's flow, but is unable to
interrupt him. By contrast Michael Sheen (Daniels, 1997) looked uncertainly around his
noblemen as if seeking guidance.

Make claim and title to the crown of France.
Hugh Capet also, who usurped the crown
Of Charles the Duke of Lorraine, sole heir male   70
Of the true line and stock of Charles the Great,
To fine his title with some shows of truth,
Though in pure truth it was corrupt and naught,
Conveyed himself as th'heir to the Lady Lingard,
Daughter to Charlemagne, who was the son   75
To Louis the emperor, and Louis the son
Of Charles the Great. Also King Louis the Ninth,
Who was sole heir to the usurper Capet,
Could not keep quiet in his conscience,
Wearing the crown of France, till satisfied   80
That fair Queen Isabel, his grandmother,
Was lineal of the Lady Ermengard,
Daughter to Charles the foresaid Duke of Lorraine;
By the which marriage the line of Charles the Great
Was reunited to the crown of France.   85
So that, as clear as is the summer's sun,
King Pepin's title, and Hugh Capet's claim,
King Louis his satisfaction, all appear
To hold in right and title of the female.
So do the kings of France unto this day.   90
Howbeit, they would hold up this Salic law
To bar your highness claiming from the female,
And rather choose to hide them in a net

86 In Olivier's film the camera draws back to a mid shot from the centre of the forestage,
    showing the whole group with 'Canterbury in the centre still kneeling amidst the chaos of
    literature, Exeter, Ely and the King and the remaining courtiers having risen to their feet in a
    semi-circle around him' (O, Fol). For the BBC, Hayes has a shot of noblemen nodding in
    agreement, playing the Archbishop's exposition entirely straight, but laughter at this line has
    often been a relief for the audience. In Hands' production the first half speech was slow,
    emphatic, easy to follow. Lines 56–64 were cut, and from then the exposition became faster,
    impossible to follow, so the line gave the audience the reassurance that 'it was not *expected*
    to make sense of the speech' (*Moment*, p. 114). The Globe production also prompted
    laughter at this line, but in the Branagh film it has a different edge of 'uneasy laughter and
    nervous looks' (Branagh, p. 23).

Than amply to embar their crooked titles
Usurped from you and your progenitors.   95
KING May I with right and conscience make this claim?
CANTERBURY The sin upon my head, dread sovereign,
For in the Book of Numbers is it writ
'When the man dies, let the inheritance
Descend unto the daughter.' Gracious lord,   100
Stand for your own, unwind your bloody flag,
Look back into your mighty ancestors.
Go, my dread lord, to your great-grandsire's tomb,
From whom you claim. Invoke his warlike spirit,
And your great-uncle's, Edward the Black Prince,   105
Who on the French ground played a tragedy,
Making defeat on the full power of France,
Whiles his most mighty father on a hill
Stood smiling to behold his lion's whelp
Forage in blood of French nobility.   110
O noble English, that could entertain

96 Olivier 's film has Henry forcibly block Canterbury's mouth with his hand in order to get a word in edgeways and ask the fundamental question. In Hands' version, complicity between the audience and Henry was created by speaking this line in a tone of bewilderment: the King, like the audience, has been totally befuddled by the lengthy and confusing explication. Hands' Archbishop answered with a comic shrug. Branagh delivers this in a very slow and deliberate tone, stressing each word, fixing Canterbury 'with an unflinching, penetrating stare' (Branagh, p. 23). Close-ups of Henry are unfathomable, his expression blank and opaque.

97 Olivier's Henry and Exeter provide from behind the throne a large open bible as a prompt to Canterbury. At the Globe, Canterbury's speech began sombrely but gathered momentum to a rousing climax.

100 Macready allocated the rest of the speech from the words 'Gracious lord' to Exeter: perhaps its explicit militarism was thought unsuitable for a churchman.

102 From this point on, Hands' Henry became 'isolated from a baying group' (Beauman, p. 111) of noblemen advocating war with France. Hayes' BBC production cut lines 103–24.

105 Hands felt that Henry's sense of his inheritance was a significant factor in his decision to go to war, and, in a return to the heraldic researches characteristic of Victorian productions, signalled this by basing Henry's war armour on that of the Black Prince (Beauman, p. 112). Hands and Noble also cut 106–14.

> With half their forces the full pride of France,
> And let another half stand laughing by,
> All out of work and cold for action.

ELY Awake remembrance of these valiant dead,   115
> And with your puissant arm renew their feats.
> You are their heir, you sit upon their throne.
> The blood and courage that renownèd them
> Runs in your veins, and my thrice-puissant liege
> Is in the very May-morn of his youth,   120
> Ripe for exploits and mighty enterprises.

EXETER Your brother kings and monarchs of the earth
> Do all expect that you should rouse yourself,
> As did the former lions of your blood.

WESTMORLAND They know your grace hath cause, and means,
> and might;   125
> So hath your highness. Never king of England
> Had nobles richer and more loyal subjects,
> Whose hearts have left their bodies here in England
> And lie pavilioned in the fields of France.

CANTERBURY Oh, let their bodies follow, my dear liege,   130
> With blood and sword and fire, to win your right.
> In aid whereof we of the spirituality
> Will raise your highness such a mighty sum
> As never did the clergy at one time
> Bring in to any of your ancestors.   135

KING We must not only arm t'invade the French
> But lay down our proportions to defend
> Against the Scot, who will make road upon us
> With all advantages.

CANTERBURY They of those marches, gracious sovereign,   140
> Shall be a wall sufficient to defend
> Our England from the pilfering borderers.

---

115 Macready and Calvert both gave this speech to Westmorland, cutting 117–21. At the Globe,
Henry was positioned downstage, facing the audience rather than the speakers, and his lack
of immediate response added to the opacity of his characterisation.

130–220 Bell, Kemble, Phelps, Calvert, Olivier and Hayes cut all mention of the Scots and domestic
factionalism. Branagh's film cut 136–224; Kean cut 143–213; Macready cut 137b–45, 150–2,
163–220; Hands cut 155–65; Noble cut 138b–65.

138–42 The Globe audience murmured in agreement.

KING We do not mean the coursing snatchers only,
        But fear the main intendment of the Scot,
        Who hath been still a giddy neighbour to us.   145
        For you shall read that my great-grandfather
        Never went with his forces into France
        But that the Scot on his unfurnished kingdom
        Came pouring like the tide into a breach
        With ample and brim fullness of his force,   150
        Galling the gleanèd land with hot assays,
        Girding with grievous siege castles and towns,
        That England, being empty of defence,
        Hath shook and trembled at th'ill neighbourhood.
CANTERBURY She hath been then more feared than harmed,
        my liege.   155
        For hear her but exampled by her self:
        When all her chivalry hath been in France
        And she a mourning widow of her nobles,
        She hath herself not only well defended
        But taken and impounded as a stray   160
        The king of Scots, whom she did send to France
        To fill King Edward's fame with prisoner kings,
        And make their chronicle as rich with praise
        As is the ooze and bottom of the sea
        With sunken wreck and sumless treasuries.   165
WESTMORLAND But there's a saying, very old and true,
        '*If that you will France win,*
        Then with Scotland first begin.'
        For once the eagle England being in prey,
        To her unguarded nest the weasel Scot   170
        Comes sneaking, and so sucks her princely eggs,
        Playing the mouse in absence of the cat
        To tame and havoc more than she can eat.
EXETER It follows, then, the cat must stay at home.
        Yet that is but a crushed necessity,   175

166 F gives this speech to Ely; Gurr opted for Holinshed's attribution of Westmorland (Gurr, p. 83n). Kemble cut 166–213; Bell and Kemble cut 183–213. Hands chose to divide the speech at 169, giving the first part to Clarence and the second to Gloucester in order 'to introduce Henry's two brothers at this point', having decided to focus attention on the brothers and to lose Bedford (Beauman, p. 114).

Since we have locks to safeguard necessaries
And pretty traps to catch the petty thieves.
While that the armèd hand doth fight abroad
Th'advisèd head defends itself at home.
For government, though high and low and lower,   180
Put into parts, doth keep in one consent,
Congreeing in a full and natural close
Like music.

CANTERBURY   Therefore doth heaven divide
The state of man in diverse functions,
Setting endeavour in continual motion,   185
To which is fixèd as an aim or butt
Obedience. For so work the honey bees,
Creatures that by a rule in nature teach
The act of order to a peopled kingdom.
They have a king, and officers of sorts,   190
Where some like magistrates correct at home,
Others like merchants venture trade abroad,
Others like soldiers, armèd in their stings,
Make boot upon the summer's velvet buds,
Which pillage they with merry march bring home   195
To the tent royal of their emperor,
Who, busied in his majesties, surveys
The singing masons building roofs of gold,
The civil citizens kneading up the honey,
The poor mechanic porters crowding in   200
Their heavy burdens at his narrow gate,
The sad-eyed justice with his surly hum
Delivering o'er to executors pale
The lazy yawning drone. I this infer,
That many things, having full reference   205
To one consent, may work contrariously.
As many arrows loosèd several ways
Come to one mark; as many ways meet in one town,
As many fresh streams meet in one salt sea,
As many lines close in the dial's centre,   210

186 Hands, cutting 204b–13a, described this speech as 'the full mediaeval statement of paternal fascism', and made it clear in this note that it is exactly such hierarchical relations that Henry will circumvent in his creation of a 'band of brothers' (Beauman, p. 114).

So may a thousand actions, once afoot
End in one purpose, and be all well borne
Without defeat. Therefore to France, my liege.
Divide your happy England into four,
Whereof take you one quarter into France,   215
And you withal shall make all Gallia shake.
If we with thrice such powers left at home
Cannot defend our own doors from the dog
Let us be worried, and our nation lose
The name of hardiness and policy.   220

KING   Call in the messengers sent from the Dauphin.

                                        [*Exit attendant*]

Now are we well resolved, and by God's help
And yours, the noble sinews of our power,
France being ours, we'll bend it to our awe,
Or break it all to pieces. Or there we'll sit,   225
Ruling in large and ample empery

223   At the Globe, Henry sat on his throne at this line.

225–33   Cut by Hands, who commented that 'the lines reinforce the naivety of Henry's
grandiloquence and emphasise the conventionality of his thinking' (Beauman, p. 116).
Noble cut 225b–33.

225   This threat is delivered quietly, almost as an afterthought, in Branagh's film.

233   Kean's 'treasure chest' was carried in with a large delegation including 'Herald, Lords,
Ambassador, French bishops' (Kean pbk), stressing the solemnity of the visit. Macready
combined the roles of the Ambassador and Montjoy, as did Noble and the Olivier and
Branagh films; Phelps combined the Ambassador and Constable roles, as did Coleman.
At the entry of the Ambassador and his attendants, Phelps introduced some comically
choreographed stage business as French and English solemnly removed their hats and
bowed in turn. Similarly, the entry of the Ambassador was greeted with some hissing and
laughter from the audience at the Globe in 1997. On a more serious note, Hands made the
Ambassador a Bishop, thus implicating him in the clerical conspiracy of 1.1, and again
citing the 'sources' as authorities for interpretive interpolations in true Victorian style.
Perhaps the most menacing interpretation of the entry comes from the BBC production, in
which Hayes shot the scene from behind the Ambassadors. The screen is filled with the
blurred bulk of their backs in the foreground, maces pointed towards Henry, who seems
cornered and dwarfed by the composition, thus suggesting a real threat from France at this
point.

225–33   Cut in Branagh's film; 230–4 cut by Hayes.

O'er France and all her almost kingly dukedoms,
Or lay these bones in an unworthy urn
Tombless, with no remembrance over them.
Either our history shall with full mouth   230
Speak freely of our acts, or else our grave
Like Turkish mute shall have a tongueless mouth,
Not worshipped with a waxen epitaph.

Enter AMBASSADOR *of France* [*with attendants*]

Now are we well prepared to know the pleasure
Of our fair cousin Dauphin; for we hear   235
Your greeting is from him, not from the king.

AMBASSADOR May't please your majesty to give us leave
Freely to render what we have in charge,
Or shall we sparingly show you far off
The Dauphin's meaning, and our embassy?   240

KING We are no tyrant, but a Christian king,
Unto whose grace our passion is as subject
As are our wretches fettered in our prisons.
Therefore with frank and with uncurbèd plainness
Tell us the Dauphin's mind.

AMBASSADOR   Thus then in few: 245
Your highness lately, sending into France,
Did claim some certain dukedoms, in the right
Of your great predecessor, King Edward the Third.
In answer of which claim the prince our master
Says that you savour too much of your youth,   250
And bids you be advised: there's naught in France
That can be with a nimble galliard won;
You cannot revel into dukedoms there.
He therefore sends you, meeter for your spirit,
This tun of treasure, and in lieu of this   255
Desires you let the dukedoms that you claim
Hear no more of you. This the Dauphin speaks.

236–43 Cut by Noble; 242–5a cut by Hayes.

251–2 In Calvert's version this insult caused an immediate reaction: 'all start and put hands on
swords and look at the king' (Calvert pbk). Hands' treasure chest opened to reveal a real
hand holding the tennis balls.

KING What treasure, uncle?

EXETER   [*Opens tun*] Tennis balls, my liege.

KING We are glad the Dauphin is so pleasant with us.

His present and your pains we thank you for.   260
When we have matched our rackets to these balls
We will in France, by God's grace, play a set
Shall strike his father's crown into the hazard.
Tell him he hath made a match with such a wrangler
That all the courts of France will be disturbed   265
With chases. And we understand him well,
How he comes o'er us with our wilder days,
Not measuring what use we made of them.

258 Macready's stage direction reads: 'Having opened chest and holding them up, low murmurs and movement throughout the court' (Macready pbk). In Phelps' production, '2 attendants open the Chest – Exeter takes out a Tennis ball holding it up to view. All express surprise' (Sprague, p. 117.) Olivier cuts to a medium close-up of Henry, whose smile drops, gaining 'an appreciative laugh from the audience' (O, Fol). Hayes held a long pause as all wait, silently, for Henry's reaction. Branagh's film shows Henry's slow, deliberate, straight stare in extreme close-up. At the Globe there was laughter from the audience and a sense of expectation about how Henry would respond. Similarly, there is 'a slight flutter of excitement and giggling' from Olivier's on-screen theatre audience (O, Fol).

259 Hands felt that the spirit of Hal 're-emerges suddenly from the persona of kingship that Henry has been experimenting with – not totally successfully – earlier in the scene' (Beauman, p. 117). Branagh's film continues with Henry's slow, low, urgent delivery.

264 Robert Hardy, in Hayes' BBC production, here stands. He motions the nobles to remain seated, thus taking personal command of the frame composition and of the situation.

266–88 The length and the extended punning of this speech have often been pruned, sometimes to protect the character of Henry from disapproval. In the eighteenth century, the speech was filleted to the first lines up to 268, then 273–4, then 279–80, then 291–4 (*Henry 1780*, pp. 4–5). Kemble cut 281–8, as did Macready. Kean cut 264–6a, 269–72, 276–7, and 281–8. Calvert cut the entire speech. At the Globe Henry picked out three balls from the tun and began to juggle them, to the great approval of the audience. Sheen (Daniels, 1997), delivered the speech holding himself very upright, like a politician under the spotlight.

We never valued this poor seat of England,
And therefore, living hence, did give ourself   270
To barbarous licence, as 'tis ever common
That men are merriest when they are from home.
But tell the Dauphin I will keep my state,
Be like a king, and show my sail of greatness
When I do rouse me in my throne of France,   275
For that I have laid by my majesty
And plodded like a man for working days.
But I will rise there with so full a glory
That I will dazzle all the eyes of France,
Yea, strike the Dauphin blind to look on us.   280
And tell the pleasant prince this mock of his
Hath turned his balls to gun-stones, and his soul
Shall stand sore chargèd for the wasteful vengeance
That shall fly with them; for many a thousand widows
Shall this his mock mock out of their dear husbands,   285
Mock mothers from their sons, mock castles down,
And some are yet ungotten and unborn
That shall have cause to curse the Dauphin's scorn.
But this lies all within the will of God,
To whom I do appeal, and in whose name   290
Tell you the Dauphin I am coming on
To venge me as I may, and to put forth
My rightful hand in a well-hallowed cause.
So get you hence in peace. And tell the Dauphin
His jest will savour but of shallow wit   295

273 Having cut 269–72 (as does Hayes), Olivier amends 273 to 'keep *our* state', and turns on this
   line to include the rest of the stage and the audience. The rest of the speech sees him
   walking around the stage and the treasure chest that is placed in the centre, with fluid
   camera movement following him.

284 In Branagh's film, 'Henry's anger has built into an explosion of outrage undeniable in its
   force' (Branagh, p. 26). This links Branagh's film with Noble's stage production, in which
   Irving Wardle described Branagh's performance 'exploding into paroxysms of psychotic
   rage' (*T* 30 March 1984).

285 Warchus' Henry emphasised the repeated 'mock' by bouncing one of the tennis balls.

289–93 Cut by Hands, as was 304–7. Hayes' production has Henry shouting the final lines of the
   speech.

When thousands weep more than did laugh at it.

[*To attendants*] Convey them with safe conduct. Fare you
well.

Exeunt Ambassador [and attendants]

EXETER This was a merry message.

KING We hope to make the sender blush at it.

Therefore, my lords, omit no happy hour   300
That may give furtherance to our expedition,
For we have now no thought in us but France,
Save those to God that run before our business.
Therefore let our proportions for these wars
Be soon collected, and all things thought upon   305
That may with reasonable swiftness add
More feathers to our wings. For, God before,
We'll chide this Dauphin at his father's door.
Therefore let every man now task his thought
That this fair action may on foot be brought.   310

Flourish. Exeunt

297 In Branagh's film, Henry's tone suddenly changes to one of extreme gentleness.

299 When the Ambassadors have left, Olivier takes off his crown and throws it casually so it
lands on the back of the throne.

303 'He moves off, urgent and determined, followed by the now united court' (Branagh,
p. 27).

309–10 Kean's scene ended with 'The characters group around the King'; Mansfield offered a
similar tableau. Olivier leads a small procession of courtiers and soldiers off through
the left-hand door of the stage, and the curtains are smartly drawn behind them by
two soldiers. The BBC/Giles scene ends with some horseplay with the tennis balls.
'As they sweep out of the chamber, Canterbury and Ely at the back of the group turn to each
other and share a smile of dark relief' (Branagh, p. 27), thus reminding us of the clerical
conspiracy. At the Globe, Henry was positioned downstage, addressing 'every man'
directly to the audience. In Warchus' production, sets of swords descended on strings
from the flies at the announcement of the expedition, for the noblemen to choose their
weapons.

2.0 *Enter* CHORUS

CHORUS Now all the youth of England are on fire
             And silken dalliance in the wardrobe lies.

2.0 One of the difficulties of this Chorus speech for directors is its range and its apparent
        inconsistency. The speech reveals the treachery of Scroop, Gray and Cambridge and
        urges the audience to consider itself transported to Southampton and from thence over
        the sea to France. But this imaginative journey is immediately curtailed, as Southampton is
        postponed until 'the king come forth' (41), thus introducing the London scene and the
        characters of Bardolph, Nym and Pistol. Terry Hands' Chorus, Emrys James, was
        interrupted by Bardolph and Nym 'before he could complete his announcement. After one
        attempt to continue he shrugged and left them to it, returning to announce the change of
        scene after they had done' (David, p. 213). This awkwardness has often been negotiated by
        breaking the Chorus speech, either to literalise, in tableau form, its account of the English
        traitors receiving French gold, or deploying it in part to introduce 2.1, reserving the
        remainder of the speech about Southampton as a preface to 2.2. This division of the Chorus
        speech is part of Olivier's and Branagh's films, and the productions directed by Bogdanov
        and Noble. Macready made use of dioramic illustration to show the English fleet at anchor
        in Southampton. Olivier's Chorus delivers lines 1–11, followed by: 'Linger your patience on,
        for if we may/We'll not offend one stomach with our play.' Ron Daniels moved 2.1 to
        precede 2.0.
            At the Globe, the speech was spoken by the Duke of Exeter actor. Branagh's film delivers
        a 'gently ironic' voice-over as the scene of the 'Boar's Head Tavern: Day' is revealed: 'Closed
        shutters are opened. Sunlight floods onto the face of an old man fighting a monstrous
        hangover. He turns and moves into the tavern, revealing the filth and debris of the place'
        (Branagh, p. 27). Branagh introduces 2.1 after line 11, combining it with 2.3. The rest of the
        speech is reserved to introduce 2.2, set on the sea shore, with the Chorus 'standing on a
        grassy cliff edge, looking out to sea' and set against a coastline which recalls the outline of a
        map in its two-dimensionality. He delivers the speech to camera, except at lines 23–5, when
        the three noblemen pass through the frame as he names them. Branagh cuts 29, 30b–33a,
        and 36–42, ending the speech on line 35 with an iconic image of Englishness: as the Chorus
        'walks away along the cliff edge, wrapping his scarf around him against the cold sea air,
        beyond him we see the dramatic white cliffs of the English coastline' (Branagh, p. 36).
        Olivier's Chorus enters the Globe stage through curtains representing a London street,
        delivering lines 1–11, 31a, 39b–40 to introduce 2.1, with other lines from the speech reserved
        until 2.2.

  1 The BBC/Giles Chorus catches a tennis ball from the frivolous mayhem which ends 1.2 to
        make the scenes into continuous action.

Now thrive the armourers, and honour's thought
Reigns solely in the breast of every man.
They sell the pasture now to buy the horse,   5
Following the mirror of all Christian kings
With wingèd heels, as English Mercuries.
For now sits expectation in the air,
And hides a sword from hilts unto the point
With crowns imperial, crowns and coronets   10
Promised to Harry and his followers.
The French, advised by good intelligence
Of this most dreadful preparation,
Shake in their fear, and with pale policy
Seek to divert the English purposes.   15
O England: model to thy inward greatness,
Like little body with a mighty heart,
What mightst thou do, that honour would thee do,
Were all thy children kind and natural?
But see, thy fault France hath in thee found out,   20
A nest of hollow bosoms, which he fills
With treacherous crowns, and three corrupted men –

3–7 Cut by Branagh.

7 Hands' production introduced its great heraldic canopy, a cannon and costumes for the preparations for war outlined in the first lines of the speech. The rehearsal time registered by the casual everyday clothing of the first act was replaced by the decisiveness of Henry's expedition and of the thoroughgoing engagement with the play world. Thus the non-naturalistic narrative authority of the Chorus was literally challenged and defeated by the ribald, anti-heroic Bardolph and Nym, who interrupted the speech at line 7 and forced Chorus to concede to them. 'It is a change of acting style. Having heard the "rhetoricks" we are now confronted by the "mechanicals" ' (Beauman, p. 120).

9–15 Cut by Kean.

11 The implicit irony of the Chorus' description of Henry's followers was pointed up in the English Shakespeare Company production, when, on this line, the shabbily comic Bardolph and Nym, entered dressed in army surplus uniforms. Noble's Chorus exited via the trapdoor in the stage, to allow 2.1 to unfold.

22 Showing the three conspirators as they are named by the Chorus has been a common device. Macready showed a picture of them through the cloud-framed diorama; Kean included 'a tableau representing the three conspirators receiving Bribe from the Emissaries of France' (Kean pbk) and listed it on the playbill; the BBC/Hayes production shows each of the conspirators in close-up as he is named, showing them meeting together in a room and

One, Richard, Earl of Cambridge, and the second
Henry, Lord Scroop of Masham, and the third
Sir Thomas Gray, knight of Northumberland –   25
Have for the gilt of France (oh, guilt indeed)
Confirmed conspiracy with fearful France,
And by their hands this grace of kings must die,
If hell and treason hold their promises,
Ere he take ship for France, and in Southampton.   30
Linger your patience on, and we'll digest
Th'abuse of distance, force perforce a play.
The sum is paid, the traitors are agreed,
The king is set from London, and the scene
Is now transported, gentles, to Southampton.   35
There is the playhouse now, there must you sit,
And thence to France shall we convey you safe
And bring you back, charming the narrow seas
To give you gentle pass, for if we may

clasping hands in an agreement. At the Globe, the three entered, to some audience booing and the Chorus pointed to them in 23–5. The same gesture was enacted by the English Shakespeare Company, although by putting the conspirators in the clichéd attitudes of *film noir* plotters – a shadowy huddle of overcoats and homburg hats – the production suggested that the episode is a trope of authoritarian control rather than a genuine threat. Hands also played the exposures, moved to immediately before 2.2, non-naturalistically, picking the traitors out with spotlights as they were named; 'they are figures rather than people' (Beauman, p. 127). Daniels' production pulled the officers, dressed in WWI khaki and with kitbags, out into a blinding light that shone into the audience. Morse code signalling suggested how the conspiracy had been revealed. The BBC/Giles production chose not to show the conspirators, but the Chorus' tone slows down to clear, expository style to make sure that the sense is understood. Olivier's film cuts all mention of the traitors in the Chorus, just as he cuts 2.2.

30 Calvert cut the speech here, adding the concluding lines: 'The sum is paid: the traitors are agreed;/ The King is set from London, and the scene/ Is now transported to Southampton', followed by a curtain drop.

34a Numerous productions (see headnote to 2.0) cut the speech here to lead into 2.1.

36 The Globe Chorus sat on a stool; Phelps cut the rest of the speech.

37 The Globe's 'bring you back' was played for, and got, laughs.

39–40 Richard David wrote of Byam Shaw's production with Roger Livesey as Chorus: 'From the start he won our complete sympathy and loyalty. We enjoyed the irony of his lame excuses, the homely jokes about sea-sickness' (*SS* 1952, p. 125).

We'll not offend one stomach with our play.   40
But when the king come forth, and not till then,
Unto Southampton do we shift our scene.   *Exit*

2.1 *Enter Corporal* NYM *and Lieutenant* BARDOLPH

BARDOLPH Well met, Corporal Nym.

NYM Good morrow, Lieutenant Bardolph.

BARDOLPH What, are Ancient Pistol and you friends yet?

NYM For my part, I care not. I say little, but when time shall serve
there shall be smiles, but that shall be as it may. I dare not fight,   5
but I will wink and hold out mine iron. It is a simple one, but
what though? It will toast cheese, and it will endure cold as
another man's sword will, and there's an end.

BARDOLPH I will bestow a breakfast to make you friends, and we'll

---

40 The BBC/Giles Chorus is revealed to be standing in a street with the tavern sign of the Boar's
Head visible. He suddenly comes nose to nose with Bardolph as the camera pulls back to
reveal his proximity. The Chorus is visibly startled and exits as the scene begins. At the Globe
Nym entered through the trapdoor in the stage, catching a handkerchief thrown by the
Chorus to pull back from Southampton.

41–2 Cut by Kean, who cut 2.1, following the Chorus with 2.2, as did Phelps.

2.1 Cut by Kemble, Kean and Phelps. Calvert combined this scene and 2.3, to serve as 1.2.
Olivier's film sets this scene on the stage of the Globe, as the rain begins to drench the
spectators in the yard. A board brought on indicates the setting of the Boar's Head, which is
then hooked on a pillar to serve as the inn sign. Branagh sets the scene inside the tavern
with the lugubrious duo of 'middle-aged soldiers of misfortune' (Branagh, p. 29) in
hangover mood. The Folio is careful to identify the men by rank: 'Enter Coporall Nym, and
Lieutenant Bardolfe', and the specificity of the stage direction is echoed by the men's
greetings in lines 1–2 and 33.

1 For the BBC/Hayes version, Bardolph and Nym are both drunkenly lachrymose. Olivier's
film has Nym make 'an elaborately furtive entrance' on to the balcony, from which he looks
suspiciously up and down the imaginary street below. He climbs over the balcony rail,
blowing a kiss up towards the balcony, and drops on to the stage, not knowing that
Bardolph is watching this scene with mild interest. 'He starts guiltily round as Bardolph
addresses him' (O, Fol). By contrast to this surreptitious entry, the Globe production
immediately introduced a shouting exchange between Nym and Bardolph.

be all three sworn brothers to France. Let't be so, good Corporal   10
Nym.

NYM Faith, I will live so long as I may, that's the certain of it, and
when I cannot live any longer I will do as I may. That is my rest,
that is the rendezvous of it.

BARDOLPH It is certain, corporal, that he is married to Nell Quickly,   15
and certainly she did you wrong, for you were troth-plight to
her.

NYM I cannot tell. Things must be as they may. Men may sleep, and
they may have their throats about them at that time, and some
say knives have edges. It must be as it may. Though patience be a   20
tired mare, yet she will plod. There must be conclusions. Well, I
cannot tell.

Enter PISTOL *and* QUICKLY

BARDOLPH Here comes Ancient Pistol and his wife. Good corporal,
be patient here.

20 Hayes has Nym begin to strop his knife against the sole of his boot.

23 The Folio identifies the woman as 'Quickly' in the stage directions but uses 'Host.' for the
speech prefixes in the scene, and 'Hostess' at line 92sd. The audience in Olivier's theatre
grow restive and excited at the thought of Pistol's arrival: he is clearly a great favourite, and
appreciative laughter punctuates the scene. The camera cuts to show a full-length shot of
'Pistol and Mrs Pistol sunning themselves in their applause' (O, Fol). For the English
Shakespeare Company production, Pistol and Quickly entered to the strains of
Mendelsohn's Wedding March, covered in confetti; confetti was also in evidence in Hayes'
and Hands' productions. Daniels' Pistol and Quickly were also getting married: Bardolph,
dressed in purple velvet with a floral buttonhole, entered carrying a large parcel wrapped in
bright pink paper. A fat, red-faced cockney Pistol wore a top hat and white tailcoat with
leather trousers; Quickly wore a short white dress with a veil, and there was a guard of
honour with swords. The backdrop was a grubby concrete wall with barbed wire and red
lights. Branagh introduces the pair with 'a squeal of pleasure from Mistress Quickly as Pistol
chases her lasciviously round a ladder, to be brought up short by seeing Nym, now
standing, sword in hand, facing them' (Branagh, p. 29). Richard Moore, who played Pistol in
Hands' production, observed that 'Nym, Pistol and Bardolph don't take their quarrelling and
brawling seriously. They all know full well that they will never really fight, or damage each
other – they just play a game of threatened fights that is understood as such between them'
(Beauman, p. 125). The Globe Quickly entered through the stage trapdoor, revealing herself

NYM How now, mine host Pistol?   25

PISTOL Base tyke, call'st thou me host? Now by this hand I swear I
scorn the term, nor shall my Nell keep lodgers.

HOSTESS No, by my troth, not long, for we cannot lodge and board a
dozen or fourteen gentlewomen that live honestly by the prick
of their needles but it will be thought we keep a bawdy house   30
straight. [*Nym draws his sword*] Oh, welladay, Lady, if he be not
hewn now, we shall see wilful adultery and murder committed.

[*Pistol draws his sword*]

BARDOLPH Good lieutenant, good corporal, offer nothing here.

NYM Pish.

PISTOL Pish for thee, Iceland dog, thou prick-eared cur of Iceland.   35

HOSTESS Good Corporal Nym, show thy valour, and put up your
sword.

[*They sheathe their swords*]

NYM Will you shog off? [*To Pistol*] I would have you *solus*.

PISTOL *Solus*, egregious dog? O viper vile! The *solus* in thy most
mervailous face, the *solus* in thy teeth, and in thy throat, and in   40
thy hateful lungs, yea, in thy maw, perdy, and, which is worse,
within thy nasty mouth! I do retort the *solus* in thy bowels, for I
can take, and Pistol's cock is up, and flashing fire will follow!

NYM I am not Barbason, you cannot conjure me. I have an humour
to knock you indifferently well. If you grow foul with me, Pistol,   45
I will scour you with my rapier, as I may, in fair terms. If you
would walk off I would prick your guts a little in good terms, as
I may, and that's the humour of it.

PISTOL O braggart vile, and damnèd furious wight, the grave doth
gape and doting death is near. Therefore exhale!   50

[*They draw their swords*]

BARDOLPH Hear me, hear me what I say. [*Draws his sword*] He that
strikes the first stroke, I'll run him up to the hilts, as I am a
soldier.

(played by a male actor) to be very tall, much to the amusement of the audience. Noble also
had Quickly and Pistol enter from the trapdoor in the stage.

26 Olivier's Pistol gives 'a dangerous intensity' to the possessive '*my* Nell' and the camera cuts
to a close-up of Nym 'looking elaborately innocent' (O, Fol).

33 The rest of the scene was cut by Hayes.

PISTOL An oath of mickle might, arid fury shall abate. Give me thy
fist, thy forefoot to me give. Thy spirits are most tall.   55
NYM I will cut thy throat one time or other in fair terms, that is the
humour of it.
PISTOL Couple a gorge, that is the word. I defy thee again! O hound
of Crete, thinkst thou my spouse to get? No, to the Spital go, and
from the powdering tub of infamy fetch forth the lazar kite of   60
Cressid's kind, Doll Tearsheet, she by name, and her espouse. I
have, and I will hold the quondam Quickly for the only she, and
pauca, there's enough. Go to.

Enter the BOY.

BOY Mine host Pistol, you must come to my master, and your
hostess. He is very sick, and would to bed. Good Bardolph, put   65
thy face between his sheets and do the office of a warming pan.
Faith, he's very ill.
BARDOLPH Away, you rogue.
HOSTESS By my troth, he'll yield the crow a pudding one of these
days. The king has killed his heart. Good husband, come home   70
presently.

Exeunt [*Hostess and Boy*]

BARDOLPH Come, shall I make you two friends? We must to France
together. Why the devil should we keep knives to cut one
another's throats?
PISTOL Let floods o'erswell, and fiends for food howl on!   75
NYM You'll pay me the eight shillings I won of you at betting?
PISTOL Base is the slave that pays.
NYM That now I will have. That's the humour of it.
PISTOL As manhood shall compound. Push home.

[*They*] *Draw* [*their swords*]

59 In Noble's production Pistol and Nym wrestled, and then Pistol chased Nym across the
stage, stopping, uxoriously, to embrace Quickly *en route*.

64 Branagh's Boy speaks in serious tone.

69 By cutting the phrase about the pudding, Branagh stresses the poignant melancholy of the
moment. Quickly goes upstairs with the Boy to Falstaff's room, and the film shows us a
close-up of Falstaff's face 'eyes closed, not moving' (Branagh, p. 32).

70 Calvert cut all reference to Falstaff. A pregnant pause was left before 'The king has killed his
heart' in Noble's production.

BARDOLPH [*Draws his sword*] By this sword, he that makes the first   80
    thrust, I'll kill him, by this sword I will.

PISTOL Sword is an oath, and oaths must have their course.

[Sheathes his sword]

BARDOLPH Corporal Nym, an thou wilt be friends, be friends. An
    thou wilt not, why then be enemies with me too. Prithee put up.

[Nym sheathes his sword]

PISTOL A noble shalt thou have, and present pay, and liquor likewise   85
    will I give to thee, and friendship shall combine, and
    brotherhood. I'll live by Nym and Nym shall live by me; is not
    this just? For I shall sutler be unto the camp, and profits will
    accrue. Give me thy hand.

NYM I shall have my noble?   90

PISTOL In cash, most justly paid.

NYM Well, then that's the humour of it.

Enter HOSTESS [and BOY]

HOSTESS As ever you come of women, come in quickly to Sir
    John. Ah, poor heart, he is so shaked of a burning quotidian
    tertian that it is most lamentable to behold. Sweet men, come to   95
    him.

NYM The king hath run bad humours on the knight; that's the even
    of it.

PISTOL Nym, thou hast spoke the right, his heart is fracted and
    corroborate.   100

NYM The king is a good king, but it must be as it may. He passes
    some humours and careers.

PISTOL Let us condole the knight, for, lambkins, we will live.

Exeunt

93 Judi Dench, in Branagh's film, tells them of Falstaff's sickness in a voice breaking with
emotion, and leaves the three men in melancholic mood. Pistol speaks 'for all of them:
"Poor Sir John, a good portly man i'faith" ' (a description Falstaff gives himself, talking about
himself in the third person, in *1 Henry IV* 2.4.347), and this introduces a flashback scene, as
through Pistol's eyes as he stares at the fire, intended to 'make clear [Falstaff's] former
relationship and estrangement from the young monarch', partly to stress Henry's isolation
in turning away from his tavern companions and partly to maximise the impact of the report
of Falstaff's death (Branagh, p. 12). The interpolated sequence comprises Falstaff's lines
from *1 Henry IV*: 'Ay, and of a cheerful look, a pleasing eye and a most noble carriage'

2.2 *Enter* EXETER, BEDFORD *and* WESTMORLAND

BEDFORD 'Fore God, his grace is bold to trust these traitors.
EXETER They shall be apprehended by and by.

(2.4.348–9) delivered as a voice-over, and then a flashback to the Boar's Head, with Falstaff
'standing by the roaring fire, laughing and throwing wide his arms to greet the now happy
Pistol, Nym and Bardolph' (Branagh, p. 33). He exclaims, again from *I Henry IV* 'But do I not
dwindle? My skin hangs about me like an old lady's loose gown' (3.3.2–3), to much laughter
from the assembled group, then his next lines are from the same scene: 'Company,
villainous company hath been the spoil of me' (7–8) to further merriment. At this point a
newcomer arrives, greeted by a smiling Falstaff: 'Hal! Hal!', and Falstaff hugs Henry. Falstaff
gives the speech of self-promotion from *I Henry IV* ending with the serious plea 'banish
plump Jack and banish all the world' (2.4.393–8). During the speech, Henry is shown in
profile, smiling, but at the conclusion there is a cut to focus on 'the King-to-be, the smiling
features turn cold. He holds his look and we hear, in a chilling and ghostly tone' (Branagh,
p. 34), the voice-over 'I do, I will.' Falstaff's face registers the hurt of this snub, which is
followed by a collage of lines from *2 Henry IV*, including Falstaff's words of fellowship to
Shallow made the keynote of Orson Welles' film of Falstaff's career, 'We have heard the
chimes at midnight' (3.2.177), this time addressed to 'Master Harry'. 'Then, almost inaudibly,
with the last painful ounce of pleading' (Branagh, p. 34), 'Jesus, the days that we have seen'
(3.2.180). These are followed, inevitably, by Henry's cold words of rejection, delivered as a
voice-over against Henry's evident emotional discomfort, 'I know thee not, old man'
(5.5.43). The film dissolves the flashback, and cuts to the present day with 2.1.97–103. At the
Globe, the Hostess and the Boy were up on the balcony. At the Globe the pantomimic
qualities of the male actor's performance prompted much audience laughter. In Hands'
production the tone of the scene suddenly changed: in place of the performance of
innuendo and mock-fighting, 'something real is happening [. . . a] reminder of mortality
draws the swaggerers out of caricature and into the play' (Beauman, p. 25).

104 Macready's promptbook notes that the three exit 'hand in hand quite good friends'. Pistol's
attempt to change the mood in Branagh's film is met with doubts from the others.

2.2 In many productions this scene opens Act 2, following immediately from (some parts of)
2.0 with this edition's 2.1 amalgamated with 2.3. Macready opened Act 2 with this scene,
after the prompbook's estimation of '25 minutes wait for dressing'. It was set in front of 'The
Gates of the City – the sea with fleet at anchor seen through. Barges in front', with a good

WESTMORLAND How smooth and even they do bear themselves,
    As if allegiance in their bosoms sat,
    Crownèd with faith and constant loyalty.   5
BEDFORD The king hath note of all that they intend
    By interception which they dream not of.

deal of activity: 'Preparations for the expedition seen without. Distant Trumpets R & L.
Soldiers etc passing with arms and baggage. Persons passing out with luggage etc. –
cannon. Knights with banners etc. passing behind' (Macready pbk). Macready's blocking
diagram shows Henry flanked by heralds with banners upstage and ranks of guards stage
right and left. Kean set this scene, following immediately from the Chorus to Act 2, in the
'council chamber in Southampton Castle'. Kemble was criticised in *The Monthly Mirror*,
December 1801, for presenting Southampton with 'a wretched daub . . . of modern ships, a
light-house &c.'. Hands transposed 2.0.12–40 to lead into this scene, Olivier 2.0 31–2, and
34–9b, Branagh and Noble 11–30. The 'tense and expectant' (Branagh, p. 37) atmosphere of
this scene of military preparations is suggested by Branagh's film, which opens with a view
through a spy-hole in a partition wall, showing the noblemen grouped around a table in a
small room looking at a map. Michael Kahn titled the scene 'Ruses. The First Victims. The
emergence of the Warrior King.' Noble's direction of the scene was described by Branagh as
'Hitchcockian', 'which drew out every ounce of the demonic showman that also lies in
Henry' (*Players*, p. 103). The trio of Exeter, Bedford and Westmorland entered the Globe on
the balcony. The BBC/Giles production sets the scene outside, near the quayside, with the
sound of seagulls and the distant sight of the sea framed by an arch. Hands' production
tented the ceiling with a richly decorated royal standard. Hands used music to suggest 'a
pier-side band. Farewell to Blighty' (Beauman, p. 127). Olivier's Chorus is still in the Globe
Theatre against a curtain depicting Southampton, but during 2.0.37, transposed to begin
2.2., the scene shifts to a model of medieval Southampton, showing the Archbishop of
Canterbury 'giving benediction to the kneeling king Henry and his knights' (*Masterworks*, p.
217), then the Chorus delivers the last lines of his speech as a voice-over, continuing the
film's movement away from the theatrical setting so firmly established for Act 1. Olivier cuts
the whole of the traitors' scene, leaving only the evidence of Henry's mercy to the drunken
prisoner (39–47), with Scroop's lines spoken by Exeter. Henry comes straight from the
Archbishop's blessing on the deck of his ship on to the quay, 'happily inspecting the
activities surrounding him, namely, loading of stoves, casks, horses etc' (O, Fol) to deliver
the rousing lines which conclude the scene, 184–8, to the accompaniment of the soldiers'
cheers.

6–7 Having cut Bedford, Hands reassigned these lines to Clarence.

EXETER Nay, but the man that was his bedfellow,
        Whom he hath dulled and cloyed with gracious favours;
        That he should for a foreign purse so sell   10
        His sovereign's life to death and treachery!

Sound trumpets. Enter the KING, SCROOP, CAMBRIDGE *and* GRAY
[and OFFICERS*]*

KING Now sits the wind fair, and we will aboard.
      My lord of Cambridge and my kind lord Masham,
      And you my gentle knight, give me your thoughts.
      Think you not that the powers we bear with us   15
      Will cut their passage through the force of France,
      Doing the execution and the act
      For which we have in head assembled them?
SCROOP No doubt, my liege, if each man do his best.
KING I doubt not that, since we are well persuaded   20
      We carry not a heart with us from hence
      That grows not in a fair consent with ours,
      Nor leave not one behind that doth not wish
      Success and conquest to attend on us.
CAMBRIDGE Never was monarch better feared and loved   25

12. Kean's promptbook includes a sketch of Henry radiating light in the darkness of the interior, and the blocking diagrams indicate that he was always positioned centre stage. The three conspirators were grouped at one side of the stage, as in Phelps' production, where they were 'all RH conversing together' (Phelps pbk). For the English Shakespeare Company production, Henry wore camouflage fatigues and a leather coat with large lapels. When Branagh enters in his film, wearing the quartered fleur-de-lys tunic and a studded collar and gauntlets and carrying maps and papers, all the noblemen leap to their feet. 'He stops at the centre table, surrounded by his men, the three traitors nearest to him. He signals for the doors to be bolted. He is calm and decisive, apparently unworried' (Branagh, p. 37). Hands' Henry 'enters costumed for war, but without his heraldic surcoat which will be the banner of war and mark his full acceptance of leadership' (Beauman, p. 127).

12 Branagh's Henry seems friendly and conversational; for the BBC, David Gwillim is smiling and open-faced.

19–50 Branagh's film shoots this sequence as a series of close-ups on the faces of the speakers. Their facial expressions give little away, but the probing interrogative camera-work is implicitly asking questions about its subjects.

        Than is your majesty. There's not I think a subject
        That sits in heart-grief and uneasiness
        Under the sweet shade of your government.

GRAY True. Those that were your father's enemies
        Have steeped their galls in honey, and do serve you   30
        With hearts create of duty and of zeal.

KING We therefore have great cause of thankfulness,
        And shall forget the office of our hand
        Sooner than quittance of desert and merit,
        According to the weight and worthiness.   35

SCROOP So service shall with steelèd sinews toil
        And labour shall refresh itself with hope,
        To do your grace incessant services.

KING We judge no less. Uncle of Exeter,
        Enlarge the man committed yesterday   40
        That railed against our person. We consider
        It was excess of wine that set him on,
        And on his more advice we pardon him.

SCROOP That's mercy, but too much security.
        Let him be punished, sovereign, lest example   45
        Breed by his sufferance more of such a kind.

KING Oh, let us yet be merciful.

CAMBRIDGE So may your highness, and yet punish too.

GRAY Sir, you show great mercy if you give him life
        After the taste of much correction.   50

KING Alas, your too much love and care of me
        Are heavy orisons 'gainst this poor wretch.
        If little faults, proceeding on distemper,
        Shall not be winked at, how shall we stretch our eye
        When capital crimes, chewed, swallowed, and digested,   55
        Appear before us? We'll yet enlarge that man,
        Though Cambridge, Scroop and Gray, in their dear care
        And tender preservation of our person

33 For the BBC/Giles Henry looks down at his gloved hand and his ring of office.

39 The BBC/Giles Henry stands, informally, issuing the order apparently casually. In Calvert's production the bound prisoner was on stage. He fell to his knees at the King's pardon, and was released from his shackles during the following lines.

55–6 Branagh is casual, relaxed, smiling as he takes off his gloves. He touches Scroop's chin in a gesture of comfortable intimacy.

Would have him punished. And now to our French causes.
Who are the late commissioners?

CAMBRIDGE   I one, my lord.   60
Your highness bade me ask for it today.

SCROOP So did you me, my liege.

GRAY   And I, my royal sovereign.

KING Then Richard, Earl of Cambridge, there is yours.
There yours, Lord Scroop of Masham, and sir knight,
Gray of Northumberland, this same is yours.   65
        [*Gives them papers*]
Read them and know I know your worthiness.
My lord of Westmorland and uncle Exeter,
We will aboard tonight. Why, how now, gentlemen?
What see you in those papers, that you lose
So much complexion? Look ye how they change.   70
Their cheeks are paper. Why, what read you there,
That have so cowarded and chased your blood
Out of appearance?

CAMBRIDGE   I do confess my fault,
And do submit me to your highness' mercy.   [*Kneels*]

GRAY *and* SCROOP To which we all appeal. [*They kneel*]   75

KING The mercy that was quick in us but late

---

59 Michael Sheen slammed his fist into his palm at this point, then laughed with the slightly
    maniacal edge indicative of stress throughout his performance (Daniels, 1997). Standing
    downstage, he faced the audience, with the conspirators behind him.

63–5 Kean delegated the job of handing over the commissions to Exeter. Branagh shoots this
      scene from behind the King, so that the faces of the traitors are in full view. The BBC/Giles
      also chooses a close-up of their aghast expressions as they kneel in front of the King.

66 Branagh's tone changes to a deliberate, steely indictment.

68 Kean's stage direction reads 'conspirators start from their places'.

70 Noble cut 71–3, and the promptbook notes that Henry 'draws sword' (Noble pbk).

76 Kean as Henry rose at this point, causing all the noblemen to rise to their feet also, making a
    strong visual contrast with the abject conspirators still on their knees. The three remained
    on their knees until they were led off by Exeter and the guards at 176.

76 Hands noted the extremity of the effects of Scroop's betrayal on Henry in relation to its
    position between the news of Falstaff's illness and his death, suggesting that Scroop stands
    as a substitute for the Falstaff who promised, jestingly, in *1 Henry IV*, 'I'll be a traitor, then
    when thou art king' (1.2.119).

By your own counsel is suppressed and killed.
You must not dare for shame to talk of mercy,
For your own reasons turn into your bosoms,
As dogs upon their masters, worrying you.   80
See you, my princes and my noble peers,
These English monsters. My lord of Cambridge here,
You know how apt our love was to accord,
To furnish him with all appurtenants
Belonging to his honour, and this man   85
Hath for a few light crowns lightly conspired
And sworn unto the practices of France
To kill us here in Hampton. To the which
This knight, no less for bounty bound to us
Than Cambridge is, hath likewise sworn. But oh,   90
What shall I say to thee, Lord Scroop, thou cruel,
Ingrateful, savage and inhuman creature?

80 After a slow, static build-up the scene abruptly changes pace in Branagh's film, when the
    conspirators 'panic in the realisation that their position is hopeless. They make a sudden
    move for their swords. The nobles are ready. Exeter grabs Scroop as he lunges for the King,
    violently pushing him back against the wall. Gloucester deals with Cambridge. York forces
    Gray to his knees, a knife at his throat' (Branagh, p. 40).

82 Macready used this moment to isolate the traitors on stage: 'all on the stage shrink away
    and leave the conspirators alone' (Macready pbk).

85 Calvert's promptbook notes that all the noblemen put their hands on their swords, as the
    conspirators made a momentary attempt to escape. In Bogdanov's production, one of the
    conspirators did make a run for it, and was shot and wounded in the attempt.

90 In the Globe production, this marked the first flash of anger from Henry.

92 Calvert's performance was noted for 'the tone of melancholy sadness' with which Henry
    rebuked Scroop (contemporary review quoted by Foulkes, p. 27); Rignold's acting was also
    praised here: 'his reproaches against Lord Scroop had infinite tenderness . . . The pause
    that he made before he addressed this friend of his youth, as well as the impulse that he
    betrayed to stop him as he was being led off for execution, were artistically suggestive' (*The
    Era* 2 November 1879). In the BBC/Giles version, the King's voice trembles with emotion.
    Emotion reveals itself differently in Branagh's film, where Henry 'throws himself at Scroop,
    grabbing him and throwing him down onto the table, to deliver the following face to face'. It
    is a gesture at once intimate and threatening, and the rest of the speech, cutting lines
    103–33, fluctuates between Henry bitterly railing at his former friend and addressing him
    with tenderness (Branagh, p. 40). Hands also opted for a physical assault on Scroop, with

> Thou that didst bear the key of all my counsels,
> That knew'st the very bottom of my soul,
> That almost mightst have coined me into gold,   95
> Wouldst thou have practised on me for thy use?
> May it be possible that foreign hire
> Could out of thee extract one spark of evil
> That might annoy my finger? 'Tis so strange
> That though the truth of it stands off as gross   100
> As black on white my eye will scarcely see it.
> Treason and murder ever kept together,
> As two yoke-devils sworn to either's purpose,
> Working so grossly in a natural cause
> That admiration did not whoop at them.   105
> But thou 'gainst all proportion didst bring in
> Wonder to wait on treason and on murder,
> And whatsoever cunning fiend it was
> That wrought upon thee so preposterously
> Hath got the voice in hell for excellence.   110
> All other devils that suggest by treasons
> Do botch and bungle up damnation
> With patches, colours, and with forms being fetched
> From glistering semblances of piety;
> But he that tempered thee bade thee stand up,   115
> Gave thee no instance why thou shouldst do treason,
> Unless to dub thee with the name of traitor.
> If that same demon that hath gulled thee thus
> Should with his lion gait walk the whole world

Alan Howard demonstrating his 'wild agony' (David, p. 198). By contrast, at the Globe the unmasking of the traitors was handled as a piece of management through theatre: Henry was totally in control of the situation both politically and emotionally. 'What principally mattered was the way their self-disclosure could be rhetorically managed by Henry for the benefit of a larger national audience, for which the playhouse audience deputised' (Cordner, *SS* 51, 1998, p. 210). For the BBC production, Hayes cut the speech to just 76–8, 81–2, 86–92, 123, 137a–141.

95 Kean's edition noted 'Scroop drops face in hands' (Sprague, p. 117).

101 Sheen took Scroop's pistol from its holster and offered it to him to see if he would shoot, then held it to his head.

102–22 Cut by BBC/Giles version; 102–7 and 111–17 by Hands and Noble; 102–37 cut by Kean; 102–17 and 122–39a cut by Macready; 102–17, 111–17, 123–37a cut by Phelps; 102–41 cut in Bell's edition and by Kemble.

He might return to vasty Tartar back   120
And tell the legions 'I can never win
A soul so easy as that Englishman's.'
Oh, how hast thou with jealousy infected
The sweetness of affiance? Show men dutiful?
Why, so didst thou. Seem they grave and learnèd?   125
Why, so didst thou. Come they of noble family?
Why, so didst thou. Seem they religious?
Why, so didst thou. Or are they spare in diet,
Free from gross passion, or of mirth or anger,
Constant in spirit, not swerving with the blood,   130
Garnished and decked in modest complement,
Not working with the eye without the ear,
And but in purgèd judgement trusting neither?
Such and so finely bolted didst thou seem.
And thus thy fall hath left a kind of blot   135
To mark the full fraught man, and best endowed
With some suspicion. I will weep for thee,
For this revolt of thine, methinks, is like
Another fall of man. Their faults are open.
Arrest them to the answer of the law,   140
And God acquit them of their practices.
EXETER I arrest thee of high treason, by the name of Richard, Earl

123–28 In the BBC/Giles production, Henry kneels with Scroop, weeping with bewildered pain at his friend's treachery. Cedric Messina, producer of the BBC Shakespeare series, identified this moment as exemplary of televisual Shakespeare: '[Henry's] moving "why, why?" to Scroop is played on Scroop's face, a tortured traitor unable to explain his actions to a tortured king' (*BBC*, p. 7).

134 At the Globe, Henry embraced Scroop, his voice breaking with emotion.

138 For the BBC/Giles, Henry gets to his feet here, shifting into his public role and addressing not the individual but the company.

142 Macready's Exeter prompted 'animated movement of indignation and surprise' (Macready pbk). Phelps' stage direction gives the conspirators some dignity: 'Cambridge draws his sword and presents it to Exeter, and each Lord as he is addressed does the like. Exeter passes the several swords to Herald' (Phelps pbk). Calvert had Gower take the conspirators' swords one by one. In Richard Mansfield's acting edition, Exeter 'touches the shoulder of each with his baton. Gower draws the sword of each' (Sprague, p. 117). Hayes had the conspirators give up their swords and cut their lines of self-justification, 146–60; in the Globe production, Exeter took each of their swords as he named them. Daniels' production had a soldier train a rifle on the traitors as they were stripped of their officers' stripes. Noble

of Cambridge. I arrest thee of high treason, by the name of
Henry, Lord Scroop of Masham. I arrest thee of high treason,
by the name of Thomas Gray, knight of Northumberland.   145

SCROOP Our purposes God justly hath discovered,
    And I repent my fault more than my death,
    Which I beseech your highness to forgive,
    Although my body pay the price of it.

CAMBRIDGE For me, the gold of France did not seduce   150
    Although I did admit it as a motive
    The sooner to effect what I intended.
    But God be thankèd for prevention,
    Which I in sufferance heartily will rejoice,
    Beseeching God and you to pardon me.   155

GRAY Never did faithful subject more rejoice
    At the discovery of most dangerous treason
    Than I do at this hour joy o'er myself;
    Prevented from a damnèd enterprise.
    My fault, but not my body, pardon, sovereign.   160

KING God quit you in His mercy. Hear your sentence.
    You have conspired against our royal person,
    Joined with an enemy proclaimed, and from his coffers
    Received the golden earnest of our death;
    Wherein you would have sold your king to slaughter,   165
    His princes and his peers to servitude,
    His subjects to oppression and contempt,
    And his whole kingdom into desolation.
    Touching our person seek we no revenge,
    But we our kingdom's safety must so tender,   170

rearranged the speech so that Scroop's arraignment was the last of the three. In Branagh's
film, Exeter 'tears the insignia from around their necks' as he formally arrests them, and, as
he arrests Scroop last, he hits him suddenly and brutally across the face in disgust (Branagh,
p. 42). By contrast, the BBC/Giles production cut the lines of the formal arrest, 142–5.
Michael Kahn's production at Stratford, Connecticut enacted a stylised execution with
wooden sticks thrust against the traitors' chests.

146 While Scroop knelt to Henry at the Globe, the King kept his back to him.

161 Iain Glen's zeal was demonstrated as he 'wags his finger and delivers the line to suggest that
while God may do it, he will not. His Henry is not just a zealot but a sophist too' (*STel* 15 May
1994). Hayes cut 161a. At the Globe, Henry was solemn and quiet.

Whose ruin you have sought, that to her laws
We do deliver you. Get you therefore hence,
Poor miserable wretches, to your death,
The taste whereof God of His mercy give
You patience to endure, and true repentance   175
Of all your dear offences. Bear them hence.
>   *Exeunt Cambridge, Scroop and Gray [and Officers]*
Now lords, for France, the enterprise whereof
Shall be to you as us, like glorious.
We doubt not of a fair and lucky war,
Since God so graciously hath brought to light   180
This dangerous treason lurking in our way
To hinder our beginnings. We doubt not now
But every rub is smoothèd on our way.
Then forth, dear countrymen. Let us deliver

171 A close-up on Robert Hardy's face in BBC/Hayes' production shows the personal and emotional cost of the betrayal and of the sentence.

174–6 Cut by the Globe.

175 In Branagh's film, Scroop begins to cry.

176 As the conspirators exited under Gower's arrest in Calvert's production, Scroop made a mute appeal for Henry's pardon, but the King 'motions him off' (Calvert pbk). The close-up on the King in the BBC/Hayes production shows him shaking his head with terrible regret; a similar shot in the BBC/Giles version shows him visibly swallowing, moved. In Bogdanov's production, the conspirators were shot upstage. These actors, summarily despatched early on in the play, would doubtless have returned in other roles, and doubling has produced some interesting correspondences. In Hands' production, the actors playing Williams and Bates had doubled as Scroop and Gray, thus establishing a subtle parallel between these two different types of challenge to Henry's leadership. A different parallel was suggested through the doubling at the Globe, where the traitors were recast as the principal nobles of the French court.

177 Hayes has his Henry climb steps to deliver his speech from above, amid fluttering pennants which almost obscure his face. Hands argued that 'it is unthinkable that a man who has gone through the previous holocaust of emotions should now be cheerfully contemplating war', and that instead he 'tries to pull himself together, but the omens are hardly auspicious'. It is his brothers Clarence and York who silently offer him his sword and tabard, symbols of warfare, 'and push him towards commitment' (Beauman, p. 133). Branagh's screenplay glosses the transition: 'he somewhere finds the force to galvanise his generals. This latest test has been passed with flying colours, as far as they're concerned, but at a great personal cost, which we can read on the strained features' (Branagh, p. 42). At the Globe this abrupt change of tone prompted some audience laughter.

Our puissance into the hand of God,   185
Putting it straight in expedition.
Cheerly to sea, the signs of war advance.
No king of England if not king of France!

Flourish. Exeunt

2.3 *Enter* PISTOL, NYM, BARDOLPH, BOY *and* HOSTESS

HOSTESS Prithee, honey-sweet husband, let me bring thee to
    Staines.
PISTOL No, for my manly heart doth yearn. Bardolph, be blithe.

187 Macready ended the scene with the English standard centre stage. Calvert's scene ended
    with shouting and waving of spears and swords as the King set out on to his ship, unfurling a
    standard. Martin-Harvey's 1916 production punctuated the final line of the scene: 'the great
    gate of embarkation swung open to reveal on a blazing backcloth the English fleet . . . The
    sight moved us to applaud with its sudden shock' (M.W. Disher, *The Last Romantic: the
    Authorised Biography of Sir John Martin-Harvey*, London and New York: Hutchinson, p.
    230). Olivier places the seal on a document proffered by his secretary. The BBC/Giles
    production pans out to show the King framed in a doorway, with the flags and banners of
    the ships visible behind him. His speech is formal oratory, stressed by the close-up of him
    looking around his audience, who respond with an ordered 'God save the King' at the end
    of the scene. At the Globe, all knelt as Henry exited. Hayes has the noblemen smiling
    confidently and shaking hands. The King's ship, glorious in gold and scarlet, is revealed at
    the quay. Branagh ends the scene leading the way out of the hostelry and to the waiting
    ship. Terry Hands ended the scene with Henry in sudden heroic pose, leaping on to the
    cannon cart to spur his army with the final couplet, followed by the 'Deo Gracias' marching
    tune, which was to be a refrain throughout the production. Noble had Gloucester whisk
    aside the midstage curtain to reveal the upstage space symbolically representing France and
    battle in the production. Matthew Warchus revitalised the nineteenth-century tradition of
    ending a scene with a tableau, by incorporating Henry into 'a heroic tableau of the spirit
    adventure, a photo-pose waiting for the court painter to capture it for posterity, and then, as
    the pose was held throughout the narrative of Falstaff's death, Henry turned out of the static
    image, glancing back at his old companions' (Holland, p. 197.) Ron Daniels' production
    raised the houselights to the sound of helicopters and trumpets.

2.3 This scene was cut by Calvert. Branagh's film introduces the scene with the profile of the
    dead Falstaff and a close-up of a lit candle. The mood is disconsolate, as the group clusters

on the stairs for the farewells. In Olivier's film, the scene dissolves from the Southampton quayside of 2.2 to the Boar's Head, but this time not the theatrical representation of it as seen in 2.1. As the Chorus delivers his last lines off-camera, the film turns to 'the real upper window of an inn as it is opened by Mistress Quickly'. A tracking shot through the window reveals an old man lying in bed within, and a close-up of him sitting up in bed speaking in a delirium. Here Olivier interpolates from *2 Henry IV* to suggest the ending of the relationship between Falstaff and Henry, thus effectively replacing Henry's dismissal of one old friend, Scroop, with another, Falstaff. Falstaff speaks his lines of welcome to the newly crowned King from 5.5: 'God save thy Grace – King Hal – my royal Hal . . . God save thee my sweet boy . . . My King, my Jove, I speak to thee my heart.' Henry's voice-over 'off and distant' delivers his rejection: (*Masterworks*, p. 219):

> I know thee not, old man. Fall to thy prayers.
> How ill white hairs becomes a fool and jester!
> I have long dreamt of such a kind of man,
> So surfeit-swell'd, so old, and so profane;
> But being awak'd I do despise my dream.
> Make less thy body hence, and more thy grace;
> Leave gormandizing; know the grave doth gape
> For thee thrice wider than for other men.
> Reply not to me with a fool-born jest;
> Presume not that I am the thing I was;
> For God doth know, so shall the world perceive,
> That I have turn'd away my former self;
> So will I those that kept me company. *2 Henry IV*, lines 48–60

Oliver does not include the final lines of this speech, the actual words of banishment on pain of death, which might be seen to represent Henry's actions in too harsh a light. On hearing Henry's words, 'Falstaff sinks back on to the pillow, fumbling convulsively with the sheets' (O, Fol). The memory of Falstaff also dominated the opening of the scene in the English Shakespeare Company production, which began with a shadow play depicting the carrying of Falstaff's coffin, to the melancholic tromboning accompaniment of Nym; Falstaff's (not very large) coffin was carried by black-leathered Pistol, Nym and Bardolph in Ron Daniels' production where it served as a centre-piece, sometimes a bench, for the scene, and was left for Mistress Quickly to drag off on her own at the end. At the Globe the courtly flourish which ended 2.2 was continued to greet the tavern crew, flattening into comic trumpet note as they entered. Luggage was thrown up through the trapdoor in Noble's production, as the three loaded up an old pram carriage covered with dirty rags.

1 BBC/Hayes begins the scene with mournful cello music and a close-up of a young boy, crying, with someone's hand ruffling his hair.

Nym, rouse thy vaunting veins. Boy, bristle thy courage up, for
Falstaff he is dead, and we must earn therefore.   5

BARDOLPH Would I were with him, wheresome're he is, either in
heaven or in hell.

HOSTESS Nay, sure, he's not in hell. He's in Arthur's bosom if ever
man went to Arthur's bosom. A made a finer end, and went away
an it had been any christom child. A parted e'en just between   10
twelve and one, e'en at the turning o'the tide, for after I saw him
fumble with the sheets, and play with flowers, and smile upon
his finger's end, I knew there was but one way. For his nose was
as sharp as a pen, and a babbled of green fields. 'How now, Sir
John,' quoth I, 'what man, be o' good cheer!' So a cried out   15
'God, God, God' three or four times. Now I, to comfort him,
bid him a should not think of God; I hoped there was no need to
trouble himself with any such thoughts yet. So a bade me lay
more clothes on his feet. I put my hand into the bed, and felt
them, and they were as cold as any stone. Then I felt to his   20
knees, and so up-peered and upward, and all was as cold as any
stone.

NYM They say he cried out of sack.

HOSTESS Ay, that a did.

BARDOLPH And of women.   25

HOSTESS Nay, that a did not.

BOY Yes, that a did, and said they were devils incarnate.

HOSTESS A could never abide carnation, 'twas a colour he never
liked.

BOY A said once, the Devil would have him about women.   30

HOSTESS A did in some sort, indeed, handle women. But then he
was rheumatic, and talked of the Whore of Babylon.

---

8 The BBC versions by Hayes and by Giles make the speech a serious and poignant elegy, and
by using a gradual zoom to a close-up of Mistress Quickly's tear-filled eyes, Branagh invests
the speech with real emotion. Productions of the play as part of a sequence, such as Hands',
have often been able to rely on the kind of audience memory of and affection for Falstaff
that both Branagh and Olivier try to manufacture in their films. Under Hands' direction, the
speech was 'powerfully moving because of all that we had seen before'. The blocking of this
scene was also praised: 'with Quickly and the broken Bardolph in the foreground, Nym
crouched in dejection stage-right behind Quickly, a bedraggled Pistol and the sobbing Boy
further up stage behind Bardolph' (David, p. 210). By contrast, at the Globe, all sat wearily
on luggage. The Hostess' speech was comic, hammy, and provoked laughter.

BOY Do you not remember a saw a flea stick upon Bardolph's nose, and a said it was a black soul burning in hell?

BARDOLPH Well, the fuel is gone that maintained that fire. That's all   35
the riches I got in his service.

NYM Shall we shog? The king will be gone from Southampton.

PISTOL Come, let's away. My love, give me thy lips. Look to my
chattels and my moveables. Let senses rule: the word is, pitch
and pay. Trust none, for oaths are straws, men's faiths are wafer   40
cakes, and Hold-fast is the only dog, my duck. Therefore *caveto*
be thy counsellor. Go, clear thy crystals. Yoke-fellows in arms,
let us to France, like horseleeches, my boys, to suck, to suck, the
very blood to suck!

BOY And that's but unwholesome food, they say.   45

PISTOL Touch her soft mouth, and march.

BARDOLPH Farewell, hostess. [*Kisses her*]

NYM I cannot kiss, that is the humour of it, but adieu.

PISTOL Let housewifery appear. Keep close, I thee command.

HOSTESS Farewell, adieu.   50

Exeunt

38 Phelps instructed Nym to 'turn away whimpering' (Phelps pbk). Branagh's Mistress Quickly
gives the Boy a maternal hug; Nym avoids her embrace but takes off a leather bracelet and
gives it to her; her farewell to Pistol is melancholic.

48 Olivier has Pistol step forward warningly as Nym moves to embrace Quickly, so he gives
up his attempt to kiss her and takes his leave by raising his cap to her from a distance.
Mansfield included a similar piece of stage business, as did Calvert and Hayes: these
productions all have Pistol indicate that Nym should watch his step. Pistol, as played by
his eighteenth-century embodiment Theophilus Cibber, offered 'a laughable importance
of deportment, extravagant grimaces, and speaking it in the sonorous cant of old
tragedizers' (quoted by Taylor, p. 64); chief among these was Marlowe. To emphasise
this point, although it was probably lost on audiences largely ignorant of Marlowe's
plays, Olivier has Pistol declaim lines from *Tamburlaine Part 1*, 2.3: 'Farewell, farewell,
divine Zenocrate/ Is it not passing brave to be a King/ And ride in triumph through
Persepolis?'.

50 Branagh's film leaves Quickly alone at the end of the scene 'in her own quiet despair'
(Branagh, p. 47). In this the film follows Olivier, whose Mistress Quickly is also left alone
in the frame: 'in great loneliness she looks up left towards first floor window. Camera pans
up to this window, following her glance. Within, a light is flickering out, and as it finally
dies away we fade out' (O, Fol). Noble's production also focused on the sadness of the
separation: 'Quickly whispered her farewell to the men, crossed herself, and descended

2.4 *Flourish, Enter the* FRENCH KING, *the* DAUPHIN, *the Dukes of* BERRI
and BOURBON, [*the* CONSTABLE *and other Lords*]

FRENCH KING   Thus comes the English with full power upon us,
              And more than carefully it us concerns
              To answer royally in our defences.
              Therefore the Dukes of Berri and of Bourbon,

into the hatch' (Loehlin, p. 91). The men moved upstage into the darkness. After a
poignant and affectionate leave-taking, the mood of the English Shakespeare Company
production changed abruptly. Nym, Bardolph and Pistol opened their jackets to reveal
Union Jack T-shirts, and fell immediately into a loud, football-terrace chant of 'Here we go,
here we go', joined by others in the balcony who unrolled Union Jack bunting and a
banner inscribed 'Fuck the Frogs'. The Chorus entered with a football rattle and a placard
bearing the word 'Gotcha', in reference to the *Sun*'s infamous headline on the sinking of
the Argentinian cruiser the *General Belgrano* during the Falklands War. This was
accompanied by the rousingly patriotic strains of Hubert Parry's 'Jerusalem'. A number of
productions transpose the Boy's speech from 3.2.24–45 to the end of this scene, including
Macready, Phelps, Calvert and Mansfield. Macready and Mansfield ended the first act at
this point.

2.4   The first glimpse of the French is important for establishing them. Calvert sets the scene in 'A
      Room in the Palace of Charles the VI' (Calvert pbk). Phelps specified the presence of 'the
      Dauphin, Duke of Burgundy, Constable, 6 other lords, 2 heralds' (Phelps pbk): most
      productions make some rationalisation of the named French noblemen. Benson presented
      the French King as insane: a detail lifted from Holinshed and picked up by a number of
      productions, most notably Olivier's film. Ron Daniels' King wore his crown with a pale
      dressing gown, and seemed weak and infirm. Olivier introduces the scene with some
      transposed pieces of the Choruses of Acts 2 and 3, beginning the scene with a view of a
      beach, and then the Chorus is a voice-over delivering 3.0.1–25 above a stormy sea, into
      which the fleet appears. The mist clears to show the French palace; the Chorus speaks
      2.0.12–15 as we follow the camera into the throne room. The initial image is that of the
      symbolically empty throne: the King himself is sitting on a cushion leaning against one of
      the pillars, gazing vacantly around him, apparently disturbed by imaginary noises. Geduld
      describes the effect: it is 'as if the figures in a medieval illuminated manuscript had suddenly
      quickened into life. At first the characters in the French court are seen motionless,
      apparently mere elements of the setting. Then they begin to move as if in separate panes of
      a large picture' (Geduld, p. 35). The stylised, two-dimensional composition of the French
      court scenes serves to emphasise their lack of depth and reality.

For the English Shakespeare Company production, the French seemed part of a bygone, perhaps Edwardian, era of social niceties, wearing pale summer suits and drinking wine, with women sitting on a picnic rug. Ron Daniels gave the French blue frock-coats and hair in neat pigtails, in sharp contrast to Exeter in battle-khaki. The BBC/Giles production sets the French court in a setting covered with gold fleur-de-lys designs on heavy dark blue velvet, using a clear colour contrast with the browns and reds of the English scenes. A moral contrast was implied by Hands, who costumed the French in blue, grey and gold medieval garb, unlike the twentieth-century dress of the English: 'Theatrically, period costume is an outmoded convention. Used here it helps to accentuate the fact that the French are frozen in an era that has already passed' (Beauman, p. 137). The French thus were presented as adhering to strict social etiquette and other outdated behaviours, unlike the increasingly companionable English 'band of brothers'. Fancy costuming has become a cliché of the representation of the French: one review of Warchus' RSC production noted that he 'falls into the trap, like Olivier, of presenting the French court as ineffectual fops. It makes for some gorgeous costumes but detracts from Henry's achievement' (*STel* 15 May 1994), echoed elsewhere with 'the French are as overdressed as usual, but it is a relief to have a Dauphin not as camp as a row of his over-decorated tents' (*TLS* 20 May 1994). In Hall's production the French noblemen's costumes were padded out with foam.

Hayes introduces the new location by showing a map of the French Channel coast in close-up, with the French King's fingers tracing the route. Branagh also uses a map with the route of the English ships to Rouen, over which the Chorus speaks 3.0.17b, and 22–4. The camera then focuses on the 'haunted face of the King of France', moving away from him to reveal the nobles assembled around him in the candlelit court.

1   Iden Payne cast the role as an urbane diplomat, in contrast to the established image of the idiot King. Olivier's King speaks querulously. The opening line of the scene was greeted in the English Shakespeare Company production, given the behaviour of the English that ended the previous scene, with laughter. Many productions have made some play of the contrast between the ragtag soldiery depicted in 2.3 and the French King's opening lines. Terry Hands' souvenir edition quotes the actors playing Bardolph and Nym: 'We go off right at the back of the stage in a thin straggly line, with tattered clothes, beaten-up equipment . . . We are part of the "full power" – three aging men, marching off, with the Boy beating a drum' (Beauman, p. 137). By contrast, at the Globe, this was greeted with clapping and booing and a couple of impromptu 'hooray's from the audience. In Michael Kahn's production, the French spoke in French throughout, which 'was simultaneously translated into Shakespearean English, UN style, by a young man and young woman talking into microphones at either side of the stage' (Cooper, p. 151.)

4–5   Olivier pans to the individual noblemen as they are mentioned: all seem to be in languid attitudes, leaning on a pillar, playing with a cup and ball, looking up in surprise from an illuminated book.

Of Brabant and of Orléans, shall make forth,   5
And you, Prince Dauphin, with all swift despatch
To line and new repair our towns of war
With men of courage and with means defendant,
For England his approaches makes as fierce
As waters to the sucking of a gulf.   10
It fits us then to be as provident
As fear may teach us, out of late examples
Left by the fatal and neglected English
Upon our fields.

DAUPHIN   My most redoubted father,
It is most meet we arm us 'gainst the foe,   15
For peace itself should not so dull a kingdom,
Though war nor no known quarrel were in question,
But that defences, musters, preparations
Should be maintained, assembled and collected
As were a war in expectation.   20
Therefore I say 'tis meet we all go forth
To view the sick and feeble parts of France.
And let us do it with no show of fear,
No, with no more than if we heard that England
Were busied with a Whitsun morris dance.   25
For, my good liege, she is so idly kinged,
Her sceptre so fantastically borne,
By a vain, giddy, shallow, humorous youth,
That fear attends her not.

CONSTABLE   Oh peace, Prince Dauphin,
You are too much mistaken in this king.   30
Question, your grace, the late ambassadors,
With what great state he heard their embassy,
How well supplied with noble counsellors,

6a On the mention of his name, Branagh's Dauphin – 'young, intelligent and arrogant –
     interrupts his father: the rest of the King's lines are cut, stressing his impotence and the
     son's rise' (Branagh, p. 49).
9–14a Cut by Phelps, as were 16–20 and 31–5.
14b The Globe's Dauphin wore foppish, pale clothes and hat. In Giles' BBC production, the
     Dauphin is urbane, rhetorically effective, delivering a performance of oratory received with
     murmurs of agreement from the court.

How modest in exception, and withal
How terrible in constant resolution,   35
And you shall find his vanities, forespent,
Were but the outside of the Roman Brutus,
Covering discretion with a coat of folly,
As gardeners do with ordure hide those roots
That shall first spring and be most delicate.   40

DAUPHIN   Well, 'tis not so, my Lord High Constable.
But though we think it so, it is no matter.
In cases of defence, 'tis best to weigh
The enemy more mighty than he seems,
So the proportions of defence are filled,   45
Which of a weak and niggardly projection
Doth like a miser spoil his coat, with scanting
A little cloth.

FRENCH KING   Think we King Harry strong,
And, princes, look you strongly arm to meet him.
The kindred of him hath been fleshed upon us,   50
And he is bred out of that bloody strain
That haunted us in our familiar paths.
Witness our too-much memorable shame
When Crécy battle fatally was struck,
And all our princes captived, by the hand   55
Of that black name, Edward, black Prince of Wales,
Whilst that his mountant sire, on mountain standing,
Up in the air, crowned with the golden sun,
Saw his heroical seed, and smiled to see him
Mangle the work of nature and deface   60
The patterns that by God and by French fathers
Had twenty years been made. This is a stem

45–47a Cut by Globe and Olivier. 45–64 was cut by Calvert, thereby minimising the French King's
        expressed awe of the English at this early stage. Branagh's King is 'teetering on the thin line
        between fear and madness' (Branagh, p. 50). Olivier's is probably the wrong side of the line,
        sitting hunched up on the bottom step and 'addressing his lines to no-one in particular'
        (O, Fol).

  56   The Globe audience cheered at this memory. In the BBC/Giles production, the court shuffle
        with embarrassment at the memory of Crécy; Branagh's Constable looks uncomfortable.
        Hayes cuts 56–62a.

Of that victorious stock, and let us fear
The native mightiness and fate of him.

Enter a MESSENGER

MESSENGER Ambassadors from Harry, king of England,   65
                Do crave admittance to your majesty.
FRENCH KING We'll give them present audience.
                Go, and bring them.

                                                   [*Exit Messenger*]

                You see this chase is hotly followed, friends.
DAUPHIN Turn head and stop pursuit, for coward dogs   70
                Most spend their mouths when what they seem to threaten
                Runs far before them. Good my sovereign,
                Take up the English short, and let them know
                Of what a monarchy you are the head.
                Self love, my liege, is not so vile a sin   75
                As self neglecting.

64 In Phelps' production a trumpet call offstage heralded the entrance of the Messenger;
    Macready, Kean, Calvert, Noble and Branagh all made the Messenger Montjoy. In
    Branagh's production the King sinks into a reverie on this remembrance of past defeats,
    and buries his head in his hands. The Globe emended here to 'the native heaviness and
    might of him'.
67 In the BBC/Giles production, the French King's decision to hear the embassy is greeted with
    an outcry from the noblemen. There is the sense that the Dauphin is more in line with the
    general opinion of the court. By contrast, Branagh, like Hands, stresses friction between the
    noblemen and the Dauphin.
69 At the Globe this was spoken in a discomfited tone.
70b–72a Cut by the Globe. Hayes has the English embassy enter accompanied by a smartly marching
    military guard.
72b During the Dauphin's speech, Olivier's King is busily burrowing in a casket for his crown
    and other ornaments.
75 Branagh's Constable stands up as if to intervene in the Dauphin's words, but cannot stop
    him delivering the final wounding piece of advice.
76 Macready had Exeter enter with 'two English Lords with pedigree'. Kean had the King
    sit on his throne to receive the embassy. Phelps included '2 French heralds, 2 French
    lords, Exeter and 6 English Lords' in this stage direction (Phelps pbk). At the Globe the
    Dauphin ostentatiously kept his hat on during bows of greeting. Branagh's Exeter, the
    corpulent actor Brian Blessed, is a stout presence among the slender noblemen of the

Enter EXETER

FRENCH KING   From our brother of England?
EXETER   From him, and thus he greets your majesty:
        He wills you in the name of God almighty
        That you divest yourself, and lay apart
        The borrowed glories that by gift of heaven,   80
        By law of nature and of nations, 'longs
        To him and to his heirs, namely, the crown,
        And all wide-strechèd honours that pertain
        By custom and the ordinance of times
        Unto the crown of France. That you may know   85
        'Tis no sinister nor no awkward claim
        Picked from the wormholes of long vanished days,
        Nor from the dust of old oblivion raked,
        He sends you this most memorable line
              [*Delivers scroll*]
        In every branch truly demonstrative,   90
        Willing you overlook this pedigree,
        And when you find him evenly derived
        From his most famed of famous ancestors,
        Edward the Third, he bids you then resign
        Your crown and kingdom, indirectly held   95
        From him, the native and true challenger.

French court, and his appearance in armour stresses the martial bearing of the English in contrast to the luxury of the French. Ron Daniels' effete King shies away from the Messenger.

77   Branagh's Exeter is calm, polite and assertive; Ron Daniels has Exeter cool, even ironic, amid the foppish French.

82   On the mention of the 'crown', the French noblemen in the BBC/Giles production, already discomfited by Exeter's remarks, break out in protest.

83–96   Cut by Hayes.

89   Macready's Exeter gave the pedigree to Montjoy, who presented it to the King. There is a marginal instruction: 'Montjoy must not kneel' (Macready pbk). In Phelps' production, Exeter handed over a 'genealogical tree on scroll to Herald who kneels and presents it to [King of] France' (Phelps pbk). Branagh's Montjoy delivers the document to his King, who hands it back unread, 'knowing its contents' (Branagh, p. 51).

FRENCH KING Or else what follows?
EXETER Bloody constraint, for if you hide the crown
        Even in your hearts, there will he rake for it.
        Therefore in fierce tempest is he coming,   100
        In thunder and in earthquake, like a Jove,
        That if requiring fail, he will compel,
        And bids you, in the bowels of the Lord,
        Deliver up the crown, and to take mercy
        On the poor souls for whom this hungry war   105
        Opens his vasty jaws, and on your head
        Turning the widow's tears, the orphan's cries,
        The dead men's blood, the privèd maiden's groans,
        For husbands, fathers, and betrothèd lovers
        That shall be swallowed in this controversy.   110
        This is his claim, his threatening, and my message –
        Unless the Dauphin be in presence here,
        To whom expressly I bring greeting to.
FRENCH KING For us, we will consider of this further.
        Tomorrow shall you bear our full intent   115
        Back to our brother of England.
DAUPHIN   For the Dauphin,
        I stand here for him. What to him from England?
EXETER Scorn and defiance, slight regard, contempt,
        And anything that may not misbecome
        The mighty sender, doth he prize you at.   120
        Thus says my king, and if your father's highness

---

97 Branagh's production had the French princes 'surprised by this question [and] look around nervously waiting for the reply' (Branagh, p. 51).

103–10 Cut by Macready, Phelps, Olivier and Hayes, perhaps because Exeter's belligerence is damaging to the English cause. The BBC/Giles production accompanies the lines with a close-up on the King to see his reaction to this image of catastrophe.

116 Phelps' King made 'a sign to French lords, they surround the Thone and appear to confer with the King' (Phelps pbk). The BBC/Giles King decisively overrides the dissent of the nobles in agreeing to consider the proposal further, showing both his personal authority and the opposition to it.

116b Branagh's Dauphin stands defiantly, arms folded, although Exeter's reply wipes the smile off his face. Hayes has Exeter approach Princess Katherine at this line.

118 The Globe's audience laughed at this.

Do not, in grant of all demands at large,
Sweeten the bitter mock you sent his majesty,
He'll call you to so hot an answer of it
That caves and womby vaultages of France   125
Shall chide your trespass and return your mock
In second accent of his ordinance.
DAUPHIN Say, if my father render fair return
It is against my will, for I desire
Nothing but odds with England. To that end,   130
As matching to his youth and vanity,
I did present him with the Paris balls.
EXETER He'll make your Paris Louvre shake for it,
Were it the mistress-court of mighty Europe.
And be assured, you'll find a difference,   135
As we his subjects have in wonder found,
Between the promise of his greener days
And these he masters now. Now he weighs time
Even to the utmost grain. That you shall read
In your own losses, if he stay in France.   140
FRENCH KING Tomorrow shall you know our mind at full.
                Flourish
EXETER Despatch us with all speed, lest that our king
Come here himself to question our delay,

128 The BBC/Giles Dauphin delivers 128–30 in confidential tone to Exeter, turning to deliver lines 131–2 more publicly to the court.

133 When Exeter, at the Globe, took a step towards the Dauphin, he stepped nervously backwards. Hayes cut 134–40, leaving Exeter's single-line threat more decisive and more hostile.

141 At the Globe the French King stood as if to take control and made to exit. Exeter called him back, stressing his control of the situation. By contrast, the BBC/Giles King refuses to bow to the advice of his courtiers, decisively deferring the question until the next day.

143 Olivier confirms the weakness of the King by having him faint at this threat. The scene closes with the 'king being supported by the Dauphin, who looks down at him in slight irritation' (O, Fol).

142–7 Cut by Branagh, who closes the scene with a visual echo of its opening: a close-up on the haunted expression of the French King, who slowly closes his eyes.

>   For he is footed in this land already.
> FRENCH KING You shall be soon dispatched, with fair conditions.   145
>   A night is but small breath and little pause
>   To answer matters of this consequence.

> *[Flourish] Exeunt*

3.0 *Enter* CHORUS

> CHORUS Thus with imagined wing our swift scene flies
>   In motion of no less celerity
>   Than that of thought. Suppose that you have seen
>   The well-appointed king at Hampton Pier
>   Embark his royalty, and his brave fleet   5
>   With silken streamers the young Phoebus feigning.
>   Play with your fancies, and in them behold

145–7 The scene ends in the BBC/Giles production with consternation in the court; Macready maintained courtly decorum, ending with a flourish of drums and trumpets. Hands ended the scene on an ominous note: 'the stage darkens; drums roll' (Beauman, p. 142).

3.0 Macready's dioramic illustrations were well suited to this scene: 'Music – As the Drop rises – it continues, as the scene opens, presenting the embarkation of the King, and the sailing of the fleet; it gradually dies away, as the night appears to come on, and the single ship is left on the scene' (Macready pbk). For the BBC, Hayes has the Chorus turn from the previous action in which he has been an anonymous bystander to deliver the speech. Similarly, the BBC/Giles Chorus steps out from the French court of the preceding scene, and takes off a blue cloak decorated with fleur-de-lys, as if he were a chameleon shedding the colours of his previous backdrop. Ron Daniels had the Chorus in khaki uniform, among the camouflaged soldiers and explosions of battle. This time it was the turn of the Llewellyn actor to take the part of the Chorus in the Globe production, dressed as a nobleman, and using a long stave for expression and emphasis.

1–3 Olivier uses much of 3.0 to introduce 2.4, but retains 3.0.25–7 here, delivered off-screen over 'English soldiers storming Harfleur beach. Then dissolve again to: A few soldiers are hauling a cannon ashore up a beach' (*Masterworks*, p. 228). Branagh's Chorus begins as a voice-over, with a quick dissolve to a scene of 'Walls and Breach, Harfleur: Night'. The screen is filled with movement and noise of battle, and the Chorus' speech 'is urgent, breathless as if he too were caught up in the battle' (Branagh, p. 53). Cutting lines 3b–24 locates the scene firmly and immediately in the battle for Harfleur.

Upon the hempen tackle ship-boys climbing.
Hear the shrill whistle, which doth order give
To sounds confused. Behold the threaden sails, 10
Borne with the invisible and creeping wind,
Draw the huge bottoms through the furrowed sea,
Breasting the lofty surge. O do but think
You stand upon the rivage, and behold
A city on th'inconstant billows dancing, 15
For so appears this fleet majestical,
Holding due course to Harfleur. Follow, follow!
Grapple your minds to sternage of this navy,
And leave your England as dead midnight, still,
Guarded with grandsires, babies and old women, 20
Either past or not arrived to pith and puissance.
For who is he whose chin is but enriched
With one appearing hair that will not follow
These culled and choice-drawn cavaliers to France?
Work, work your thoughts, and therein see a siege. 25
Behold the ordnance on their carriages
With fatal mouths gaping on girded Harfleur.
Suppose th'ambassador from the French comes back,
Tells Harry that the king doth offer him
Katherine his daughter, and with her to dowry 30
Some petty and unprofitable dukedoms.
The offer likes not, and the nimble gunner

15 Macready's diorama revealed the English fleet at sea, a visual effect praised for the quality of the moonlit sea.

19–21 Cut by the Globe.

25 Macready's diorama advances: 'when the French coast begins to appear, very distant shouts and alarums are heard [a marginal note reminds 'signal flag for shouts at distance'], which continue very faintly through the remainder of the speech' (Macready pbk). The BBC/Giles Chorus is encouraging, urging, speaking directly to the camera. Branagh's Chorus is in the middle of the battlefield, 'caught up wildly in the excitement of the gunfire, smoke and explosions' (Branagh, p. 53), and his speech is punctuated with the noise of shells.

30 At the Globe, there was audience appreciation and some laughter.

32 Hayes introduces a dissolve from the figure of the Chorus to the lighting of a fuse, as the Chorus' tone gains in excitement.

With linstock now the devilish cannon touches
                    Alarm, and chambers go off
And down goes all before them. Still be kind,
And eke out our performance with your mind.   *Exit*   35

3.1 *Enter the* KING, EXETER, BEDFORD *and* GLOUCESTER

Alarm. [Enter soldiers with] scaling ladders at Harfleur

33 At this point, Macready's painted diorama melted into the scene of the siege with such precision that reviewers remarked how difficult it was to tell where one ended and the other began.

sd The Folio stage direction, 'Alarum, and Chambers goe off' is the first time that the Chorus was clearly identified as present and thus involved in the action he/she describes. Kean's stylised depiction suggests that the Chorus was located amid the battle by a crescendo of music during the speech, and the curtain opened to discover a tableau of the opposing French and English armies. Branagh locates the Chorus clearly amid the battle, his words sometimes drowned out by massive explosions.

3.1 For many productions, the revelation of the battle for Harfleur for this scene was the *coup de théâtre* – so far. The Folio mentions 'Alarum: Scaling Ladders at Harfleur', presumably placed against the *frons scenae* or back wall of the stage to allow access to the balcony above. Macready's promptbook gives extensive instructions:

> scene passing on presents the landing and assault of Harfleur – as it moves away, it discloses on stage the walls and gate of Harfleur, manned with combatants; the English on the scaling ladders attaching them – others with cannon – some behind with the long and cross bows. The English repulsed come rushing on – the assailants on the stage leave their attack, when the king enters last. Many of the English pass off the stage and exit R. (Macready pbk)

Macready's Henry was flanked by six named and four unnamed noblemen, two heralds, twelve guards and a captain, all with 'spears and weapons pointed toward the walls' (Macready pbk), although the *Spectator*'s reviewer had some harsh words about the representation:

> the scene before Harfleur becomes ludicrous by trying to represent the assault on the town: the French are quietly looking over the walls while the English king is urging his

soldiers on to the breach, and when they rush forward the stage is left clear for the buffoonery of Pistol and his brother cowards – with only an uncouth piece of ordnance, which once being fired, once and no more, had made a most abortive explosion. (*The Spectator*, 15 June 1839)

At least some of this bathos, however, is surely a feature of the play, anticipated by the Chorus and structured by, for example, the juxtaposition of 3.1 and 3.2, rather than a shortcoming of Macready's production. Down the margin of 3.0 in Kean's promptbook is an extensive list of those required for the next scene, numbering fifteen named English and French participants and a further two hundred extras as standard-bearers, axemen, double axemen, archers, cannoneers, lancemen, hatchet men, harpooners, spear carriers, knights, trumpeters, body guards and, later to be symbols of French treachery, '20 English boys'. The scene is 'The Siege of Harfleur. The Walls are Manned by the French. The English are Repulsed from an Attack on the Breach' (Kean pbk). Kean was praised in *The Saturday Review* for 'the first genuine battle ever seen on theatrical boards – a noisy, blazing, crowding, smoking reality' in which the army could have been 'a hundred thousand strong' since its tail was never seen (2 April 1859). Phelps similarly calls out 'the whole of the English troops – soldiers – officers' against a panoramic background, with troops 'seen fighting through opening in panorama' (Phelps pbk). Phelps' King entered 'on a platform' to rally the troops, who redoubled their attack, but the speech of 3.1. is transposed to 3.4.

Whereas Shakespeare juxtaposes Henry's heroics with Bardolph's version of the speech at the opening of 3.2, Phelps began the Harfleur sequence with 3.2. Calvert's scene took place in 'The English Intrenchments. Within Bowshot of Harfleur. The English repulsed from an attack on the breach. Enter King Henry hastily, attended' (Calvert pbk). Calvert's production was praised for its 'realism' in 'the horrors of the battlefield, with the bodies of the slain, begrimed, blood-stained, tumbled helter-skelter with broken engines of warfare and ruined masonry all over the stage' (unattributed press cutting, bound with 1879 edn). Waller's production revealed the breach as 'a grim, sweaty place reeking of death, slippery with blood, and beginning to be filled with a sense of fear, panic and defeat . . . Then came the King, panting and out of breath, but with a face of granite' (Walter Macqueen-Pope, *Ghosts and Greasepaint: a Story of the Days that Were*, London: R. Hale, 1951, p. 101). Olivier ends 2.4 with the French King's swoon, then dissolves to the Chorus' voice-over of 3.0.25–7 above an image of a turbulent sea, then a beach where a few soldiers are hauling a cannon ashore. 'The fears that storm through the French king's mind give way to a glimpse of the stormy waters of the English Channel, and the ornamentations and artificialities of the French court give way to the realities of the English invasion' (Geduld, pp. 36–7). The English foot soldiers appear round the cliff in retreat; Henry on (white) horseback, takes off his helmet to address his men.

KING Once more unto the breach, dear friends, once more,
        Or close the wall up with our English dead!
        In peace there's nothing so becomes a man
        As modest stillness and humility.

Branagh's film begins the scene by stressing the messy, muddied and frightened confusion of the rout, as the English retreat in a panic from the breached city wall. Henry emerges as a mythic figure, silhouetted against the centre of the breach and dramatically backlit by the burning city, on the rearing white horse that had been associated with stage Henrys for a century. The sense of physical exertion and effort associated with this victory was suggested in Hands' production by increasing the rake of the angled stage to become the walls of Harfleur. Hands' entry had 'the English soldiers come crashing over the breach, some falling to the ground, others clinging to the scaling ladders. Henry comes over the breach last' (Beauman, p. 143). Warchus conducted the siege 'with pounding gunfire and thrilling pillars of fire, with Henry swinging from a rope onto the parapets like an early Errol Flynn' (*STel* 15 May 1994). Robert Hardy delivers his lines from a ladder over a sea of the helmets of his troops in Hayes' BBC production. Michael Kahn's sceptical reading of the play produced for the scene the title 'Siege of Harfleur; Propaganda of the Machine; the People Follow.' By contrast with lavish nineteenth-century stagings, Ron Daniels' production was without supernumeraries in this scene, stressing the heroic few of Henry's army, numbering ten including their leader; Noble's promptbook indicates that seventeen characters, in addition to Bardolph, Nym and Pistol, were on stage during the scene. At the Globe, Henry entered in quartered red and blue fleur-de-lys; the pace of the action speeding up. The BBC/Giles King is seen on some exterior steps to the walls of Harfleur.

1 Phelps interpolated the scene of Henry's victory at this point. Music accompanied the first two lines of 3.1 as Henry 'ascends bridge heading the whole of the army with colours speaking through music . . . Omnes keep the bridge with shouts during dialogue on stage' (Phelps pbk). This speech has become one of the most famous in the canon: and the difficulties of delivering it, in context, to a knowing audience were illustrated at the Globe, where the opening words were greeted with cheers of familiarity. Here, Henry moved around the stage, shouting, against a background of rumbling drums. The speech in its entirety has not always been a well-known and reiterated set piece, however. Bell's acting edition cut 7–17a and 22–30; lines 7–25a were cut by Kean; Kemble delivered only the first two lines, followed by a new line 'Beat in the rondure of their rampar'd walls', and then a line from *1 Henry VI* 1.5.28, as Talbot is urging the English forces at Orléans to renew the fight against the French, led by Joan la Pucelle, 'Or tear the lions out of England's coat'. (Lines 17b–34 were transposed to the end of 4.3.) This adapted and much-reduced version of the speech was also preferred in Macready's production, followed by

But when the blast of war blows in our ears,   5
Then imitate the action of the tiger:
Stiffen the sinews, conjure up the blood,
Disguise fair nature with hard-favoured rage.
Then lend the eye a terrible aspect,
Let it pry through the portage of the head,   10
Like the brass cannon. Let the brow o'erwhelm it
As fearfully as doth a gallèd rock
O'erhang and jutty his confounded base,
Swilled with the wild and wasteful ocean.
Now set the teeth and stretch the nostril wide,   15
Hold hard the breath, and bend up every spirit

an adapted line 33, 'Bend up every spirit . . .' and the final exhortation of line 34. A contemporary review observed astutely that this adaptation 'suits [Macready's] purpose to convert a deliberate exhortation into a sudden rallying cry' (*The Spectator,* 15 June 1832). For the BBC/Giles production, Henry moves among the coughing and groaning men, exhausted from their efforts, giving the speech the quality of an extemporary rather than set-piece oration. In addressing particular phrases to individual soldiers, something of the personal element of his leadership is conveyed, although Loehlin describes him as 'trying to *tease* his men into battle' (Loehlin, p. 79). Branagh's opening lines are screamed out from horseback as the English soldiers run in different directions to escape the battle. He gallops to join them in the trenches, delivering the rest of the speech to a gradually increasing group, who crowd round to listen. Olivier uses the characteristic backwards zoom, so that rather than focusing on the speaker, the camera pulls back and up to frame him among his soldiers. Anthony Davies suggests this high-angled distant camera position serves 'to stress Henry's relative smallness' (Davies, p. 28); Geduld observes that 'despite his obvious valour, he has begun his campaign as the underdog' (Geduld, p. 37) (cf. the comparable speech before Agincourt, Commentary, p. 191). Olivier's delivery of the speech is described in considerable detail in his *On Acting*, pp. 61–3, in which the self-conscious oratory of the lines is explained, in interspersed glossing such as 'now we're really motoring, climbing vocally but in complete control. The politician and the hero' (after line 17a) or 'Got them . . . now hold them. Remember never give them everything' (after line 28). Iain Glen as Henry was here 'clearly a decent man playing a hard-hearted, politically expedient role which he finds almost intolerable' (*Tel* 12 May 1994). Alan Howard, in Hands' production, delivered the speech from a scaling ladder on the walls of Harfleur; Pennington, in Bogdanov's production, threatened rather than persuaded, waving a machine gun from his vantage point on a tank amid his unwilling foot soldiers.

To his full height. On, on, you noble English,
Whose blood is fet from fathers of war-proof,
Fathers that like so many Alexanders
Have in these parts from morn till even fought,   20
And sheathed their swords for lack of argument.
Dishonour not your mothers. Now attest
That those whom you called fathers did beget you.
Be copy now to men of grosser blood,
And teach them how to war. And you, good yeomen,   25
Whose limbs were made in England, show us here
The mettle of your pasture. Let us swear
That you are worth your breeding, which I doubt not,
For there is none of you so mean and base
That hath not noble lustre in your eyes.   30
I see you stand like greyhounds in the slips,
Straining upon the start. The game's afoot.
Follow your spirit, and upon this charge
Cry 'God for Harry, England and Saint George!'

Alarm, and chambers go off [*Exeunt*]

22 The following lines in the Globe production were addressed to the audience, with
    some laughter at 23. Laughter is also provoked in the BBC/Giles version, and
    indicates that the troops are rallying, coming round to their leader's demands.
    Michael Sheen, in Daniels' production, turned to address the audience as the soldiery.
    The stage was raised to form a ramp upstage, over which the renewed troops
    stormed.

25 At this line, Hayes has all the soldiers turn to look directly at the camera, thus
    simultaneously suggesting more troops out of sight, and implicating the audience as
    members of Henry's army.

34 Macready's productions before 1839 ran this scene immediately into the Governor's
    surrender in 3.4: 'When the Gates are open a bridge is seen. French captain and 12
    guards are on it. They salute the king as he passes. The Governor and 2 citizens enter at
    the gates and kneel. Exeter takes the keys from the Governor' (Macready pbk). Kean also
    ran the scene straight into the capitulation of Harfleur. The BBC/Giles soldiers give a great
    shout of renewed determination. In Olivier's film, the soldiers repeat the line, cheering,
    and rush renewed up to the breach. These words were punctuated with drums in the
    Globe.

3.2 *Enter* NYM, BARDOLPH, PISTOL *and* BOY

BARDOLPH On, on, on, on, on, to the breach, to the breach!

NYM Pray thee, corporal, stay. The knocks are too hot, and for mine
    own part I have not a case of lives. The humour of it is too hot,
    that is the very plain-song of it.

PISTOL 'The plain-song' is most just, for humours do abound.   5
    Knocks go and come, God's vassals drop and die,
        [*Sings*] And sword and shield,
        In bloody field,
        Doth win immortal fame.

BOY Would I were in an ale-house in London. I would give all my   10
    fame for a pot of ale, and safety.

PISTOL And I.
        [*Sings*] If wishes would prevail with me,
        My purpose should not fail with me,
        But thither would I hie.   15

BOY [*Sings*] As duly

3.2 The contrast between this scene and 3.1 stresses the contrast, or perhaps the proximity,
between heroism and cowardice. Macready's 1839 production introduced the miscreants as
slapstick comedy: 'in excessive trepidation, each striving to get behind and hold the others
before him, they come on holding the boy and stooping to shield themselves; at every fresh
alarm, their fear increases' (Macready pbk). Kean cut the scene altogether. Phelps
overturned this contrast by placing 3.2 at the beginning of the third act, probably, given the
marginalia of the promptbook, to give more time to set up the elaborately staged parley.
Calvert set the scene in 'The Neighbourhood of the Mines. The Duke of Gloster's Quarters.
Enter, alarmedly, Bardolph, Nym, Pistol and the Boy.'

    Olivier's Bardolph stood on a rock, recalling and contrasting his leader urging the troops
on. Gary Taylor argues that in Terry Hands' production this juxtaposition 'did not . . . simply
pop the heroic balloon; in a subtler way [it] sustained it' (*Moment*, p. 135), although Hands
noted in the published text of his production: 'Not everybody is convinced [by Henry's
speech in 3.1]. Not everybody is heroic' (Beauman, p. 145). Noble cut lines 1–4 and had
Bardolph enter from the audience, with Pistol and Nym trying to pull him back. Hayes kept
only a much-reduced final speech from the Boy. In Daniels' production, Nym seemed about
to offer help to an apparently injured Bardolph, but recoiled, stagily, at the smell, to
audience laughter.

1 Like Macready, the Globe played the entrance for comic value.

7 Macready cut the song; the Globe delivered it in tap-room style.

> But not as truly
> As bird doth sing on bough.

Enter LLEWELLYN

LLEWELLYN Up to the preach, you dogs! Avaunt, you cullions!
PISTOL Be merciful, great duke, to men of mould! Abate thy rage, 20
  abate thy manly rage! Abate thy rage, great duke! Good bawcock,
  bate thy rage. Use lenity, sweet chuck.
NYM These be good humours! Your honour wins bad humours!

Exeunt [Pistol, Bardolph and Nym, pursued by Llewellyn]

BOY As young as I am, I have observed these three swashers. I am
  boy to them all three, but all they three, though they would serve 25
  me, could not be man to me, for indeed three such antics do not
  amount to a man. For Bardolph, he is white-livered and red-
  faced, by the means whereof a faces it out but fights not. For
  Pistol, he hath a killing tongue and a quiet sword, by the means
  whereof a breaks words and keeps whole weapons. For Nym, 30
  he hath heard that men of few words are the best men, and
  therefore he scorns to say his prayers lest a should be thought a
  coward, but his few bad words are matched with as few good
  deeds, for a never broke any man's head but his own, and that

18 The Globe's Llewellyn entered from the yard among the audience, chasing the reprobates with a stave so they exited to audience laughter. Daniels had a more sombre entry, with Llewellyn supporting a wounded comrade. The reprobate Nym, Bardolph and Pistol were drunk: Nym, apparently from a combination of booze and fear, vomits. Noble's production introduced an elaborate slapstick sequence: 'Fluellen enters . . . Pistol holds staff across Bardolph and Nym, all crouching on floor. Nym stands and falls over staff. Bardolph steps on Nym and crashes against thunder sheet. Pistol stands, falls over Nym who rises and beats Pistol. Nym grasps other end of staff, pivots on Pistol. Swings [upstage] onto iron. Both end up against iron' (Noble pbk).

22 Phelps' promptbook gives some details of stage business: 'Pistol makes a bolt and gets to R. Fluellen fetches him back and beats them off.'

24 Many productions having deployed this speech elsewhere, it is cut from its position here by Kemble, Bell, Phelps, Macready and Olivier. Daniels' production put the Boy at the front of the stage, addressing the audience. The Globe Boy entered through the trapdoor. Olivier dissolves to a close-up of 'a flaming linstock touching the powder box of a cannon. Track with its recoil from the explosion' (*Masterworks*, p. 238). The Chorus off-screen delivers 3.0 32b–33, then cuts to a wall of masonry crashing, at line 34, thus using the Chorus speeches as immediate commentary on unfolding events rather than prefatory explication.

was against a post when he was drunk. They will steal anything   35
and call it purchase. Bardolph stole a lute-case, bore it twelve
leagues and sold it for three halfpence. Nym and Bardolph are
sworn brothers in filching, and in Calais they stole a fire-shovel.
I knew by that piece of service the men would carry coals. They
would have me as familiar with men's pockets as their gloves or   40
their handkerchiefs, which makes much against my manhood if
I should take from another's pocket to put into mine, for it is
plain pocketing up of wrongs. I must leave them and seek some
better service. Their villainy goes against my weak stomach, and
therefore I must cast it up.   45

Exit

3.3 *Enter* GOWER [*and* LLEWELLYN]

GOWER Captain Llewellyn, you must come presently to the mines.
The Duke of Gloucester would speak with you.

1–9 Phelps only kept these lines, after which the parley is sounded for the scene between Henry
and the Governor of Harfleur, following events in Q, which does not include the characters
of Jamy and Macmorris. The Folio text makes the point that this is an interchange between
national types rather than individualised characters by using 'Irish', 'Scot' and 'Welch' as
speech prefixes. The whole scene was cut by Kean and Phelps. Macready kept
Macmorris – replacing the references to 'Chrish' with 'St Patrick' with the double benefit
of banishing blasphemy and adding an 'Irish' touch – but cut all reference to Jamy. Bell's
acting edition notes: 'The Irish and Scotch captains, are exceeding meagre characters;
very faintly drawn, and poor cyphers, when best represented; scarce any traces of
nationality, in dialogue or dialect, is preserved' (Bell, p. 36), and the evidence of mid-
eighteenth-century playbills seems to suggest that Jamys and Macmorrises were often
omitted in performance. Kemble, following this, preserved only lines 1–19. Despite the
enduring comic popularity of national stereotypes for British audiences – in, for example,
the long-running television comedy series *'Allo 'Allo* (BBC, 1982–94) – the representation
of these characters has been an awkward aspect of the play in the theatre. Terry Hands'
acceptance of current stereotypes is rather unsettling, despite the parenthetic
explanation:

In rehearsal the actors added to Shakespeare's indications those elements of
contemporary attitude which still (sometimes affectionately) define our island peoples.
Barrie Rutter emphasised the aggression, Catholicism and delight in carnage of

LLEWELLYN To the mines? Tell you the Duke it is not so good to
come to the mines, for, look you, the mines is not according to
the disciplines of the war, the concavities of it is not sufficient.   5
For, look you, th'athversary, you may discuss unto the Duke,
look you, is digged himself, four yard under the countermines!
By Cheshu, I think a will plow up all, if there is not better
directions.

GOWER The Duke of Gloucester, to whom the order of the siege is   10
given, is altogether directed by an Irishman, a very valiant
gentleman, i'faith.

LLEWELLYN It is Captain Macmorris, is it not?

GOWER I think it be.

LLEWELLYN By Cheshu, he is an ass, as in the world. I will verify as   15
much in his beard. He has no more directions in the true
disciplines of the wars, look you, of the Roman disciplines, than
is a puppy dog.

Enter MACMORRIS *and Captain* JAMY

GOWER Here a comes, and the Scots captain, Captain Jamy, with
him.   20

LLEWELLYN Captain Jamy is a marvellous falorous gentleman, that
is certain, and of great expedition and knowledge in th'anchient
wars, upon my particular knowledge of his directions. By
Cheshu, he will maintain his argument as well as any military

> Macmorris, the Irish captain – in charge of explosives. Ken Stott (a Scotsman) pointed
> out the northern addiction to whisky of Jamy, the Scots captain of infantry. Trevor
> Peacock brought to the fiery Welshman Fluellen the pedantic bookmanship of the
> valleys and Derek Smith the phlegmatic English captain chewed sweets like Shaw's
> 'chocolate soldier'. (Beauman, p. 147)

Olivier's film chooses a 'stagey' style: 'an episode removed in spirit and substance from the
more serious main action is not inappropriately played against a painted landscape'
(Geduld, p. 3), although this increased artificiality identifies the captains with the anti-
illusionistic aesthetics of the film's representations of the French. Warchus also highlighted
the incongruity of the scene, which one reviewer judged 'so overdone as to remove the four
captains from the realistic convention in which the army was presented and place them in a
music-hall category of their own' (David, p. 214). Branagh prunes the scene heavily. Daniels
introduced Llewellyn and Gower eating from mess tins; Hayes has Jamy and Macmorris
climb out of a trench.

man in the world, in the disciplines of the pristine wars of the   25
Romans.

JAMY I say guidday, Captain Llewellyn.

LLEWELLYN Goodden to your worship, good Captain James.

GOWER How now, Captain Macmorris, have you quit the mines?
Have the pioneers given o'er?   30

MACMORRIS By Chrish law, 'tish ill done. The work ish give over,
the trumpet sound the retreat. By my hand I swear, and my
father's soul, the work ish ill done. It ish give over. I would have
blowed up the town, so Chrish save me law, in an hour. O, 'tish ill
done, 'tish ill done. By my hand, 'tish ill done.   35

LLEWELLYN Captain Macmorris, I beseech you now, will you
vouchsafe me, look you, a few disputations with you, as partly
touching or concerning the disciplines of the war, the Roman
wars, in the way of argument, look you, and friendly
communication? Partly to satisfy my opinion, and partly for the   40
satisfaction, look you, of my mind, as touching the direction of
the military discipline, that is the point.

JAMY It sall be vary guid, guid faith, guid captains baith, and I sall
'quite you with guid leave, as I may pick occasion, that sall I,
marry.   45

MACMORRIS It is no time to discourse, so Chrish save me. The day
is hot, and the weather, and the wars, and the king, and the
dukes. It is no time to discourse, the town is besieched! An the
trumpet call us to the breach, and we talk and be Chrish do
nothing, 'tis shame for us all! So God sa' me, 'tis shame to stand   50
still, it is shame, by my hand. And there is throats to be cut, and
works to be done, and there ish nothing done, so Christ sa' me
law.

JAMY By the mess, e'er these eyes of mine take themselves to
slumber I'll dee guid service, or I'll lig i'the grund for it. I owe   55

---

27 At the Globe Jamy was dressed in beret and tartan cloak; Hayes goes for the stereotype by
introducing Jamy swigging spirits from a bottle.

31 The Globe's Macmorris was dressed in short 'savage' cloak and entered shouting.
Branagh (himself an Irishman) identifies Macmorris as 'wild and apparently deranged' at
this point (Branagh, p. 58). Daniels' Macmorris entered blackened with the soot from his
explosions; Noble had him enter through the trapdoor following a large explosion, like a
stage-devil.

50 Noble's Macmorris threw a grenade into the pit.

Got a death, and I'll pay't as valorously as I may, that sall I surely do, that is the breff and the long. Marry, I wad full fain hear some question 'tween you twae.

LLEWELLYN Captain Macmorris, I think, look you, under your correction, there is not many of your nation –   60

MACMORRIS Of my nation? What ish my nation? Ish a villain, and a bastard, and a knave, and a rascal. What ish my nation? Who talks of my nation?

LLEWELLYN Look you, if you take the matter otherwise than is meant, Captain Macmorris, peradventure I shall think you do   65
not use me with that affability as in discretion you ought to use me, look you, being as good a man as yourself, both in the disciplines of war, and in the derivation of my birth, and in other particularities.

MACMORRIS I do not know you so good a man as myself. So Chrish   70
save me, I will cut off your head!

GOWER Gentlemen both, you will mistake each other.

JAMY Ah, that's a foul fault.

A parley

GOWER The town sounds a parley.

LLEWELLYN Captain Macmorris, when there is more better   75
opportunity to be required, look you, I will be so bold as to tell you I know the disciplines of war, and there is an end.

Exeunt

60 Hayes presents Llewellyn as deliberately needling Macmorris, with sideways glances at Gower. By contrast Hands' production showed Llewellyn insulting Macmorris 'quite unintentionally [. . . with] an interrupted sentence as the syntax suggests, rather than a deliberate provocation followed by a long pause to let the point sink in' (*Moment*, p. 127).

61 In the BBC/Hayes production, Macmorris' splenetic response is greeted with laughter from the other captains. Olivier has 'Ish a villain . . .' delivered as a question, to which the other captains shake their head in sympathetic reply. At the Globe Macmorris' fury caused audience laughter. In Daniels' production the other captains were laughing behind his back.

64 In the general hilarity of the audience response at the Globe, Llewellyn's accent was also a source of comedy.

71 Branagh's Macmorris is ominously quiet and steely, then suddenly lunges for Llewellyn. Hayes ends the scene with a comic scuffle in which both combatants end up falling flat on their faces. In Daniels' production, Macmorris went for Llewellyn with a shovel, with serious aggression, but was interrupted by the entrance of Henry, in the same battle-stained dress as his men.

3.4 *Enter the* KING [, EXETER] *and all his train before the gates*

KING How yet resolves the governor of the town?
       This is the latest parle we will admit,

3.4 Bell had 'Enter King Henry, and his train, before the gates; Governor and Citizens, on the
Ramparts'. Macready's Governor was already at the gate with a white flag at the opening of
the scene. Calvert set this scene: 'The Siege of Harfleur. At the Breach. Signs of a Severe
Conflict' where 'The Governor of the Town appears on the walls with a Flag of Truce'
(Calvert pbk). Kean ran the scene straight on from 3.1, having cut 3.2 and 3.3 in their
entirety. Thus the victory is swiftly won: 'The English charge upon the breach, headed by
the King. Alarums. The Governor of the town appears on the walls with flag of truce' (Kean
pbk). Phelps situated the Governor centre upstage, in an opening in the flat. The citizens of
Harfleur looked down from the city walls on the encircling English. Drums and trumpets
signalled the start of the scene, and the stagehands were reminded to 'attend to Rattling of
Chains' (Phelps pbk). Geduld observes that Olivier's film 'contrasts the English in their
"real" armor with the French inside their "artificial" city' (Geduld, p. 38). Both sides were
involved in gameplaying in Michael Kahn's production, as Harfleur was constructed of
brown wrapping paper and cardboard, and besieged with a salvo of small balls. At the
Globe, the curtains at the rear of the stage were drawn back for the first time in the
performance, to reveal a wooden door in the centre. The army entered to a drum beat. By
contrast, Branagh plays the scene as if he has a last chance to take the town through
rhetorical, rather than military, prowess: 'the resilience of Harfleur seems unbreakable' and
the King stands before it 'bloodstained, filthy, and as if possessed by some demon'
(Branagh, p. 59). Terry Hands' production let 'a wall and the empty space between armies'
stand for the city of Harfleur: this 'made the words possible', and Henry's ultimatum was
thus delivered uncut (*Moment*, p. 140), with Alan Howard directing it out to the upper
balcony of the theatre on which the Governor stood. 'The impact of Henry's lines is directly
received by the audience. They become Harfleur' (Beauman, p. 150). One reviewer noted
that this required the audience to change sides – as they had been positioned as reserve
English troops in 3.1, with the back of the stage the point of attack (David, p. 196). Warchus
cast a woman as the Governor, thus providing 'a direct response to the horrendous
language of rape and murder that Henry had offered, his language and her body directly
connected' (Holland, p. 197).

1 At the Globe, Henry was low-key and quiet; the Governor was above in the balcony.
Henry spoke as if the audience were his army. By contrast, Alan Howard in Terry Hands'
production spoke to the audience as if it comprised the citizens of Harfleur. Like the
BBC/Giles and Hayes Henrys at this point, Olivier was filmed from a high angle, as if the
point-of-view of the Governor. As in the camerawork of 3.1, this works to diminish him, to

Therefore to our best mercy give yourselves,
Or like to men proud of destruction
Defy us to our worst. For as I am a soldier,   5
A name that in my thoughts becomes me best,
If I begin the battery once again
I will not leave the half-achieved Harfleur
Till in her ashes she lie burièd.
The gates of mercy shall be all shut up   10
And the fleshed soldier, rough and hard of heart,
In liberty of bloody hand shall range
With Conscience wide as hell, mowing like grass
Your fresh fair virgins and your flowering infants.

stress his position as underdog, although the cutting of Henry's speech after line 2 eliminates both the King's problematic threats and the sense of a hard-won victory over the town. A similar shot in Branagh's film, showing the King, his face bloodstained and filthy, alone on horseback amid the eerie post-battle calm of the breach, works to emphasise his personal leadership. For the RSC, Ron Daniels gave his Henry 'a microphone and crude loudspeakers, the reproduction seeming to flatten out the sound into a merciless coldness' (Smallwood, p. 238). He directed his tirade into the audience: the Governor was not seen. The audience were no longer being addressed as comrades-in-arms, as at the end of 3.1. By contrast, in Bogdanov's production Pennington as Henry did not stand and shout, but sat coldly at a folding camp table and delivered his speech to his prisoner the Governor, 'a proud, beaten old man with a black coat and an accent . . . accompanied by a silent comrade with beret and moustache', in a scene evocative of the Nazi Occupation of France during the Second World War (Loehlin, p. 117).

3–6 The Globe cut these lines. As Branagh speaks to the Governor, he is joined by the citizens on the ramparts: 'frightened children, women, old men' (Branagh, p. 59), and these cue Henry's increasingly threatening speech.

9–41 These threats were cut by Kemble, Kean, Phelps and Macready, who also cut line 43. 11–27a, 30–2 and 38–41 were cut by Bell; 15–41 in the BBC/Giles version; 10–27a in Branagh and Hayes; Olivier kept only lines 1–2 and the Governor's speech at line 44. Daniels retained this escalating catalogue of barbarity in full, to chilling effect: 'his brother Gloucester became appalled at the savagery of his threats and tried to switch off the microphone; Henry smashed him to the ground and went on' (Smallwood, p. 238). Gloucester's quiet weeping could be heard throughout the rest of the speech. In Branagh's film, the soldiers watch their leader's ultimatum uneasily.

11–14 Cut by the Globe.

What is it then to me if impious war,   15
Arrayed in flames like to the prince of fiends,
Do with his smirched complexion all fell feats
Enlinked to waste and desolation?
What is't to me, when you yourselves are cause,
If your pure maidens fall into the hand   20
Of hot and forcing violation?
What rein can hold licentious wickedness
When down the hill he holds his fierce career?
We may as bootless spend our vain command
Upon th'enragèd soldiers in their spoil   25
As send precepts to the Leviathan
To come ashore. Therefore, you men of Harfleur,
Take pity of your town and of your people
Whiles yet my soldiers are in my command,
Whiles yet the cool and temperate wind of grace   30
O'erblows the filthy and contagious clouds
Of heady murder, spoil and villainy.
If not, why, in a moment look to see
The blind and bloody soldier with foul hand
Defile the locks of your shrill-shrieking daughters,   35
Your fathers taken by the silver beards,
And their most reverend heads dashed to the walls,
Your naked infants spitted upon pikes
Whiles the mad mothers with their howls confused
Do break the clouds, as did the wives of Jewry   40
At Herod's bloody-hunting slaughtermen.
What say you? Will you yield, and this avoid?

15–21 Cut by Calvert, in a less substantial editing of this speech than was the nineteenth-century norm. Richard Foulkes suggests this 'did not remove sympathy for [Henry], but revealed his earnest desire to save the citizens of Harfleur from such extremities' (Foulkes, p. 29).

30–41 Cut by BBC/Hayes.

37 Rylance in the Globe production rises to a pitch of anger at this point.

42a Branagh allows a final pause for the Governor to submit, before the final questioning of 42–3.

42 At the Globe, at the end of the line, Rylance paused, and in the expectant quiet, some of the audience laughed.

> Or guilty in defence be thus destroyed?

Enter GOVERNOR [*above*]

GOVERNOR Our expectation hath this day an end.
          The Dauphin, whom of succours we entreated,   45
          Returns us that his powers are yet not ready
          To raise so great a siege. Therefore, great king,
          We yield our town and lives to thy soft mercy.
          Enter our gates, dispose of us and ours,
          For we no longer are defensible.   50
KING Open your gates. Come, uncle Exeter,   [*Exit Governor above*]
          Go you and enter Harfleur. There remain
          And fortify it strongly 'gainst the French.
          Use mercy to them all. For us, dear uncle,

---

43 At the Globe this was intoned as a genuine question, an appeal, and greeted with audience laughter. Daniels changed the lighting here, to reveal the Governor, absent earlier in the scene, in the balcony above the stage.

44 Cut by the Globe. Macready's Governor spoke as the French flag was lowered. Howard, in Hands' production, wept with relief at the surrender. In Hayes' production the Governor's speech is delivered as a voice-over so that nothing detracts from the focus on Henry's face. Similarly, the surrender is played over a shot of Henry in Branagh's film, his face, almost imperceptibly, seeming to relax. Daniels' Henry, facing the audience, closed his eyes in relief. Bogdanov had the Governor give over his keys and sign the surrender with a fountain pen. As he left under armed guard, Henry began to whistle with relief at his victory.

51 Macready, Kean and Phelps all had the gates of the city opened at Henry's command. Macready's promptbook includes the detail that the defeated citizens formed a passage for Henry's triumphant entrance. The march included about eighty individuals. Kean's soldiers 'enter the town through the breach' (Kean pbk). Phelps enacted Henry's command, and the heavy city gates were opened with the 'rattling of heavy chains' (Phelps pbk). The Governor entered, bearing the keys of the city on a cushion, and he and his citizen escort knelt before Henry. Branagh's Henry 'closes his eyes in exhaustion and relief' (Branagh, p. 60) and then returns slowly to his men. The tone is of relief rather than celebration, as Henry speaks quietly to Exeter and the army begins slowly to enter the city.

54 In Phelps' production the exit was to the tune of the military march 'British Grenadier' as the English army marched through the gates. Branagh's Henry 'stumbles with sudden pain' (Branagh, p. 61) and has to be helped away by Exeter, as a bluish smoke fills the frame. By contrast, the soldiers in Olivier's film and in Hayes' BBC production look cheerfully unscathed. Hands had Henry remain on stage, his sadness and loneliness highlighted by

The winter coming on, and sickness growing   55
Upon our soldiers, we will retire to Calais.
Tonight in Harfleur will we be your guest,
Tomorrow for the march are we addressed.

Flourish, and enter the town

3.5 *Enter* KATHERINE *and* [ALICE,] *an old gentlewoman*

KATHERINE Alice, tu as été en Angleterre, et tu bien parles le
    langage.

music. Slowly, at the end of the scene in Daniels' production, Henry's men saluted him, but Gloucester remained on the ground where the King had knocked him. The Globe Henry's tone was thoughtful. The scene ended with the drum beat as the army passed through the door in the back of the stage.

3.5 The scene is introduced in Folio: 'Enter Katherine and an Old Gentlewoman'. Gary Taylor points out that nowhere in the scene is Katherine named, and thus the scene is 'domestic and apolitical', an intrusion of private comedy into a public historical world (*Moment*, pp. 118–19). As such, it has often seemed expendable, even an embarrassment. At the end of 3.4, Bell has the dismissive note 'After this scene, we meet in the original, to wound our patience, a French one, of the most trifling, childish nature; disgraceful to the author, and the piece' (Bell, p. 39). There is no mention of Alice in any of the cast lists which survive from the eighteenth century, and thus Johnson's speculation about the scene's appeal in the theatre was probably not based on seeing it acted: 'The scene is indeed mean enough, when it is read, but the grimaces of two French women, and the odd accent with which they uttered the English, made it divert upon the stage' (Johnson, p. 547). Kemble, Macready, Kean and Waller cut it. Others, including Calvert and Mansfield, moved it to the more comfortable comic, post-battle location of Act 5. (The ease with which the scene has been excised from the play was exploited in reverse by the all-female cabaret act *Fascinating Aida*, who included a skit on 'The English Lesson' in performances during the 1980s. The sketch is reprinted in *The Shakespeare Revue*, London: Nick Hern Books, 1994.) Coleman's production included the Princess and Alice along with 'Charles the King, Isabelle of Bavaria, the Queen, Duke of Orleans, Audette playing at cards. Ladies of the Court embroidering', perhaps to suggest the general triviality of French courtly life and also to include more women. The language lesson stopped, discreetly, at '*de elbow*' (43). Hands, by contrast, had Katherine appear alone, as the upstage wall declined, 'like a Venus rising from the waves' (Beauman, p. 149) so that her 'beauty and the elegance of her dress are for a moment the

ALICE Un peu, madame.

KATHERINE Je te prie, m'enseignez. Il faut que j'apprenne à parler.
Comment appelez-vous la main en anglais?   5

ALICE La main. Elle est appelée *de hand*.

KATHERINE *De hand*. Et les doigts?

ALICE Les doigts, ma foi, j'ai oublié les doigts, mais je me
souviendrai les doigts. Je pense qu'ils sont appelés *de fingres*.
Oui, *de fingres*.   10

KATHERINE La main, *de hand*. Les doigts, les *fingres*. Je pense que je
suis le bon écolier. J'ai gagné deux mots d'anglais vitement.
Comment appelez-vous les ongles?

ALICE Les ongles, nous les appelons de *nails*.

---

sole objects of our interest', and by overlapping her entrance with Henry's exit, the production's choreography linked them (*Moment*, p. 118). Noble's promptbook signals the abrupt change in mood: 'Cut the smoke. Music goes pretty' (Noble pbk). In an American Repertory Theatre production of 1995 in Cambridge, Massachusetts, Ron Daniels prompted Katherine's desire to learn English by playing a radio broadcast of Henry's Harfleur threats at the beginning of the scene (Loehlin, p. 164). Olivier includes the scene, with Renée Asherson as Katherine, who 'seems in face, form and manner to have stepped out of the pages of *Les Très Riches Heures*. She is a story-book princess cutting story-book flowers in a story-book palace' (Geduld, p. 39). In the BBC/Giles production, the Princess and her companion are talking in 'A Bower in the Garden' of the Palace of Rouen, framed by garden arches in an idyllic, sunny setting with birdsong. It is more serious than bawdy, and the accompanying text of the play provides a translation, noting gravely that 'the words "foot" and "count" (Alice's attempt at "gown") resemble in pronunciation two French obscenities' (*BBC*, p. 59). In Branagh's film, the contrast of the bright morning light from the smoky darkness of the previous scene is striking. Princess Katherine, probably known to many of the film's first viewers as Kenneth Branagh's then off-screen wife, Emma Thompson, is waking caged doves in her room – in a symbol of the peace which will be ultimately ratified with her marriage to the King. The conversation with Alice takes place as Katherine sits at her dressing-table having her hair combed. In the only professional production of the play directed by a woman, Dorothy Green's at Stratford in 1946, this scene was pronounced 'first-rate' in a production noted for its preference for small details over 'purple patches' (*Birmingham Evening Despatch*, 11 May 1946). In the all-male production at the Globe, the exaggerated performance of femininity, complete with slightly mincing steps and strained voices, replaced the bawdy wordplay as the main vehicle for the scene's humour. Toby Cockerell as Katherine was greeted with raucous wolf whistling on his entrance, although some audience members at the Globe were apparently unaware that the Princess was played by a man.

KATHERINE *De nails.* Écoutez! Dites-moi si je parle bien: *de hand, de*   15
fingres, et *de nails.*

ALICE C'est bien dit, madame. Il est fort bon anglais.

KATHERINE Dites-moi l'anglais pour le bras.

ALICE *De arm*, madame.

KATHERINE Et le coude.   20

ALICE *D'elbow.*

KATHERINE *D'elbow.* Je m'en fais la répétition de tous les mots que
vous m'avez appris dès à présent.

ALICE Il est trop difficile, madame, comme je pense.

KATHERINE Excusez-moi, Alice. Écoutez, *d'hand, de fingre, de nails,*   25
d'arma, de bilbow.

ALICE *D'elbow*, madame.

KATHERINE O Seigneur Dieu, je m'en oublié *d'elbow*! Comment
appelez-vous le col?

ALICE *De nick*, madame.   30

KATHERINE *De nick.* Et le menton?

ALICE *De chin.*

KATHERINE *De sin.* Le col, *de nick.* Le menton, *de sin.*

ALICE Oui. Sauf votre honneur, en vérité vous prononcez les mots
aussi droit que les natifs d'Angleterre.   35

KATHERINE Je ne doute point d'apprendre, par la grâce de Dieu, et
en peu de temps.

ALICE N'avez-vous pas déjà oublié ce que je vous ai enseigné?

KATHERINE Non, et je réciterai à vous promptement: *d'hand, de*
fingre, de mailés –   40

ALICE *De nails*, madame.

KATHERINE *De nails, de arma, de ilbow –*

ALICE Sauf votre honneur, *de elbow.*

KATHERINE Ainsi dis-je. *D'elbow, de nick,* et *de sin.* Comment
appelez-vous les pieds et la robe?   45

ALICE *De foot*, madame, et *de count.*

KATHERINE *De foot* et *de count*? O Seigneur Dieu, ils sont les mots
de son mauvais, corruptible, gros et impudique, et non pour
les dames d'honneur d'user! Je ne voudrais prononcer ces mots
devant les seigneurs de France pour tout le monde! Foh! *De foot*   50
et *de count*! Néanmoins, je réciterai une autre fois ma leçon
ensemble: *de hand, de fingre, de nails, d'arma, d'elbow, de nick, de*
sin, de foot, le count.

ALICE Excellent, madame!

KATHERINE C'est assez pour une fois. Allons-nous à dîner.   55

Exeunt

3.6 *Enter the King of* FRANCE, *the* DAUPHIN, *the* CONSTABLE *of France, the Duke of* BOURBON, *and others*

FRENCH KING 'Tis certain he hath passed the River Somme.
CONSTABLE And if he be not fought withal, my lord,
        Let us not live in France. Let us quit all
        And give our vineyards to a barbarous people.
DAUPHIN *O Dieu vivant!* Shall a few sprays of us,   5
        The emptying of our father's luxury,
        Our scions, put in wild and savage stock,
        Spurt up so suddenly into the clouds
        And overlook their grafters?
BOURBON Normans, but bastard Normans, Norman bastards!   10

3.6 The connection between this scene and the previous one was stressed in Hands' production, when the overlap in the women's exit and the noblemen's entrance stressed the 'political implications' of Katherine's desire to learn English (*Moment*, p. 118). BBC/Hayes, too, overlaps their exit with the sound of male voices as the next scene begins. Olivier's film links the scenes with a point-of-view shot from Katherine, which shows Montjoy galloping into the courtyard below her window and then pans to the horizon 'upon which in the distance we see the glint of the little English band riding away'. Katherine looks 'as if into the future in undismayed surmise' (O, Fol), and then takes her place, with Alice and the Queen, at the table with the other nobles. Branagh's film punctures the carefree laughter of 3.5 by overlapping it with 3.6: 'Katherine throws open the door [a visual echo of the end of 1.0] only to see her father . . . surrounded by his council of war . . . Their mood is grim and Katherine is immediately quiet and serious. The men move on towards the Council Chamber and the Princess, slowly, sadly, closes the door' (Branagh, p. 66) – left outside the council of war, unlike her counterpart in Olivier's film. Branagh's King retains his haunted, hunted expression throughout, as the fiery Dauphin tries to spur him into decisive military action. There was the customary booing and hissing at the entrance of the French nobles in the Globe production. The court in the BBC/Giles production is full of milling noblemen and an atmosphere of flustered activity. Most productions set the scene in a French palace, but Macready's French were already encamped ready for battle, attended by banners and guards. Heavy cuts to the scene minimised the French confidence. Terry Hands rationalised the French noblemen who are named in this scene, reallocating the lines between the King, Dauphin, Orléans, Constable and Montjoy.

  1 This line was given to the Constable in Hands' production.
  5 The Globe accompanied these lines with a distant and menacing drum beat, like a heartbeat.
 10 At this line in Olivier's film, a shocked shriek from Katherine and Alice is heard.

    Mort de ma vie, if they march along
    Unfought withal, but I will sell my dukedom
    To buy a slobbery and a dirty farm
    In that nook-shotten isle of Albion.
CONSTABLE *Dieu de batailles*, where have they this mettle?   15
    Is not their climate foggy, raw and dull,
    On whom, as in despite, the sun looks pale,
    Killing their fruit with frowns? Can sodden water,
    A drench for sur-reined jades, their barley-broth,
    Decoct their cold blood to such valiant heat?   20
    And shall our quick blood, spirited with wine,
    Seem frosty? Oh, for honour of our land
    Let us not hang like roping icicles
    Upon our houses' thatch whiles a more frosty people
    Sweat drops of gallant youth in our rich fields!   25
    'Poor' may we call them, in their native lords!
DAUPHIN By faith and honour,
    Our madams mock at us and plainly say
    Our mettle is bred out, and they will give
    Their bodies to the lust of English youth   30
    To new-store France with bastard warriors.
BOURBON They bid us to the English dancing-schools,
    And teach lavoltas high and swift corantos,
    Saying our grace is only in our heels,
    And that we are most lofty runaways.   35
FRENCH KING Where is Montjoy the herald? Speed him hence,
    Let him greet England with our sharp defiance.
    Up, princes, and with spirit of honour edged

15–26 Cut by BBC/Hayes.

16 This line, delivered with a nod to the open sky over the yard of the theatre, always got a laugh in the Globe production, whatever the weather.

22b–26 Cut in the Globe production.

30 Olivier shows Alice and the Queen of France covering Katherine's ears to protect her from the Dauphin's unsuitable language.

36 Hands had the King enter at this point in full armour, an imposing figure who addressed his speech into the auditorium, so that 'the audience became his warlords [having previously been addressed as the citizens of Harfleur]. His appeal is directed at them' (Beauman, p. 157.) At the Globe, the King entered in the balcony. By contrast, Olivier's Queen nudges her husband, who wakes from his lethargy to utter his lines.

More sharper than your swords hie to the field.
Charles Delabret, High Constable of France,   40
You Dukes of Orléans, Bourbon and of Berri,
Alençon, Brabant, Bar and Burgundy,
Jacques Châtillon, Rambures, Vaudemont,
Beaumont, Grandpré, Roussi and Fauconbridge,
Foix, Lestrelles, Boucicault and Charolais,   45
High dukes, great princes, barons, lords and knights,
For your great seats, now quit you of great shames.
Bar Harry England that sweeps through our land
With pennons painted in the blood of Harfleur.
Rush on his host as doth the melted snow   50
Upon the valleys, whose low vassal seat
The Alps doth spit and void his rheum upon.
Go down upon him. You have power enough,
And in a captive chariot into Rouen
Bring him our prisoner.
CONSTABLE   This becomes the great.   55
Sorry am I his numbers are so few,
His soldiers sick, and famished in their march,
For I am sure when he shall see our army
He'll drop his heart into the sink of fear
And for achievement offer us his ransom.   60
FRENCH KING Therefore, Lord Constable, haste on Montjoy,
And let him say to England that we send
To know what willing ransom he will give.
Prince Dauphin, you shall stay with us in Rouen.
DAUPHIN Not so, I do beseech your majesty.   65
FRENCH KING Be patient, for you shall remain with us.

---

40 In Hands' production 'the French King creates in our imaginations a French army of
    astounding potency' (*Moment*, p. 141). Presumably to mitigate this, Olivier and Branagh
    both cut lines 41–9. Hayes accompanies the speech with a slow track backwards to reveal
    ranks of noblemen listening to the King's exhortation.

66 Branagh's King is unexpectedly authoritative in curbing the will of his defiant heir. In the
    BBC/Giles version, the King also takes command, giving orders to the cheers of the court. The
    scene ends with a thoughtful close-up of the Dauphin. Hands gave an early indication of
    French disunity by having the Dauphin caught between following the noblemen to war and
    following his father: after a moment's indecision, he followed the Constable. In Olivier's film,
    the King slaps the face of his son, before kissing him 'to smooth his ruffled feelings' (O, Fol).

Now forth, Lord Constable and princes all,
And quickly bring us word of England's fall.

Exeunt

3.7 *Enter Captains, English and Welsh,* GOWER *and* LLEWELLYN

GOWER How now, Captain Llewellyn, come you from the bridge?
LLEWELLYN I assure you there is very excellent services committed
at the bridge.

67 The contrast between the French and the English was brought out by Ron Daniels: 'as the
exquisitely titled earls knelt in elegant obeisance to their liege, an azure silk curtain wafting as
backdrop to their lavender costumes, the vision was blasted away by the sound and smoke of
gunfire as English tommies swarmed across the stage from the siege of Harfleur' (Smallwood,
p. 238). Calvert had the French King viewing his troops and receiving the shout 'Valois'. He
returned a benediction to the army (Calvert pbk). Olivier ends the scene with the image of
Katherine eating 'some delicacy', before dissolving to the English camp for the next scene.

3.7 Victorian productions were clear that this scene required 'a view in Picardy' for its setting.
Calvert included 'distant battle heard' (Calvert pbk). Olivier's shooting script also indicates
'English camp in Picardy' as the setting. The scene is introduced in Branagh's film by a
sequence of weary boots marching through mud and rain, intercut with a map of the English
route from Harfleur towards Agincourt. The mud and filth evoke imagery of the trenches of
the First World War. Henry and the noblemen are on horseback, but the principal soldiers
are on foot, stumbling with exhaustion in the quagmire. 'This is not a victorious army on the
march but a sick and depleted band of men' (Branagh, p. 69). Here, Branagh follows
Noble's stage production, which featured a real and steady downpour, as Henry's men
crouched for shelter under tarpaulins. In the BBC/Giles version the soldiers look dirty and
battle-worn. At this point in Hands' production, the brightly coloured canopy dropped to
form a crumpled covering for the stage, representing a low point in English morale:
'symbolically their high hope – the heraldic canopy – drops to form a grey and muddy
Somme battlefield' (Beauman, p. 159). Ron Daniels' production suddenly quickened in pace
here: after two long interior scenes in the French court, a scene of battle casualties is shown.
One bleeding soldier is lying downstage; upstage another moans on a stretcher, while a
third fumbles to open a bandage. At the Globe, the actor playing Gower, carrying a longbow
and wearing a tunic with the cross of St George, acted as Chorus.
1 BBC/Hayes has Llewellyn enter carrying a wounded man into the stable where he and
Gower have a makeshift field hospital.

GOWER Is the Duke of Exeter safe?

LLEWELLYN The Duke of Exeter is as magnanimous as   5
Agamemnon, and a man that I love and honour with my soul,
and my heart, and my duty, and my life, and my living, and my
uttermost power. He is not, God be praised and blessed, any
hurt in the world, but keeps the pridge most valiantly with
excellent discipline. There is an anchient lieutenant there at the   10
pridge. I think in my very conscience he is as valiant a man as
Mark Antony, and he is a man of no estimation in the world, but
I did see him do as gallant service.

GOWER What do you call him?

LLEWELLYN He is called Anchient Pistol.   15

GOWER I know him not.

Enter PISTOL

LLEWELLYN Here is the man.

PISTOL Captain, I thee beseech to do me favours. The Duke of
Exeter doth love thee well.

LLEWELLYN Ay, I praise God, and I have merited some love at his   20
hands.

PISTOL Bardolph, a soldier firm and sound of heart, and of buxom
valour, hath by cruel fate and giddy Fortune's furious fickle wheel,
that goddess blind that stands upon the rolling restless stone –

LLEWELLYN By your patience, Anchient Pistol, Fortune is painted   25
plind, with a muffler afore her eyes to signify to you that Fortune
is plind. And she is painted also with a wheel to signify to you,
which is the moral of it, that she is turning and inconstant and
mutability and variation. And her foot, look you, is fixed upon
a spherical stone, which rolls and rolls and rolls. In good truth,   30
the poet makes a most excellent description of it. Fortune is an
excellent moral.

PISTOL Fortune is Bardolph's foe, and frowns on him. For he hath
stolen a pax, and hangèd must a be. A damnèd death! Let
gallows gape for dog, let man go free, and let not hemp his   35

10–71 Cut by BBC/Hayes.

21 In Branagh's film, Pistol pleads desperately for support for Bardolph. 22–32 was
cut by Olivier, 22–33a was cut by Noble, so Pistol and Llewellyn did not discuss
Fortune.

34 The BBC/Giles Gower crosses himself at news of the theft.

windpipe suffocate! But Exeter hath given the doom of death, for pax of little price. Therefore go speak. The Duke will hear thy voice, and let not Bardolph's vital thread be cut with edge of penny cord and vile reproach! Speak, captain, for his life, and I will thee requite. 40

LLEWELLYN Anchient Pistol, I do partly understand your meaning.

PISTOL Why then, rejoice therefore.

LLEWELLYN Certainly, anchient, it is not a thing to rejoice at. For if, look you, he were my brother I would desire the Duke to use his good pleasure and put him to execution. For discipline ought to 45 be used.

PISTOL Die and be damned, and *fico* for thy friendship!

LLEWELLYN It is well.

PISTOL The fig of Spain! *Exit*

LLEWELLYN Very good. 50

GOWER Why, this is an arrant counterfeit rascal. I remember him now: a bawd, a cutpurse.

LLEWELLYN I'll assure you, a uttered as prave words at the pridge as you shall see in a summer's day. But it is very well. What he has spoke to me, that is well, I warrant you, when time is serve. 55

GOWER Why, 'tis a gull, a fool, a rogue, that now and then goes to the wars, to grace himself at his return into London under the form of a soldier. And such fellows are perfect in the great commanders' names, and they will learn you by rote where services were done – at such and such a sconce, at such a breach, 60 at such a convoy; who came off bravely, who was shot, who disgraced, what terms the enemy stood on. And this they con perfectly in the phrase of war, which they trick up with new-tuned oaths. And what a beard of the general's cut and a horrid suit of the camp will do among foaming bottles and ale-washed 65 wits is wonderful to be thought on. But you must learn to know such slanders of the age, or else you may be marvellously mistook.

LLEWELLYN I tell you what, Captain Gower: I do perceive he is not the man that he would gladly make show to the world he is. If I 70 find a hole in his coat I will tell him my mind.

36–7 Noble cut the mention of Exeter.

48–74 Cut by Branagh; 53–68 cut by BBC/Giles.

[*A drum within*]

Hark you, the king is coming, and I must speak with him from the pridge.

Drum and colours. Enter the KING [, GLOUCESTER] *and his poor soldiers*

LLEWELLYN God pless your majesty.

KING How now, Llewellyn? Camest thou from the bridge?   75

LLEWELLYN Ay, so please your majesty. The Duke of Exeter has very gallantly maintained the pridge. The French is gone off, look you, and there is gallant and most prave passages. Marry, th'athversary was have possession of the pridge, but he is enforced to retire, and the Duke of Exeter is master of the   80
pridge. I can tell your majesty, the duke is a prave man.

KING What men have you lost, Llewellyn?

LLEWELLYN The perdition of th'athversary hath been very great, reasonable great. Marry, for my part I think the duke hath lost never a man, but one that is like to be executed for robbing a   85
church, one Bardolph, if your majesty know the man. His face is all bubuckles and whelks, and knobs, and flames o'fire, and his lips blows at his nose, and it is like a coal of fire, sometimes plue and sometimes red. But his nose is executed and his fire's out.   90

KING We would have all such offenders so cut off, and we give

---

74 The Folio gives an unusually descriptive stage direction here: 'Enter the King and his poore Souldiers', emphasising the dishevelled state of the marching army. By contrast, in the BBC/Giles production the entrance is remarkable for the extreme shininess of Henry's breastplate. Hayes has Llewellyn salute. The Globe production saw the army enter bearing the royal standard. Calvert's King was preceded by ten nobles, and 'torches and watchfires borne by soldiers. The king is in consultation with his officers' (Calvert pbk). In Branagh's film the King dismounts to speak to Llewellyn. Ron Daniels' Henry is hardly distinguishable from his men, and there is little observance of ceremony in his exchanges.

86 Samuel Johnson noted that Shakespeare was particularly taken with the idea of Bardolph's red complexion, but that 'this conception is very cold to the solitary reader, although it may be somewhat improved by the exhibition on the stage' (Johnson, p. 550). At news of Bardolph's crime, Robert Hardy in BBC/Hayes is visibly shocked, in contrast to the lighthearted account by Llewellyn.

91 Bardolph's execution is one of the more difficult aspects of Henry's conduct to assimilate into a positive reading of his character. Macready cut all mention of it. Hayes has his Henry serious, speaking to a hushed soldiery. In the BBC/Giles version, Henry pauses from

cleaning his boots to listen to the description of Bardolph, and is silent for a long moment before delivering, coldly, line 91. While Hands chose not to bring Bardolph on stage, placing Llewellyn upstage as if he could see the execution taking place offstage, he did make it clear that Henry had given his assent to the death sentence. Richard David describes Hands' depiction of the 'eye-shutting, teeth-clenching ordeal of Bardolph's execution for which (to make matters worse) this Henry had personally to give the signal' as one of the emotional highlights of Alan Howard's performance (David, p. 198), as Pistol looked him unflinchingly in the eye. Olivier shoots the scene more as a warning to the soldiery than a moment of psychological insight: Henry has his back to the camera and is surrounded by a small semi-circle of his men. Writing of his performance in Noble's stage production, Kenneth Branagh identified the thrill of having Bardolph executed on stage in front of the King: 'For me it shed a whole new light on Henry's loneliness, marking . . . the end of a chapter of events which robbed him of every real friend he had . . . He was now completely alone with a solitude so painful it must produce "Upon the King" ' (*Players*, p. 102). Noble had Bardolph kneel, with his hands tied, with Exeter in armour behind him. He fixed Henry with a long unbroken gaze. At a nod from the King, he was abruptly garrotted. A number of reviews commented on the sickeningly audible snap of his neck. A roll of drums heralded the execution in Hands' production. Bogdanov also brought Bardolph on stage, and by introducing his call 'My lord' to Henry, made clear that the King rejected an explicit appeal from his old companion. For his film, Branagh uses a flashback to show that Henry does not assent to Bardolph's execution without emotion. A cart bears him as a prisoner, his nose already split and bleeding.

> A public trial of strength is provided for the King. Watched by his sodden soldiers he must enforce his decree that any form of theft or pillage of the French countryside will be punished by death. Any favouritism or sentiment shown here will be disastrous for discipline amongst these poor soldiers. The cost to the King is enormous as he gives the nod to Exeter. (Branagh, p. 71)

Bardolph is hanged on-screen, with a sequence of shot-reverse-shot cutting between his fear and Henry's 'distressed but unflinching stare'. The scene cuts in flashback to a night at the Boar's Head tavern, where Bardolph and Falstaff are vying in a drinking game, cheered on by the others and watched by the young Hal. The bystanders fall on Bardolph and grab him by the neck in a joke after he has won the contest, and he appeals to Hal: 'Do not, when thou art king, hang a thief.' 'The smile on Hal's face drops away' (Branagh, p. 73) as he pronounces 'No, thou shalt': the exchange borrows from 1.2.48–50 of *1 Henry IV*, where the plea is spoken by Falstaff. The flashback sequence ends on the shocked face of Bardolph, resuming as Henry, eyes full of tears, gives the signal for the cart to be pulled away and Bardolph to be hanged. The focus is on Henry's tear-stained face, and the twitching feet of Bardolph's death throes. These feet are much in evidence through Montjoy's speech and the

express charge that in our marches through the country there be
nothing compelled from the villages, nothing taken but paid for,
none of the French upbraided or abused in disdainful language.
For when lenity and cruelty play for a kingdom, the gentler   95
gamester is the soonest winner.

Tucket. Enter MONTJOY

MONTJOY You know me by my habit.
KING Well then, I know thee. What shall I know of thee?
MONTJOY My master's mind.
KING Unfold it.   100
MONTJOY Thus says my king: 'Say thou to Harry of England,
though we seemed dead, we did but sleep. Advantage is a
better soldier than rashness. Tell him, we could have rebuked
him at Harfleur, but that we thought not good to bruise an
injury till it were full ripe. Now we speak upon our cue, and   105
our voice is imperial. England shall repent his folly, see his
weakness and admire our sufferance. Bid him therefore
consider of his ransom, which must proportion the losses we
have borne, the subjects we have lost, the disgrace we have
digested, which in weight to re-answer, his pettiness would bow   110
under. For our losses, his exchequer is too poor. For th'effusion
of our blood, the muster of his kingdom too faint a number.
And for our disgrace, his own person kneeling at our feet but
a weak and worthless satisfaction. To this add defiance, and

rest of the scene. In Michael Langham's production in 1966, the body of Bardolph was
dumped at the King's feet, the bloodied mark of the noose clearly visible on his limp neck. In
the Globe production, the King stepped forward to address the audience, in severe, sombre
tones; Michael Sheen, in Daniels' production, also stepped forward to deliver the warning to
the audience.

96 In Branagh's film, the sound of a horse's hooves disturbs the quiet that has fallen after the
execution of Bardolph. Montjoy, arriving alone, looks up uneasily at the hanging body, and
his speech is shot with the swinging boots clearly in view. Calvert's Montjoy arrived with his
attendants, as does Olivier's, with two heralds and a standard-bearer. Daniels had him
wearing a beret and carrying a white flag.

100 Calvert's Henry sat on a tree stump on this line.

104 The English soldiers jeer at this line in BBC/Hayes.

tell him for conclusion, he hath betrayed his followers, whose   115
condemnation is pronounced.' So far my king and master, so
much my office.

KING   What is thy name? I know thy quality.

MONTJOY   Montjoy.

KING   Thou dost thy office fairly. Turn thee back   120
          And tell thy king I do not seek him now,
          But could be willing to march on to Calais
          Without impeachment. For to say the sooth,
          Though 'tis no wisdom to confess so much
          Unto an enemy of craft and vantage,   125
          My people are with sickness much enfeebled,
          My numbers lessened, and those few I have
          Almost no better than so many French,
          Who when they were in health, I tell thee, herald,
          I thought upon one pair of English legs   130
          Did march three Frenchmen. Yet forgive me, God,
          That I do brag thus. This your air of France
          Hath blown that vice in me. I must repent.

118 Alan Howard, in Hands' production, interpreted Henry's answers to Montjoy as demonstrating 'his temporary loss of control and his uncertainty about what to do or say next' due to the 'degree of pain he has suffered at Bardolph's execution' (Beauman, p. 165). In Hayes' BBC production, Henry takes little notice of Montjoy and is preoccupied with dressing a wound on his own wrist.

120 During the speech, Macready's production gradually lowered the lights to indicate nightfall and the darkening of the mood.

127–33 Cut by Olivier.

129 Calvert's promptbook signals that Montjoy should start and rise, riled by the King's insinuations, and that Llewellyn should show his appreciation of the taunts. Branagh cut 123b–33 to produce a wearier speech of resignation rather than bravado. At the Globe these lines of patriotic bluster raised a laugh from the audience. The BBC/Giles King seems relaxed and calm, half-humorous in his jibes at the French and undeterred. Alan Howard, in Hands' production, made sense of these jokes as Henry's desperate attempt to banish the memory of the hanged Bardolph and revive his weary soldiers. Sheen, in Daniels' production, took the edge off the comedy, by bending down to the casualty on a stretcher at the words 'when . . . in health'.

Go therefore, tell thy master here I am.
My ransom is this frail and worthless trunk,   135
My army but a weak and sickly guard.
Yet, God before, tell him we will come on
Though France himself and such another neighbour
Stand in our way. There's for thy labour, Montjoy.
Go, bid thy master well advise himself.   140
If we may pass, we will. If we be hindered,
We shall your tawny ground with your red blood
Discolour. And so, Montjoy, fare you well.
The sum of all our answer is but this:
We would not seek a battle as we are,   145
Nor as we are we say we will not shun it.
So tell your master.
MONTJOY I shall deliver so. Thanks to your highness.   [*Exit*]
GLOUCESTER I hope they will not come upon us now.
KING We are in God's hand, brother, not in theirs.   150
March to the bridge. It now draws toward night.
Beyond the river we'll encamp ourselves,
And on tomorrow. Bid them march away.

                                                     Exeunt

139 Most Montjoys are given coins or a purse here. Macready gave a ring. In Bogdanov's
     production Henry's defiance was stressed by his gift of a tennis ball.

148 Branagh's Montjoy is impressed at the strength and resolve of the English King.

150 At this line, the rain resumes in Branagh's film. Calvert ended the scene here.

153 Branagh's delivery of this line was almost an afterthought, to himself, punctuated 'And on
     tomorrow bid them march away' (Branagh, p. 75). His exit requires him, like the soldiers, to
     pass under Bardolph's hanging body as the army struggles up the muddy track towards the
     bridge. The scene is followed by the Chorus, who looks up at the body before addressing
     the camera with 4.0.1–22a, pulling his overcoat more tightly around his body to suppress a
     shiver. In Hands' production, the army was momentarily mutinous, shuffling with buried
     defiance and requiring him to deliver the last line as a clear command. The army exited with
     a dejected version of their marching song 'Deo Gracias', last heard in more positive key at
     Southampton at the end of 2.2. Olivier has Gower and Henry stand in silence for a moment,
     looking in the direction of Montjoy's exit, before the King gives the orders to march. A high-
     angled shot shows the army marching over a bridge in the middle distance with the sun
     setting behind. Daniels had the interval after this scene, ending the first half of the play on a
     low and threatening note, as does Hayes, whose two-part television adaptation divides at
     this point, the end of the episode entitled 'Signs of War'.

3.8 *Enter the* CONSTABLE *of France, the Lord* RAMBURES, ORLÉANS,
BOURBON, *with others*

CONSTABLE Tut, I have the best armour of the world! Would it were
     day.
ORLÉANS You have an excellent armour, but let my horse have his
     due.
CONSTABLE It is the best horse of Europe.   5
ORLÉANS Will it never be morning?
BOURBON My lord of Orléans, and my lord High Constable, you
     talk of horse and armour?
ORLÉANS You are as well provided of both as any prince in the
     world.   10
BOURBON What a long night is this! I will not change my horse with
     any that treads but on four pasterns. *Ch'ha!* He bounds from
     the earth as if his entrails were hairs – *le cheval volant*, the
     Pegasus, *qui a les narines de feu!* When I bestride him I soar, I am

---

3.8 This scene was cut by Bell and Macready. Many productions, including Kean, Calvert,
     Hands, Noble and Branagh's film, have pasted the first half of the fourth Chorus,
     describing the French camp, to preface this speech. Throughout, almost all productions
     have given the lines here allocated to Bourbon to the Dauphin (see Gurr, pp. 224–5, for a
     discussion of the reasons for the New Cambridge emendation). Hands replaced Rambures
     with Montjoy, and reallocated a number of lines to consolidate the individualised French
     noblemen as at 3.6. Calvert set the scene in the Dauphin's tent, with the noblemen
     discovered playing at dice, to the accompaniment of boys singing. One reviewer noted that
     these madrigals were encored by a rapt audience. Branagh sets the scene in the ornate tent
     of the Constable at night, where the French noblemen drink from silver goblets in relative
     luxury, especially compared with the wearied and muddied English troops of the previous
     scene. The BBC/Giles version uses the quiet interior of the tent, with the remains of a meal
     left on the table, as the noblemen weary at the Dauphin's chatter. Daniels' noblemen played
     chess, languidly. Olivier uses the inside of the tent and has a close-up of the Constable's
     armour fastened with gold stars. Hands set the French nobles centre stage and strongly lit,
     with the 'huddled shapes of English soldiers lying at the sides of the stage' (Beauman,
     p. 168), thus stressing the proximity of the two camps. Noble's Chorus had an electric torch
     in the darkness.
10 Calvert's Orléans was 'rising and bowing obsequiously' (Calvert pbk).

a hawk! He trots the air. The earth sings when he touches it. The   15
basest horn of his hoof is more musical than the pipe of
Hermes.

ORLÉANS He's of the colour of the nutmeg.

BOURBON And of the heat of the ginger. It is a beast for Perseus. He
is pure air and fire, and the dull elements of earth and water   20
never appear in him but only in patient stillness while his rider
mounts him. He is indeed a horse, and all other jades you may
call beasts.

CONSTABLE Indeed, my lord, it is a most absolute and excellent
horse.   25

BOURBON It is the prince of palfreys. His neigh is like the bidding
of a monarch, and his countenance enforces homage.

ORLÉANS No more, cousin.

BOURBON Nay, the man hath no wit that cannot from the rising of
the lark to the lodging of the lamb vary deserved praise on my   30
palfrey. It is a theme as fluent as the sea. Turn the sands into
eloquent tongues and my horse is argument for them all. 'Tis a
subject for a sovereign to reason on, and for a sovereign's
sovereign to ride on, and for the world, familiar to us and
unknown, to lay apart their particular functions and wonder at   35
him. I once writ a sonnet in his praise, and began thus: 'Wonder
of nature! . . .'

ORLÉANS I have heard a sonnet begin so to one's mistress.

BOURBON Then did they imitate that which I composed to my
courser, for my horse is my mistress.   40

ORLÉANS Your mistress bears well.

BOURBON Me well, which is the prescript praise and perfection of a
good and particular mistress.

CONSTABLE Nay, for methought yesterday your mistress shrewdly
shook your back.   45

BOURBON So perhaps did yours.

CONSTABLE Mine was not bridled.

BOURBON Oh, then belike she was old and gentle, and you rode like
a kern of Ireland, your French hose off, and in your strait
strossers.   50

---

45 Olivier leaves an uncomfortable pause here, cuts lines 46–62, and has Orléans at line 63
trying to change the subject. Noble substituted Montjoy for Rambures.

CONSTABLE You have good judgement in horsemanship.

BOURBON Be warned by me, then. They that ride so and ride not warily fall into foul bogs. I had rather have my horse to my mistress.

CONSTABLE I had as lief have my mistress a jade. 55

BOURBON I tell thee, Constable, my mistress wears his own hair.

CONSTABLE I could make as true a boast as that, if I had a sow to my mistress.

BOURBON '*Le chien est retourné à son propre vomissement, et la truie lavée au bourbier.*' Thou makest use of anything. 60

CONSTABLE Yet do I not use my horse for my mistress, or any such proverb so little kin to the purpose.

RAMBURES My lord Constable, the armour that I saw in your tent tonight, are those stars or suns upon it?

CONSTABLE Stars, my lord. 65

BOURBON Some of them will fall tomorrow, I hope.

CONSTABLE And yet my sky shall not want.

BOURBON That may be, for you bear a many superfluously, and 'twere more honour some were away.

CONSTABLE Even as your horse bears your praises, who would trot 70
as well were some of your brags dismounted.

BOURBON Would I were able to load him with his desert. Will it never be day? I will trot tomorrow a mile, and my way shall be paved with English faces.

CONSTABLE I will not say so, for fear I should be faced out of my 75
way. But I would it were morning, for I would fain be about the ears of the English.

RAMBURES Who will go to hazard with me for twenty prisoners?

CONSTABLE You must first go yourself to hazard, ere you have them. 80

BOURBON 'Tis midnight. I'll go arm myself. *Exit*

ORLÉANS The Duke of Bourbon longs for morning.

RAMBURES He longs to eat the English.

CONSTABLE I think he will eat all he kills.

ORLÉANS By the white hand of my lady, he's a gallant prince. 85

82 At the Globe Orléans imitated the Dauphin's effeminate walk, to the delight of the audience.

CONSTABLE Swear by her foot, that she may tread out the oath.

ORLÉANS He is simply the most active gentleman of France.

CONSTABLE Doing is activity, and he will still be doing.

ORLÉANS He never did harm that I heard of.

CONSTABLE Nor will do none tomorrow. He will keep that good   90
name still.

ORLÉANS I know him to be valiant.

CONSTABLE I was told that, by one that knows him better than
you.

ORLÉANS What's he?   95

CONSTABLE Marry, he told me so himself, and he said he cared not
who knew it.

ORLÉANS He needs not, it is no hidden virtue in him.

CONSTABLE By my faith, sir, but it is. Never anybody saw it but
his lackey. 'Tis a hooded valour, and when it appears it will   100
bate.

ORLÉANS Ill will never said well.

CONSTABLE I will cap that proverb with 'There is flattery in
friendship.'

ORLÉANS And I will take up that with 'Give the devil his due.'   105

CONSTABLE Well placed. There stands your friend for the devil.
Have at the very eye of that proverb with 'A pox of the devil'.

ORLÉANS You are the better at proverbs, by how much 'a fool's bolt
is soon shot'.

CONSTABLE You have shot over.   110

ORLÉANS 'Tis not the first time you were overshot.

Enter a MESSENGER

MESSENGER My lord High Constable, the English lie within fifteen
hundred paces of your tents.

CONSTABLE Who hath measured the ground?

MESSENGER The lord Grandpré.   115

CONSTABLE A valiant and most expert gentleman. Would it were
day! Alas, poor Harry of England! He longs not for the dawning
as we do.

90 The tensions between the French nobles were highlighted in Hands' production, as the
mutual antipathies between the Dauphin and the Constable, and between the Constable
and Orléans, were made clear.

112 No messenger entered in Noble's production, and his lines were spoken by the Dauphin.

ORLÉANS What a wretched and peevish fellow is this king of
England, to mope with his fat-brained followers so far out of his   120
knowledge.

CONSTABLE If the English had any apprehension they would run
away.

ORLÉANS That they lack, for if their heads had any intellectual
armour they could never wear such heavy headpieces.   125

RAMBURES That island of England breeds very valiant creatures.
Their mastiffs are of unmatchable courage.

ORLÉANS Foolish curs, that run winking into the mouth of a
Russian bear and have their heads crushed like rotten apples.
You may as well say that's a valiant flea that dare eat his breakfast   130
on the lip of a lion.

CONSTABLE Just, just. And the men do sympathise with the mastiffs
in robustious and rough coming on, leaving their wits with their
wives. And then, give them great meals of beef and iron and
steel, they will eat like wolves and fight like devils.   135

ORLÉANS Ay, but these English are shrewdly out of beef.

CONSTABLE Then shall we find tomorrow they have only stomachs
to eat and none to fight. Now is it time to arm. Come, shall we
about it?

ORLÉANS It is now two o'clock. But let me see, by ten   140
We shall have each a hundred Englishmen!

Exeunt

119 At the Globe, these insults were directed at the audience.

120 Here Olivier cuts to a view outside the tent, with the lights of the English camp clearly visible
in the middle distance.

122 The Globe Constable cupped his hands to make a megaphone to shout this insult around
the theatre, and was greeted with booing and, at some performances, missiles from the
audience. Noble cut 122–6.

136 Audiences at Glen Byam Shaw's production in 1951, 'still heavily oppressed by meat rations',
cheered with recognition at this line (Williamson, p. 58). Hands ended the first half of the
performance after this scene.

4.0 [*Enter* CHORUS]

CHORUS Now entertain conjecture of a time
　　　　When creeping murmur and the poring dark
　　　　Fills the wide vessel of the universe.

4.0 Calvert, like Mansfield, Branagh, Hands after him, followed the Chorus with 3.8, then the rest of the Chorus with the English camp. Macready's dioramic staging opened to reveal the two opposing camps simultaneously. In Kean's version, the Chorus lines 1–22a preceded 3.8, as too in Calvert's version, where Rumour was revealed seated on the rocks with 'strong whole light as if from moon' (Calvert pbk). A tableau of monks, boys and soldiers in the English camp contrasted with dice-playing French. Religious observance was a feature of Mansfield's characterisation of the English camp too: 'chanting is heard in the distance. The monks confess and bless the soldiers. Retiring, they leave the young Duke of Bedford standing over the embers of a smouldering fire. He is joined by his brothers, King Henry and the Duke of Gloster' (Mansfield, p. 60). The proximity and contrast allowed by the Chorus' serial description of the two camps was brought out in Adrian Noble's version. His Chorus, wearing a First World War greatcoat, picked his way along a 'trench-like row of slumped, sleeping soldiers that spans the breadth of the set. His flashlight illuminates the taut, white faces of one soldier after another, who flinch or stare hopelessly into the darkness and distance' (Fitter, p. 261). In the furthest depths of the stage the French lolled on couches, playing chess in indolent expectation of their victory. In Branagh's version, the Chorus' speech to line 22a is put before 3.8 (so too in Hands' production), dissolving to the Constable's tent as the Chorus limps away into the gloom. Lines 22b–47 are used to preface a juxtaposed image of the English camp, with the nobles sitting outside by a small fire in a scene steeped in cold, cheerless blue-grey colours. The camera roves around the camp with Llewellyn and then with Henry. The BBC/Giles Chorus appears in the opening of the French tent, dressed in a brownish habit, and wanders among the fires and tents of the English encampment. Hayes' BBC version begins its second part, 'Band of Brothers', with this scene, which opens with the men standing still outside their tents as the Chorus makes his way quietly through the darkness from the background of the frame into the foreground. In Daniels' production Henry was seen behind a gauze curtain, walking among his men, who were still, downcast, and nervous. At the Globe the scene opened with the company singing, Erpingham asleep against one of the pillars, and the Chorus, played by the Michael Williams actor, in a tunic with a red St George cross.

1–2 Olivier's Chorus delivers these two lines over a blank dark screen, which fades in to a long shot of the lights of the French and English camps.

From camp to camp, through the foul womb of night,
The hum of either army stilly sounds, 5
That the fixed sentinels almost receive
The secret whispers of each other's watch.
Fire answers fire, and through their paly flames
Each battle sees the other's umbered face.
Steed threatens steed, in high and boastful neighs, 10
Piercing the night's dull ear. And from the tents
The armourers accomplishing the knights
With busy hammers closing rivets up
Give dreadful note of preparation.
The country cocks do crow, the clocks do toll, 15
And the third hour of drowsy morning name.
Proud of their numbers and secure in soul
The confident and over-lusty French
Do the low-rated English play at dice,
And chide the cripple tardy-gaited night 20
Who like a foul and ugly witch doth limp
So tediously away. The poor condemnèd English,
Like sacrifices, by their watchful fires
Sit patiently and inly ruminate
The morning's danger; and their gesture sad, 25
Investing lank-lean cheeks and war-worn coats,
Presented them unto the gazing moon
So many horrid ghosts. O now, who will behold
The royal captain of this ruined band

17 Hayes' Chorus looks across towards the French camp, although this is not shown.

22b Hands used this section of the Chorus (to line 47) to introduce 4.1, and introduced Henry, 'moving slowly downstage among his sleeping soldiers, a silhouette in the gloom' as the Chorus spoke (Beauman, p. 175).

28 At this line, Kean's set revealed 'the English camp, with a group of soldiery praying' (Kean pbk).

29 At this point in Olivier's Chorus, the camera begins to adopt the King's subjective viewpoint as he moves about the camp: 'the subjective shots increasingly emphasize Henry's intimacy with his men, his personal involvement with their fates, his identification with them: the English camp, seen through his eyes, is essentially part of him. Henry becomes, in effect, a new Chorus' (Geduld, p. 41). The camera tracks forward and Henry's shadow falls across a close-up of a soldier huddled by a fire.

Walking from watch to watch, from tent to tent?   30
Let him cry 'Praise and glory on his head!'
For forth he goes and visits all his host,
Bids them good morrow with a modest smile,
And calls them brothers, friends and countrymen.
Upon his royal face there is no note   35
How dread an army hath enrounded him,
Nor doth he dedicate one jot of colour
Unto the weary and all-watchèd night,
But freshly looks and overbears attaint
With cheerful semblance and sweet majesty,   40
That every wretch, pining and pale before,
Beholding him, plucks comfort from his looks.
A largess universal like the sun
His liberal eye doth give to everyone,
Thawing cold fear, that mean and gentle all   45
Behold, as may unworthiness define,
'A little touch of Harry in the night'.
And so our scene must to the battle fly,
Where (O for pity!) we shall much disgrace,
With four or five most vile and ragged foils   50
Right ill disposed in brawl ridiculous,
The name of Agincourt. Yet sit and see,
Minding true things by what their mockeries be.   *Exit*

31–2, 37–42 Cut by the Globe.

    34 Hayes shows Henry moving through the camp, laughing with groups of soldiers.

48–53 Cut by Olivier.

49–51 Since Kean's production was to be no 'disgrace', these lines were cut, with the word 'field'
replacing 'name' in line 52. The *Saturday Review* notice had been troubled with the
anticipation of these lines after seeing Henry's soldiers 'amply supplied with weapons';
and expressed its mock-relief when 'The heart of Mr Kean relented' and cut the lines (2
April 1859).

4.1 *Enter the* KING *and* GLOUCESTER [*and* BEDFORD *by another door*]

KING Gloucester, 'tis true that we are in great danger.
    The greater therefore should our courage be.
    Good morrow, brother Bedford. God almighty,
    There is some soul of goodness in things evil
    Would men observingly distil it out.   5
    For our bad neighbour makes us early stirrers,
    Which is both healthful and good husbandry.
    Besides, they are our outward consciences
    And preachers to us all, admonishing
    That we should dress us fairly for our end.   10
    Thus may we gather honey from the weed
    And make a moral of the devil himself.

Enter ERPINGHAM

    Good morrow, old Sir Thomas Erpingham.
    A good soft pillow for that good white head
    Were better than a churlish turf of France.   15
ERPINGHAM Not so, my liege. This lodging likes me better
    Since I may say 'now lie I like a king'.
KING 'Tis good for men to love their present pains.
    Upon example so the spirit is eased,
    And when the mind is quickened, out of doubt   20

4.1 Macready located it in 'King Henry's tent', which was decorated with 'a table, lights, ink, paper' as the headquarters of the campaign and low lit: 'very dark', notes the promptbook. Kean's night-time scenery included a moon which became obscured as a 'storm of rain heard' (Kean pbk). Calvert set this 'Within the English lines (night)', and introduced a number of soldiers on guard, sleeping, others at prayers.

    At the Globe, the King and Gloucester entered tentatively. In the BBC/Giles version, the scene takes place in the King's tent. He is drying his hands and throws the towel at Bedford – in brisk, unflappable mood. Calvert's Gloucester uttered a sigh to prompt the King's first speech.

1–81 Cut by BBC/Hayes.

3–12 Cut by Olivier.

16 In a symbolic swap, Olivier's Henry removes his crown and hands it to Erpingham, who gives his cloak as if in exchange.

18–23 Cut by Macready, Kean and Calvert. Olivier cut 18–30.

> The organs, though defunct and dead before,
> Break up their drowsy grave and newly move
> With casted slough and fresh legerity.
> Lend me thy cloak, Sir Thomas. Brothers both,
> Commend me to the princes in our camp.   25
> Do my good morrow to them, and anon
> Desire them all to my pavilion.

GLOUCESTER We shall, my liege.

ERPINGHAM Shall I attend your grace?

KING   No, my good knight.
> Go with my brothers to my lords of England.   30
> I and my bosom must debate awhile,
> And then I would no other company.

ERPINGHAM The Lord in heaven bless thee, noble Harry.

Exeunt [all but king]

KING God a mercy, old heart, thou speak'st cheerfully.

Enter PISTOL

PISTOL *Qui va là?*   35
KING A friend.

---

31 In Iain Glen's performance (Warchus), this line 'was not the usual pretext to allow a little surreptitious wandering around in disguise' but the heartfelt attempt of a deeply religious man 'who desperately wanted to find a quiet place to pray and kept being interrupted' (Holland, p. 198).

34 James Agee wrote of Olivier's performance: 'the difference in tone between [his] almost boyish "God-a-mercy" and his "Good old knight" [line 260] not long afterward, measures the King's growth in the time between with lovely strength, spaciousness and cleanness' (Eckert, p. 55).

35 Macready had a scene change here to 'Another part of the English camp' (Macready pbk), as does Branagh, placing Pistol's question as the guilty response of one caught rummaging through some of the kitbags in the shadows. Seeing the cloaked figure of Henry, he grabs a pike to threaten the stranger. Olivier's Pistol is similarly surprised as he emerges from the tent 'having clearly completed an unlawful mission' (O, Fol). The BBC/Giles Pistol brandishes a sword at the challenge. In Daniels' production it was the King who drew his gun. Bogdanov's Pistol was squatting behind a sandbag wall to defecate. Alan Howard, in Hands' production, nudged a sleeping Pistol awake. Noble's Pistol 'walks round front of HV – trying to see face. HV keeps face down so P cannot see' (Noble pbk).

PISTOL Discuss unto me, art thou officer, or art thou base, common
and popular?

KING I am a gentleman of a company.

PISTOL Trail'st thou the puissant pike?   40

KING Even so. What are you?

PISTOL As good a gentleman as the emperor.

KING Then you are a better than the king.

PISTOL The king's a bawcock and a heart of gold, a lad of life, an
imp of fame, of parents good, of fist most valiant. I kiss his dirty   45
shoe, and from heartstring I love the lovely bully. What is thy
name?

KING Harry *le roi*.

PISTOL Leroy? A Cornish name. Art thou of Cornish crew?

KING No, I am a Welshman.   50

PISTOL Knowest thou Llewellyn?

KING Yes.

PISTOL Tell him I'll knock his leek about his pate upon St Davy's
day.

KING Do not you wear your dagger in your cap that day, lest he   55
knock that about yours.

PISTOL Art thou his friend?

KING And his kinsman too.

PISTOL The *fico* for thee, then.

KING I thank you. God be with you.   60

PISTOL My name is Pistol called.   *Exit*

KING It sorts well with your fierceness.

Enter LLEWELLYN *and* GOWER [*by separate doors*]

GOWER Captain Llewellyn!

---

39 At the Globe, Henry spoke with a Welsh accent throughout the encounter with Pistol.

59 Macready's Pistol 'snaps his fingers in his face' at this line (Macready pbk).

62 The BBC/Giles King speaks this line to himself, after Pistol has gone. Calvert's King
delivered it with 'a slight chuckle' (Calvert pbk). Branagh changes the scene to 'Another
Area' (p. 85). Olivier's camera pans and tracks back until it is stopped by the sight of
Llewellyn, emerging from behind a tent and disappearing into a trench except for his head
and shoulders.

63 In Olivier's film, Gower enters calling loudly in search of Llewellyn. Daniels had him
shouting with a torch, as Llewellyn was seen reading a book by torchlight under his
cloak.

LLEWELLYN So! In the name of Jesu Christ, speak fewer. It is the
greatest admiration in the universal world when the true and   65
ancient prerogatives and laws of the wars is not kept. If you
would take the pains but to examine the wars of Pompey the
Great you shall find, I warrant you, that there is no tiddle taddle
nor pibble pabble in Pompey's camp. I warrant you, you shall
find the ceremonies of the wars, and the cares of it, and the   70
forms of it, and the sobriety of it, and the modesty of it, to be
otherwise.

GOWER Why, the enemy is loud. You hear him all night.

LLEWELLYN If the enemy is an ass and a fool and a prating
coxcomb, is it meet, think you, that we should also, look you, be   75
an ass and a fool and a prating coxcomb, in your own conscience,
now?

GOWER I will speak lower.

LLEWELLYN I pray you, and beseech you, that you will.

Exeunt [Gower and Llewellyn]

KING Though it appear a little out of fashion,   80
    There is much care and valour in this Welshman.

Enter three soldiers, John BATES, *Alexander* COURT *and Michael*
WILLIAMS

COURT Brother John Bates, is not that the morning which breaks
yonder?

64 Macready's lights gradually rose to indicate dawn breaking through the rest of the scene.
Calvert's Henry 'gets out of sight. Looking as if surveying the situation' (Calvert pbk). The
BBC/Giles Llewellyn wears camouflage branches in his tin hat. Olivier has Llewellyn jump
out of the trench to hush the noisy Gower. At the Globe, Llewellyn entered through the yard;
the King was downstage, inconspicuous and wrapped in a cloak. There is a monkish air to
Branagh in this scene, cowled in the shadows.

74 In Olivier's film, Llewellyn's speech begins in a whisper but gradually loses control and
develops into a shout at 'prating coxcomb', when Gower issues a reproving 'shh'.

82 In the BBC/Giles version, dawn is breaking as the three soldiers sit around a fire. Branagh
introduces Williams at confession. Court, who takes little part in the discussion after the first
line, is often cut, as in productions by Macready and Kean. His silence was interpreted,
however, in Noble's production, which portrayed him as 'skeletal, ghastly in pallor, clad
only in a thin grey vest and armed with a scythe, trembling incessantly and with dilated eyes
. . . Court is silent because he is imbecile with terror' (Fitter, p. 263). In Branagh's film, some

BATES I think it be. But we have no great cause to desire the
    approach of day.   85
WILLIAMS We see yonder the beginning of the day, but I think we
    shall never see the end of it. Who goes there?
KING A friend.
WILLIAMS Under what captain serve you?
KING Under Sir Thomas Erpingham.   90
WILLIAMS A good old commander, and a most kind gentleman. I
    pray you, what thinks he of our estate?
KING Even as men wrecked upon a sand, that look to be washed off
    the next tide.
BATES He hath not told his thought to the king?   95
KING No. Nor it is not meet he should. For though I speak it to
    you, I think the king is but a man as I am. The violet smells
    to him as it doth to me. The element shows to him as it doth to
    me. All his senses have but human conditions. His ceremonies
    laid by, in his nakedness he appears but a man; and though his   100

of this intensity is diluted, although Court is 'terrified. There is an air of awful resignation over them all' (Branagh, p. 87). Olivier too casts Court, only a boy, as white-faced with fear, who sleeps through most of the scene.

87 At the Globe all three pointed their staves threateningly at Henry; Daniels had them all pointing rifles. Branagh's Henry cracks a twig underfoot and Williams is ready to attack with his knife. In the firelight, the cloaked figure of Henry has a slightly sinister, even menacing, aspect. Daniels had the King sharing a drag on a cigarette and a pull from a flask with the men, under the royal standard flying above. Hayes' Henry is a hooded figure who approaches the huddle of men around the campfire. The rest of their conversation is filmed with Henry sitting on a stool and the others on the ground. In Olivier's film Williams looks up, startled, towards the camera (it is Henry's point of view). An unexpected version of this sequence, using lines 83 onwards, is performed by a computer-simulated campfire on the holodeck of the Starship Enterprise (*Star Trek: The Next Generation* 'The Defector', originally broadcast 1 September 1990), as part of an episode concerning the conscience-stricken captain, Jean-Luc Picard, who faces a decision which may lead the universe into full-scale war.

96b–104 Cut by Macready and Calvert.

97 The sophistry of the King's apparent admission of his humanity is perhaps best approached by the *Star Trek* version: Data, an android, not a human, delivers the line, and is told at the end of the sequence by the captain 'you're here to learn about the human condition, and there is no better way of doing that than by embracing Shakespeare'.

affections are higher mounted than ours, yet when they stoop
they stoop with the like wing. Therefore when he sees reason of
fears as we do, his fears, out of doubt, be of the same relish as
ours are. Yet in reason no man should possess him with any
appearance of fear, lest he by showing it should dishearten his   105
army.

BATES He may show what outward courage he will, but I believe, as
cold a night as 'tis, he could wish himself in Thames up to the
neck. And so I would he were, and I by him, at all adventures, so
we were quit here.   110

KING By my troth, I will speak my conscience of the king. I think he
would not wish himself anywhere but where he is.

BATES Then I would he were here alone. So should he be sure to be
ransomed and a-many poor men's lives saved.

KING I dare say you love him not so ill to wish him here alone,   115
howsoever you speak this to feel other men's minds. Methinks I
could not die anywhere so contented as in the king's company,
his cause being just and his quarrel honourable.

WILLIAMS That's more than we know.

BATES Ay, or more than we should seek after, for we know enough if   120
we know we are the king's subjects. If his cause be wrong our
obedience to the king wipes the crime of it out of us.

WILLIAMS But if the cause be not good the king himself hath a
heavy reckoning to make, when all those legs and arms and
heads chopped off in a battle shall join together at the latter day   125
and cry all 'We died at such a place', some swearing, some crying
for a surgeon, some upon their wives left poor behind them,
some upon the debts they owe, some upon their children rawly
left. I am afeard there are few die well that die in a battle, for how
can they charitably dispose of anything when blood is their   130
argument? Now if these men do not die well it will be a black
matter for the king that led them to it, who to disobey were
against all proportion of subjection.

111 A close-up of Henry's humorous face in BBC/Hayes confirms his identity, in the absence of
the early part of the scene which sets out his disguise.

113b–14 This implicit criticism of Henry is cut by Branagh.

115 The Globe's Henry was visibly upset at their response.

123 Olivier gives this speech to a pale Court.

124 Mention of the severed limbs of battle was omitted by Calvert.

KING So if a son that is by his father sent about merchandise
    do sinfully miscarry upon the sea, the imputation of his   135
    wickedness, by your rule, should be imposed upon his father
    that sent him. Or if a servant, under his master's command
    transporting a sum of money, be assailed by robbers and die in
    many irreconciled iniquities, you may call the business of the
    master the author of the servant's damnation. But this is not so.   140
    The king is not bound to answer the particular endings of his
    soldiers, the father of his son, nor the master of his servant, for
    they purpose not their death when they purpose their services.
    Besides, there is no king, be his cause never so spotless, if it
    come to the arbitrament of swords can try it out with all   145
    unspotted soldiers. Some, peradventure, have on them the guilt
    of premeditated and contrived murder, some of beguiling
    virgins with the broken seals of perjury, some, making the wars
    their bulwark, that have before gored the gentle bosom of peace
    with pillage and robbery. Now, if these men have defeated the   150
    law and outrun native punishment, though they can outstrip
    men they have no wings to fly from God. War is His beadle, war
    is His vengeance, so that here men are punished for before-
    breach of the king's laws in now the king's quarrel. Where they
    feared the death they have borne life away, and where they   155
    would be safe they perish. Then, if they die unprovided, no
    more is the king guilty of their damnation than he was before
    guilty of those impieties for the which they are now visited.
    Every subject's duty is the king's, but every subject's soul is his
    own. Therefore should every soldier in the wars do as every sick   160
    man in his bed, wash every mote out of his conscience. And
    dying so, death is to him advantage; or, not dying, the time was
    blessedly lost wherein such preparation was gained. And in him
    that escapes it were not sin to think that, making God so free an

137 The Globe cut the master–servant example, as had Macready, Kean, Olivier, Hayes, Hands,
     Noble and Branagh. The BBC/Giles version retains the full speech, with Henry as a
     humorous and earnest curate, reflective and persuasive.
141–59 Cut by Kean and Calvert.
144–56; 160–6 Cut by Olivier.
160–6 Cut by Noble and by Hands, who remarks wryly in the published souvenir text: 'Should
     Christianity regain its ubiquity, some argument might be countenanced for its reinclusion'
     (Beauman, p. 182).

offer, He let him outlive that day to see His greatness, and to   165
teach others how they should prepare.

WILLIAMS 'Tis certain, every man that dies ill, the ill upon his own
head; the king is not to answer it.

BATES I do not desire he should answer for me, and yet I determine
to fight lustily for him.   170

KING I myself heard the king say he would not be ransomed.

WILLIAMS Ay, he said so to make us fight cheerfully, but when our
throats are cut he may be ransomed and we ne'er the wiser.

KING If I live to see it, I will never trust his word after.

WILLIAMS You pay him then! That's a perilous shot out of an elder   175
gun, that a poor and a private displeasure can do against a
monarch. You may as well go about to turn the sun to ice with
fanning in his face with a peacock's feather. You'll never trust his
word after! Come, 'tis a foolish saying.

KING Your reproof is something too round. I should be angry with   180
you if the time were convenient.

WILLIAMS Let it be a quarrel between us, if you live.

KING I embrace it.

WILLIAMS How shall I know thee again?

KING Give me any gage of thine and I will wear it in my bonnet.   185
Then, if ever thou darest acknowledge it, I will make it my
quarrel.

WILLIAMS Here's my glove. Give me another of thine.

KING There.

[They exchange gloves]

WILLIAMS This will I also wear in my cap. If ever thou come to me   190
and say, after tomorrow, 'This is my glove', by this hand I will
take thee a box on the ear.

KING If ever I live to see it, I will challenge it.

WILLIAMS Thou darest as well be hanged.

KING Well, I will do it, though I take thee in the king's company.   195

---

167 At the Globe Williams was angry and dismissive.

180 Real aggression was evident in the Globe production. Similarly, Hayes has Williams slap
Henry disparagingly, and the King then push back with genuine anger, but by cutting
182–96, the quarrel is pre-empted. Olivier cuts 182–96 and thus also evades the full
antagonism of the scene. In Daniels' production, by contrast, the scene turned quickly ugly,
and other soldiers had to break up the scuffle between Henry and Williams. The BBC/Giles
Henry also strikes Williams.

WILLIAMS Keep thy word. Fare thee well.

BATES Be friends, you English fools, be friends! We have French
quarrels enough if you could tell how to reckon.

KING Indeed, the French may lay twenty French crowns to one they
will beat us, for they bear them on their shoulders. But it is no   200
English treason to cut French crowns, and tomorrow the king
himself will be a clipper.

Exeunt soldiers

Upon the king! 'Let us our lives, our souls, our debts, our
careful wives, our children and our sins, lay on the king.'
We must bear all.   205
O hard condition, twin-born with greatness,
Subject to the breath of every fool, whose sense
No more can feel but his own wringing.

198 Olivier has Bates and Williams rise and leave, grumbling, as Henry watches them, leaving
Court asleep in the firelight.

199–202 Cut by Kean, Olivier, Hayes and Noble. At the Globe Henry threw his cloak to the ground in
a gesture of absolute frustration.

203 Productions emphasising the spectacle of the play, especially during the nineteenth century,
had some difficulties with the speech's denunciation of outward pomp. Macready and Kean,
for example, cut the most egregious lines 235–8. Calvert seated his Henry on a cannon, and
the heading 'THE KING ALONE', stressed his solitude after a stage busy with extras throughout
the production. In Daniels' production, Henry delivered the soliloquy 'as the utterance of a
man much disorientated and angered by the conversation he had just had' (Smallwood, p.
239). By contrast, the BBC/Giles Henry is weary, low-voiced and emotional. Olivier's speech
is delivered as a voice-over, as the King is seated alongside the sleeping Court. The dawn
gradually 'haloes' his head (Geduld, p. 42). Agee described the medium close-up on
Olivier's 'deeply sad' expression during the speech as 'one of his brilliant devices for
acclimatizing Shakespeare to the screen' (Eckert, p. 56). Branagh described his stage
performance of the speech as a response to 'the terrible certainty of what Williams has said'
(*Players*, p. 103). In his film, Llewellyn comes up to him and recognises the King, but Henry
dismisses him without a word. He is alone, unhooded, and begins to whisper 'the ever-
present ache of his responsibility' (Branagh, p. 91). Branagh's delivery of the speech is
highly emotional, in contrast to his characteristically measured delivery, and the eerie light
on his face adds to the sense of a man on the edge of his self-control. Noble's production
positioned Henry in the centre forestage. At the Globe Henry knelt for the beginning of this
speech, his back to the audience.

206–8 Cut by Olivier.

What infinite heart's ease must kings neglect
That private men enjoy?   210
And what have kings that privates have not too,
Save ceremony, save general ceremony?
And what art thou, thou idol ceremony?
What kind of god art thou, that suffer'st more
Of mortal griefs than do thy worshippers?   215
What are thy rents? What are thy comings-in?
O ceremony, show me but thy worth!
What? Is thy soul of adoration?
Art thou aught else but place, degree and form,
Creating awe and fear in other men,   220
Wherein thou art less happy being feared
Than they in fearing?
What drink'st thou oft, instead of homage sweet,
But poisoned flattery? Oh, be sick, great greatness,
And bid thy ceremony give thee cure.   225
Thinkst thou the fiery fever will go out
With titles blown from adulation?
Will it give place to flexure and low bending?
Canst thou, when thou command'st the beggar's knee,
Command the health of it? No, thou proud dream,   230
That playst so subtly with a king's repose.
I am a king that find thee, and I know
'Tis not the balm, the sceptre and the ball,
The sword, the mace, the crown imperial,
The intertissued robe of gold and pearl,   235
The farcèd title running 'fore the king,
The throne he sits on, nor the tide of pomp
That beats upon the high shore of this world;
No, not all these, thrice-gorgeous ceremony,
Not all these, laid in bed majestical,   240
Can sleep so soundly as the wretched slave

210 At the Globe Henry rose, rubbing his eyes and bent double.
216–22 Cut by Olivier and BBC/Hayes.
230 At the Globe Henry knelt, rubbing his hands over his face and head wearily.
232 Robert Hardy, in the BBC/Hayes production, looks directly out at the camera here.
241 Olivier strokes the hair of the sleeping Court. The *Era* reviewer singled out these lines of George Rignold's performance for particular praise, as 'spoken in a wearied tone which laid bare the suffering of his heart' (9 November 1879).

Who, with a body filled and vacant mind,
Gets him to rest, crammed with distressful bread;
Never sees horrid night, the child of hell,
But like a lackey from the rise to set   245
Sweats in the eye of Phoebus, and all night
Sleeps in Elysium; next day after dawn
Doth rise and help Hyperion to his horse
And follows so the ever-running year
With profitable labour to his grave.   250
And but for ceremony such a wretch,
Winding up days with toil and nights with sleep,
Had the forehand and vantage of a king.
The slave, a member of the country's peace,
Enjoys it, but in gross brain little wots   255
What watch the king keeps to maintain the peace,
Whose hours the peasant best advantages.

Enter ERPINGHAM

ERPINGHAM My lord, your nobles, jealous of your absence,
       Seek through the camp to find you.
KING Good old knight,   260
       Collect them all together at my tent.
       I'll be before thee.
ERPINGHAM   I shall do't, my lord.   *Exit*
KING O God of battles, steel my soldiers' hearts.

247 Dawn begins to break in Olivier's film.

254–7 Cut by Olivier, Hayes and Globe.

257 Erpingham entered in a great hurry in Macready's production, and in some versions was replaced by Gower. Hands cut Erpingham's entry entirely. Olivier has Erpingham take back his cloak and place the crown on Henry's head, recrowning him for the events that lie ahead. They walk together through the camp, passing a tent where the sounds of a celebration of Mass are heard and the ceremony is glimpsed through the opening. On Erpingham's entry at the Globe, the King got to his feet and gathered himself.

263 Irving Wardle described Henry's prayer in Noble's production as 'a gabbled, terrified act of bribery, fully in the spirit of his guilty father' (*T* 30 March 1984). At the Globe, Rylance knelt facing the audience but seemed to hide from their gaze as if his self-confidence had left him, holding a hand in front of his face. Hayes also has Henry pray out front, this time to camera, with his rosary beads featured prominently in his hands. Olivier, apparently prompted by the Mass he overhears, kneels facing the French camp (O, Fol).

Possess them not with fear. Take from them now
The sense of reckoning ere th'opposèd numbers   265
Pluck their hearts from them. Not today, O Lord,
Oh, not today, think not upon the fault
My father made in compassing the crown.
I Richard's body have interrèd new,
And on it have bestowed more contrite tears   270
Than from it issued forcèd drops of blood.
Five hundred poor I have in yearly pay
Who twice a day their withered hands hold up
Toward heaven to pardon blood. And I have built
Two chantries where the sad and solemn priests   275
Sing still for Richard's soul. More will I do,
Though all that I can do is nothing worth
Since that my penitence comes after all,
Imploring pardon.

Enter GLOUCESTER

GLOUCESTER My liege.
KING   My brother Gloucester's voice? Ay,   280
I know thy errand. I will go with thee.
The day, my friends, and all things stay for me.

Exeunt

266b–79 Henry's acknowledgement of the guilt of Richard's death is cut by Olivier. Instead,
Gloucester enters, touches his brother on the shoulder, and they walk away into the
distance together.

267 At the Globe Henry's voice was breaking with tears.

274 One reviewer identified this as the triumph of Kemble's performance: 'As a *coup de théâtre*,
his starting up from prayer at the sound of a trumpet, in the passage where he states his
attempted atonement to Richard the Second, formed one of the most spirited excitements
that the stage has ever displayed' (Sprague, p. 119). This popular business was repeated by
Vandenhoff in 1825, and by Macready, who leapt to his feet at a trumpet sounding 'shrill and
short' (Macready pbk), cutting the reference to Richard. Kean also cut this, perhaps because
the audience would not understand the reference (although elsewhere in the text of the
play Kean refers to his own earlier production of *Richard II*), perhaps because it casts
potentially damaging doubt on the legitimacy of Henry's kingship at this crucial point.

276 At the Globe Henry almost broke down.

282 Waller had the curtain fall on Henry kneeling. Branagh ends with a tear: 'he has done and
felt all he can. He slowly closes his eyes and lowers his head' (Branagh, p. 93). Alan Howard,

4.2 *Enter* BOURBON, ORLÉANS, RAMBURES *and* BEAUMONT

ORLÉANS The sun doth gild our armour. Up, my lords!
BOURBON *Montez à cheval!* My horse, varlet lackey! Ha!
ORLÉANS Oh, brave spirit!
BOURBON *Via les eaux et terres!*
ORLÉANS *Rien puis l'air et feu?*   5
BOURBON *Cieux*, cousin Orléans!

Enter CONSTABLE

in Hands' production, lay down among his soldiers to sleep. Hayes frames Henry, crossing himself in a gesture of sincere piety, from a slightly low-angle position, subtly emphasising his growth in personal and spiritual stature. In Warchus' production Henry planted the cross given him by the Archbishop in the ground.

4.2 Despite heavy cuts, Macready's promptbook contains numerous injunctions to pace this scene slowly in order to give time for the stagehands to prepare the Agincourt spectacle. Kean introduced the scene with a flourish of trumpets, and had servants 'exeunt hastily' (Kean pbk) to give an air of bustle. Calvert set this in the Dauphin's tent as before. Again, most productions cast the Dauphin in the role this edition gives to Bourbon. Olivier presents an early morning scene in the French camp, beginning with a close-up of a flap of fabric blowing in the wind and the confident tones of Bourbon (instead of Orléans) delivering line 1. The fabric is revealed as a banner, behind which Bourbon, standing on 'a slight hillock, arms stretched above his head' (O, Fol) is being strapped into his armour. Throughout the scene, the nobles are engaged in dressing for battle, with armour being polished and strapped on. Branagh cuts 1–7, and instead of presenting the scene as the boasting of individual French noblemen in their tent, he sets it against the backdrop of the French army, with hundreds of cavalry on a hilltop viewed from a low angle to emphasise their superiority. The French noblemen are viewing their forces, and fully confident of victory. Daniels contrasted the dazzling armour of the French with the drab camouflage of the English, as the French descend, angel-like, from the flies on a golden platform and walk among the sleeping English. Hayes' television production contrasts the sombre mood of the previous scene with this image of bright cheerfulness, as the French drink from polished goblets in a composition dominated by a foreground cannon.

2 Olivier's Dauphin appears 'in his magnificent gilt armour, two varlets fussily following him from behind' (O, Fol)

5 The BBC/Giles French lords, coxcombs in bright armour, drink a toast amid much laughing and posturing.

Now, my lord Constable?
CONSTABLE Hark how our steeds for present service neigh.
BOURBON Mount them, and make incision in their hides
  That their hot blood may spin in English eyes   10
  And dout them with superfluous courage! Ha!
RAMBURES What, will you have them weep our horses' blood?
  How shall we then behold their natural tears?

Enter MESSENGER

MESSENGER The English are embattled, you French peers.
CONSTABLE To horse, you gallant princes, straight to horse! 15
  Do but behold yon poor and starvèd band
  And your fair show shall suck away their souls,
  Leaving them but the shells and husks of men.
  There is not work enough for all our hands,
  Scarce blood enough in all their sickly veins   20
  To give each naked curtal-axe a stain,
  That our French gallants shall today draw out
  And sheathe for lack of sport. Let us but blow on them,
  The vapour of our valour will o'erturn them.
  'Tis positive 'gainst all exceptions, lords,   25
  That our superfluous lackeys and our peasants
  Who in unnecessary action swarm
  About our squares of battle were enough
  To purge this field of such a hilding foe,
  Though we upon this mountain's basis by   30
  Took stand for idle speculation,
  But that our honours must not. What's to say?
  A very little little let us do
  And all is done. Then let the trumpets sound
  The tucket sonance and the note to mount,   35
  For our approach shall so much dare the field
  That England shall crouch down in fear, and yield.

Enter GRANDPRÉ

GRANDPRÉ Why do you stay so long, my lords of France?

15–63 Cut by Olivier. The scene ends with a shot of the Dauphin ready to be winched on to his
  horse by a scaffold contraption.
19–55 Cut by Hayes.

Yon island carrions, desperate of their bones,
Ill-favouredly become the morning field.   40
Their ragged curtains poorly are let loose
And our air shakes them passing scornfully.
Big Mars seems bankrupt in their beggared host,
And faintly through a rusty beaver peeps.
The horsemen sit like fixèd candlesticks   45
With torch staves in their hand, and their poor jades
Lob down their heads, dropping the hides and hips,
The gum down-roping from their pale dead eyes,
And in their pale dull mouths the gemelled bit
Lies foul with chewed-grass, still and motionless.   50
And their executors the knavish crows
Fly o'er them all, impatient for their hour.
Description cannot suit itself in words
To demonstrate the life of such a battle,
In life so lifeless, as it shows itself.   55
CONSTABLE They have said their prayers, and they stay for death.
BOURBON Shall we go send them dinners and fresh suits,
And give their fasting horses provender,
And after fight with them?
CONSTABLE I stay but for my guidon. To the field!   60
I will the banner from a trumpet take
And use it for my haste. Come, come, away!
The sun is high and we outwear the day.

                                       Exeunt

4.3 *Enter* GLOUCESTER, BEDFORD, EXETER, ERPINGHAM *with all his host,* SALISBURY *and* WESTMORLAND

GLOUCESTER Where is the king?
BEDFORD The king himself is rode to view their battle.

44–50 Cut by Kean.

45 Bogdanov began the speech at this line, and had Grandpré writing it as a poem or letter at a field typewriter, giving up on line 53.

4.3 Macready's King entered with the royal standard borne before him, and his (evidently sizeable) tent was filled with six clusters of eight soldiers and four banners each, as well as

WESTMORLAND Of fighting men they have full threescore thousand.
EXETER There's five to one. Besides, they all are fresh.
SALISBURY God's arm strike with us! 'Tis a fearful odds.   5
God be wi'you, princes all. I'll to my charge.
If we no more meet till we meet in heaven
Then joyfully, my noble lord of Bedford,
My dear lord Gloucester and my good lord Exeter,
And my kind kinsman, warriors all, adieu.   10
BEDFORD Farewell, good Salisbury, and good luck go with thee.
EXETER Farewell, kind lord. Fight valiantly today.

                                        [*Exit Salisbury*]

And yet I do thee wrong to mind thee of it,
For thou art framed of the firm truth of valour.
BEDFORD He is as full of valour as of kindness,   15
Princely in both.

                        Enter the KING

WESTMORLAND   O that we now had here
But one ten thousand of those men in England
That do no work today.
KING   What's he that wishes so?

banners and heralds behind the throne, and a large number of 'nobles etc'. according to the
diagram in the promptbook. For this scene, 'The English Position at Agincourt', Kean
presented 'the English army drawn up for battle', and the promptbook blocking diagram
shows ranks of over a hundred archers, spearmen, axeman and cannoneers, punctuated by
standards (Kean pbk). Calvert, too, added 108 extras (Calvert pbk). 'The French exit to an
anthem of brass and kettledrum. The English army wakes unwillingly to reveille – a ladle
banged on a soup-pot. They begin their day's preparations, rolling blankets, assembling
weapons etc.' (Beauman, p. 189). Olivier opens the scene with the standard of St George
blowing in the morning breeze. Gower carries a bucket of water for a horse that is being
groomed by Jamy, and as the camera moves through the camp we see the English and 'a
much less elaborate preparation going on than in the previous scene in the French camp'
(O, Fol).
    5 Noble reallocated this to Erpingham. In Hayes' production the soldiers cross themselves.
6–16 Cut by Noble; 6–11 cut in BBC/Hayes.
   18 For this St Crispin's Day speech, Branagh's camera-work frames the King with a few of his
soldiers also in view, symbolising the leader on the same plane as his men. The camera
stresses the fellowship of the speech, although the red of Henry's costume is visually

My cousin Westmorland. No, my fair cousin.
If we are marked to die, we are enough   20
To do our country loss. And if to live,
The fewer men, the greater share of honour.
God's will, I pray thee wish not one man more.
By Jove, I am not covetous for gold,
Nor care I who doth feed upon my cost.   25
It yearns me not if men my garments wear.
Such outward things dwell not in my desires.
But if it be a sin to covet honour,
I am the most offending soul alive.
No, faith, my coz, wish not a man from England.   30
God's peace, I would not lose so great an honour
As one man more, methinks, would share from me,
For the best hope I have. Oh, do not wish one more!
Rather proclaim it, Westmorland, through my host

distinguished from the greys and browns of the soldiers. In the first part of the speech he walks around the camp, men following to hear his encouragement. In essence this follows Olivier, whose earlier speech before Harfleur had been shot so as to emphasise his relative smallness, whereas 'here the camera pulls directly back, keeping a horizontal level with Henry. In eschewing the high subtended angle, the movement of the camera no longer gives Henry a sympathetic diminution, for his cause is now fully established, and he can proclaim his intentions as an equal' (Davies, p. 28). Agee describes Olivier's delivery of the speech as 'calculated yet self-exceeding improvisation, at once self-enjoying and selfless . . . rising to a situation wholly dangerous and glamorous' (Eckert, p. 56). Mansfield entered through ranks of soldiers to deliver the speech; in Noble's production Branagh 'walks slowly down stage, company follow' (Noble pbk). Iain Glen's rendition of the speech was pronounced by one reviewer 'sincere but wan. Quite why the troops stiffen their sinews and summon up the blood is a mystery' (*STel* 15 May 1994), although others admired a low-key approach to one of the play's great arias: Alan Howard began 'almost casually as the king lines up with the soldiers for his mugful of water from a keg' (David, p. 199); Burton at the Old Vic in 1955 spoke 'sitting on a drum among [his men], tousling the head of the boy at his feet' (Leiter, p. 220). Michael Kahn titled this scene 'The Machine Creates the Believable Lie. Point of No Return'. Coleman strung the two great battle speeches of the play together here, adding 3.1 for good measure. At the Globe, the speech was directed out to the audience, and 'Agincourt became paradoxically more "real" as a psychological state experienced by soldiers . . . because the place had to be created out of nothing' (Kiernan, p. 72).

23–33a Cut by Macready and Calvert; 24–33 cut by Kean, Olivier, Hayes and Branagh.

That he which hath no stomach to this fight   35
Let him depart. His passport shall be made,
And crowns for convoy put into his purse.
We would not die in that man's company
That fears his fellowship to die with us.
This day is called the Feast of Crispian.   40
He that outlives this day and comes safe home
Will stand a-tiptoe when this day is named,
And rouse him at the name of Crispian.
He that shall see this day and live old age
Will yearly on the vigil feast his neighbours,   45
And say 'Tomorrow is Saint Crispian.'
Then will he strip his sleeve and show his scars,
And say 'These wounds I had on Crispin's day.'
Old men forget, yet all shall be forgot
But he'll remember, with advantages,   50
What feats he did that day. Then shall our names,
Familiar in his mouth as household words,
Harry the king, Bedford and Exeter,
Warwick and Talbot, Salisbury and Gloucester,
Be in their flowing cups freshly remembered.   55
This story shall the good man teach his son,

35 In emending 'fight' to 'feast', the BBC/Hayes production regularises the image but evades the unpleasant truth about the battle ahead.

39 Hayes has Pistol attempt to step forward from the soldiers to take up this offer, but he is restrained by the officers and Henry is unaware of this protest.

40 Branagh stops moving among the soldiers and climbs on to a cart to deliver the rest of the speech. In the BBC/Hayes production, Hardy climbs on to a bale of hay and encourages his men to gather round. He is framed by unfurled flags, and shot from below, with the heads and helmets of his audience in the bottom of the frame, stressing his leadership. Pencil marks in the Folger Shakespeare Library copy of Kemble's promptbook suggest this speech may have been cut in its entirety.

48 Here Richard Burton's voice quavered 'with jocular senescence' (Leiter, p. 220). Branagh speaks with 'God-given certainty' (Branagh, p. 97).

51 Olivier's Henry mounts a cart here, and the camera begins to pull backwards and upwards to reveal 'as much of the army as possible' (O, Fol).

56 Here, Exeter is seen smiling broadly in Branagh's film, and the camera moves to pick out Llewellyn, Nym, the Boy and other familiar faces in the crowd of soldiers.

And Crispin Crispian shall ne'er go by
From this day to the ending of the world
But we in it shall be remembered.
We few, we happy few, we band of brothers –   60
For he today that sheds his blood with me
Shall be my brother; be he ne'er so vile
This day shall gentle his condition –
And gentlemen in England, now abed,
Shall think themselves accursed they were not here,   65
And hold their manhoods cheap whiles any speaks
That fought with us upon Saint Crispin's Day.

Enter SALISBURY

SALISBURY My sovereign lord, bestow yourself with speed.
      The French are bravely in their battles set,
      And will with all expedience charge on us.   70
KING All things are ready, if our minds be so.
WESTMORLAND Perish the man whose mind is backward now!
KING Thou dost not wish more help from England, coz?
WESTMORLAND God's will, my liege, would you and I alone,
      Without more help, could fight this royal battle!   75
KING Why, now thou hast unwished five thousand men,

---

60 The note in the Kean promptbook reads 'Great animation on the part of the soldiers'. Waller ended his speech downstage with his back to the audience addressing a semi-circle of the soldiers kneeling around him. In the BBC/Hayes production, Henry leans a hand on the shoulders of Gloucester and Bedford, thus stressing literal, consanguineous brothers rather than the idealised image of comradeship.

63 At this line in Macready's production the assembled soldiery knelt as if to accept the honour. Branagh's soldiers give a loud cheer. Most productions seem to have stressed the reaction of the soldiers, but, in contrast, the last eight lines of the speech in the BBC/Giles film are delivered against a close-up of Henry, speaking in a low voice, with no reaction shots of his men.

67 Olivier's soldiers cheer. Salisbury was replaced by Gower in Kean's acting version and by Gloucester in Noble's production.

71 Alan Howard believed that 'this line, not the St Crispin's day speech . . . was the one rallying call of the scene' (Beauman, p. 192).

73 A fine profile shot of Olivier as Henry at this point provides one of the often-reproduced publicity stills from the film.

> Which likes me better than to wish us one.
> You know your places. God be with you all.

> *Tucket. Enter* MONTJOY

MONTJOY Once more I come to know of thee, King Harry,
    If for thy ransom thou wilt now compound   80
    Before thy most assurèd overthrow.
    For certainly thou art so near the gulf
    Thou needs must be englutted. Besides, in mercy,
    The Constable desires thee thou wilt mind
    Thy followers of repentance, that their souls   85
    May make a peaceful and a sweet retire
    From off these fields where, wretches, their poor bodies
    Must lie and fester.
KING   Who hath sent thee now?
MONTJOY The Constable of France.
KING I pray thee bear my former answer back.   90
    Bid them achieve me, and then sell my bones.
    Good God, why should they mock poor fellows thus?

78 Kean's Montjoy was subservient, uncovering his head and kneeling before the English King. In Daniels' production, the soldiers knelt and prayed as they fixed bayonets to their rifles; Montjoy entered carrying a white flag. Hayes' production has King and soldiers crossing themselves. The BBC/Giles Henry shakes hands with each of his men. Olivier steps from the cart from where he has given his oration straight on to the back of his horse, brought alongside. His easy athleticism is contrasted with a cut to the French camp, where the Dauphin is being lowered by crane on to his horse, aided by several grooms supporting him and an elaborate contraption of ropes. The film cuts again, this time to a shot of Montjoy and the standard-bearer galloping towards the camera. On reaching the King, Montjoy dismounts: Henry's superiority is shown by his remaining on horseback. The cheers and smiles of Branagh's camp are stopped by the 'ominous arrival of Montjoy' on horseback (Branagh, p. 99). Henry greets him with barely contained anger. Hands' Montjoy came bearing a green branch, symbolic of peace.

82–8 Cut by Kean, Olivier and Hayes.

89 Hands decided that Montjoy's answer was a lie and that he had come of his own accord to try and stop the battle, although, as Taylor notes, this was probably not perceived by any member of the audience (*Moment*, pp. 144–5).

The man that once did sell the lion's skin
While the beast lived, was killed with hunting him.
A many of our bodies shall no doubt   95
Find native graves, upon the which, I trust,
Shall witness live in brass of this day's work.
And those that leave their valiant bones in France,
Dying like men, though buried in your dunghills,
They shall be famed, for there the sun shall greet them   100
And draw their honours reeking up to heaven,
Leaving their earthly parts to choke your clime,
The smell whereof shall breed a plague in France.
Mark then abounding valour in our English,
That being dead, like to the bullet's crazing   105
Break out into a second course of mischief
Killing in relapse of mortality.
Let me speak proudly. Tell the Constable
We are but warriors for the working day.
Our gayness and our gilt are all besmirched   110
With rainy marching in the painful field.
There's not a piece of feather in our host
(Good argument, I hope, we will not fly)
And time hath worn us into slovenry.
But by the mass, our hearts are in the trim,   115
And my poor soldiers tell me yet ere night
They'll be in fresher robes, or they will pluck
The gay new coats o'er the French soldiers' heads
And turn them out of service. If they do this –
As, if God please, they shall – my ransom then   120
Will soon be levied. Herald, save thou thy labour.
Come thou no more for ransom, gentle herald.

93–4 Hands turned this still-current phrase into a demonstration of comradeship: Henry began it, and it was completed by the soldiers, in 'a music-hall moment shared by all, whatever their rank' (Beauman, p. 193). By contrast, Olivier cut the couplet.

95–107 These lines were cut by Kean and Calvert; 104–7 by Olivier and Hayes.

113 In the BBC/Hayes production, Henry uses Montjoy's presence as an excuse for more uplifting addresses to his soldiers.

116–21 Cut by Olivier and Hayes. David Gwillim in the BBC/Giles production speaks the lines angrily.

They shall have none, I swear, but these my joints,
Which if they have, as I will leave 'em them,
Shall yield them little. Tell the Constable.   125
MONTJOY I shall, King Harry. And so fare thee well.
Thou never shalt hear herald any more.   *Exit*
KING [*Aside*] I fear thou wilt once more come again for a ransom.

Enter YORK

YORK My lord, most humbly on my knee I beg
The leading of the vanguard.   130
KING Take it, brave York. Now soldiers, march away,
And how Thou pleasest, God, dispose the day.

Exeunt

4.4 *Alarm. Excursions. Enter* PISTOL, FRENCH *soldier*, BOY

PISTOL Yield, cur!

127 In Olivier's film, Montjoy smiles, sadly, on this line. Hayes has Henry laugh confidently as
Montjoy leaves, but then stand aside to deliver the more serious line following, as if to himself.
128 The BBC/Giles Henry speaks this as a quiet aside, to himself. Noble interpolated 4.0.48–53
here.
129 York's request was cut by Kean, Calvert and Olivier. Noble developed a ritual around it: 'York
steps forward and kneels. Erpingham hands him the button. All kneel and kiss the ground.
York throws button and as [he] catches all cheer and stand' before the army charged
upstage into the void representing Agincourt (Noble pbk).
132 Macready interpolated lines from 3.1.17, 31–4 here, ending the scene on a rousing oration
rather than the sombre piety of 4.3.132. Calvert ended the scene with the assembled army
marching off left to shouts of 'St George'. A note in the promptbook alerts 'Everyone for
Agincourt Tableau'. Branagh leads his men 'as they go down on their knees to cross
themselves and kiss the ground on which they will fight' (Branagh, p. 101). Branagh then
interpolates 4.0.48–52. Hands ended the scene literalising the Chorus' 'little touch of Harry'
(4.0.47): the soldiers each touched Henry as he passed. Olivier rides into close-up to deliver
the last line of the scene quietly. The BBC/Hayes production cuts to an image of marching
feet in close-up, given a slightly slow-motion, almost abstracted representation as the frame
mists over. Again, as at lines 60–7, the BBC/Giles version eschews a shot of the army here,
focusing instead on a close-up of the King in three-quarter profile, looking out of the frame.

4.4 This scene stands as an ironic, anti-climactic, unheroic synecdoche for the entire Battle of
Agincourt: it is the only representation of fighting. It was cut by Kemble, Macready, Kean,

FRENCH *Je pense que vous êtes le gentilhomme de bon qualité.*

PISTOL Quality? 'Colin o custure me'. Art thou a gentleman? What
    is thy name? Discuss.

FRENCH *O Seigneur Dieu!* 5

PISTOL O Seigneur Due should be a gentleman. Perpend my words,
    O Seigneur Due, and mark: O Seigneur Due, thou diest on
    point of fox, except, O Seigneur, thou do give to me egregious
    ransom.

FRENCH *Oh, prenez miséricorde! Ayez pitié de moi!* 10

PISTOL Moy shall not serve. I will have forty moys, or I will fetch thy
    rim out at thy throat, in drops of crimson blood.

FRENCH *Est-il impossible d'échapper la force de ton bras?*

PISTOL Brass, cur? Thou damnèd and luxurious mountain goat,
    offer'st me brass? 15

Olivier, BBC/Hayes and Branagh; Calvert pruned it by about a fifth. Mansfield's production played the scene over 'the din of battle' (Mansfield). Other productions interpolate, either before or after the scene, a representation of the battle. In Warchus' production, 'While the battle rages – on a ramp centre-stage, before an azure sky – hooded bystanders plant poppies on the margins of the stage and disparate pieces of armour like severed limbs descend and hang eerily in the air' (*FT* 12 May 1994). The field of Agincourt was represented as a giant tombstone engraved '1387–1422', the dates of Henry's birth and death. Hands introduced a sound montage to represent the battle, introduced by the end of the Chorus' speech, 4.0.48–53. The tape, with the sound of horses charging and arrows and the cries of men in battle, was borrowed from Barton and Hall's 1964 production. This forty-second aural sequence was followed by the entrance of Le Fer in golden armour, and an 'inescapably funny scene' (Beauman, p. 196). For Bogdanov it was central to his revisionist concept of the play that 'there isn't a scene in *Henry V* about the Battle of Agincourt. The only scene there is is of Pistol kicking the shit out of some poor Frenchman called Mousieur le Fer. That's the Battle of Agincourt: it's an Englishman, a liar, a cheapskate, a thief, a murderer, a lout, a bully, kicking a wounded Frenchman in the gut' (Loehlin, p. 120). Pistol used a supermarket trolley to gather plunder from the dead, and there was no comedy in the violence of his attack on Le Fer. In Daniels' production, the Dauphin and French nobles entered the scene on magnificently camp shiny hobby-horses, with stilt legs clearly showing beneath metallic canopies. Their cantering and play-jousting was juxtaposed with the sound of ordnance and explosions offstage. They exited, and Pistol, wearing a shirt decorated with a neo-Nazi skull motif, was greeted with Gallic kisses by Le Fer, who wore blue overalls and beret. Mansfield had Le Fer dragged on in 'a halter' (pbk). In the BBC/Giles production, Pistol brandishes a sword over his prisoner, who is lying on the ground.

2–9 Cut by Calvert.

FRENCH *Oh, pardonnez-moi!*

PISTOL Sayest thou me so? Is that a tun of moys? Come hither, boy. Ask me this slave in French what is his name.

BOY *Écoutez. Comment êtes-vous appelé?*

FRENCH *Monsieur le Fer.*   20

BOY He says his name is Mr Fer.

PISTOL Mr Fer. I'll fer him, and firk him, and ferret him. Discuss the same in French unto him.

BOY I do not know the French for fer and ferret and firk.

PISTOL Bid him prepare, for I will cut his throat.   25

FRENCH *Que dit-il, monsieur?*

BOY *Il me commande à vous dire que vous faites-vous prêt, car ce soldat ici est disposé tout à cette heure de couper votre gorge.*

PISTOL *Oui, coupe la gorge, par ma foi*, peasant, unless thou give me crowns, brave crowns, or mangled shalt thou be by this my   30
sword.

FRENCH [*Kneels*] *Oh! Je vous supplie, pour l'amour de Dieu, me pardonner! Je suis le gentilhomme de bonne maison. Gardez ma vie, et je vous donnerai deux cents écus.*

PISTOL What are his words?   35

BOY He prays you to save his life. He is a gentleman of a good house, and for his ransom he will give you two hundred crowns.

PISTOL Tell him my fury shall abate, and I the crowns will take.

FRENCH *Petit monsieur, que dit-il?*

BOY *Encore qu'il est contre son jurement de pardonner aucun prisonnier.*   40
Néanmoins, pour les écus que vous l'ayez promis, il est content à vous donner la liberté, le franchisement.

FRENCH *Sur mes genoux je vous donne mille remerciements, et je m'estime heureux que je suis tombé entre les mains d'un chevalier – je pense le plus brave, vaillant, et très distingué seigneur d'Angleterre.*   45

PISTOL Expound unto me, boy.

BOY He gives you upon his knees a thousand thanks, and he esteems himself happy that he hath fallen into the hands of one (as he thinks) the most brave, valorous and thrice-worthy seigneur of England.   50

PISTOL As I suck blood, I will some mercy show. Follow me.

BOY *Suivez-vous le grand capitaine.*

[Exeunt Pistol and French soldier]

40–5 Cut by Calvert.

I did never know so full a voice issue from so empty a heart. But
the saying is true, the empty vessel makes the greatest sound.
Bardolph and Nym had ten times more valour than this roaring   55
devil i'th'old play, that everyone may pare his nails with a
wooden dagger, and they are both hanged, and so would this be
if he durst steal anything adventurously. I must stay with the
lackeys with the luggage of our camp. The French might have a
good prey of us if he knew of it, for there is none to guard it but   60
boys.   *Exit*

53 The BBC/Giles Boy delivers this speech, conspiratorially, direct to camera (the only other
    character to do this in the production is the Chorus).

61 In Noble's production the Boy 'hoists the French knight's double-handed sword over his
    shoulders. Hooking a hand casually over each end, he makes to exit. He is encircled
    suddenly by a knot of French soldiers, and frozen thus in a crucifixion position, he is
    butchered. The lights dim over his corpse, as a distant boy's voice sings "Would I were in an
    alehouse . . ." ' (Fitter, pp. 262–3). The Chorus concealed the tableau by pulling the half-
    curtain across: it was smeared with blood. (In Branagh's film, a similar visual image is
    evoked by the encircling of York, slowed down to maximise its sacrificial impact: 'York is . . .
    cornered. His assailants rush towards him, plunging their knives in' (Branagh, p. 105), and
    blood runs from his open mouth.) Hands had the Boy murdered at this point by three
    unidentifiable French soldiers with their visors down: thus absolving the French nobility who
    appear in the play from direct blame. They trap him by the cart and kill him. Daniels brought
    on the French golden hobby-horses, which encircle the Boy, their unreality suddenly
    menacing like automata. They rear to knock the Boy down.
        After this scene Calvert interpolated a tableau of the battle, with the French soldiers
    stage left and the English right, accompanied by 'guns and shouts'. Henry stood
    between Grandpré and Alençon (enacting 4.7.137). One review remarked on this in
    detail:

    > In the centre was seen the Dauphin of France, seated upon a rearing steed, and the
    > entire stage was filled with combatants, while upon the drop-scene at the back of the
    > stage other figures were so skilfully painted that they appeared lifelike, and blending
    > with those in front, presented a very realistic picture of a vast army in deadly conflict.
    > The only action that took place was the striking of a death blow to the Dauphin by King
    > Henry who grasps the steed by the bit as the former partially falls from his saddle. The
    > tableau was many times redemanded. (unattributed press cutting of Booth's Theatre
    > production, 8 February 1879, PR 2812 A35 c 1 Shakespeare Col. Folger Shakespeare
    > Library, Washington D.C.)

4.5 *Enter* CONSTABLE, ORLÉANS, BOURBON, *and* RAMBURES

CONSTABLE *O diable!*
ORLÉANS *O Seigneur! Le jour est perdu, tout est perdu!*
BOURBON *Mort de ma vie*, all is confounded, all!
        Reproach and everlasting shame
        Sits mocking in our plumes.   5
                A short alarm
        O méchante fortune! Do not run away.

This last sentence shows how readily the admiration for spectacular stage effects could override the desire for narrative progression. With the possibilities of cinematic technology, Branagh creates a montage sequence for the battle, including hundreds of galloping horsemen charging towards the terrified English. Henry, mounted on his white horse, 'raises his sword in the air, and, as he swirls it above his head, he gives a great yell, and brings the sword down. The blood-curdling cry is echoed by many of the men as they rush into battle and we cut to find ourselves in the middle of the filthy, vicious scrum' (Branagh, p. 103). Shots of arrows hitting targets, the tightly packed combatants and the mud of the battlefield are edited to produce an effect of exhilaration and confusion. Pistol and Nym are picked out crawling through the mud to pillage the dead for valuables, 'Bates is drowning a French soldier in one of the huge muddy puddles', Nym is stabbed in the back while taking a purse from a corpse, 'Henry is fighting ferociously, surrounded by French horsemen' (Branagh, p. 104). Loehlin notes astutely that in this method 'nearly every shot in Branagh's battle sequence features a recognisable character whose actions continue his personal story' (Loehlin, p. 140). Olivier begins the scene with a shot of birds gathering in the treetops, then an aerial shot shows the two armies on the battlefield, with the French outnumbering the English by four or five to one and accompanied by coloured banners and uniforms. The battle is represented by a montage sequence of successive waves of French cavalry with reverse-shots of the English bowmen, and an episode in which English infantrymen drop, Robin Hood-style, from the branches of trees to unhorse French cavalry beneath. William Walton's music adds substantially to the excitement of the sequence.

4.5 Kean identified 'Another Part of the Field of Battle', into which the French noblemen entered 'hastily and in confusion' (Kean pbk). Macready set it in 'The Field of Battle' (Macready pbk). BBC/Hayes cut the scene. Most productions reallocate Bourbon's lines in this scene to the Dauphin.
  6 At the Globe the Dauphin directed his appeal to the audience, who, having been earlier exhorted as the English soldiers, were now addressed as the French army.

CONSTABLE Why, all our ranks are broke.
BOURBON O perdurable shame, let's stab ourselves.
        Be these the wretches that we played at dice for?
ORLÉANS Is this the king we sent to for his ransom?   10
BOURBON Shame, and eternal shame, nothing but shame!
        Let us die! In once more, back again,
        And he that will not follow Bourbon now
        Let him go hence, and with his cap in hand
        Like a base pander hold the chamber door,   15
        Whilst by a slave, no gentler than my dog,
        His fairest daughter is contaminate.
CONSTABLE Disorder, that hath spoiled us, friend us now.
        Let us on heaps go offer up our lives.
ORLÉANS We are enough yet living in the field   20
        To smother up the English in our throngs,
        If any order might be thought upon.
BOURBON The devil take order now, I'll to the throng.
        Let life be short, else shame will be too long.
                                              Exeunt

4.6 *Alarm. Enter the* KING *and his train, with prisoners*

KING Well have we done, thrice-valiant countrymen.
        But all's not done, yet keep the French the field.

13–17 Cut by Kean.
  23 The BBC/Giles production ends the scene with a close-up of the frightened, sweating face
      of the Dauphin.

4.6 Directorial decisions around the killing of the French prisoners in this scene have been
      crucial in challenging the nineteenth-century view of a heroic Henry: Taylor was the
      first editor to include a stage direction despatching the prisoners on stage (Taylor,
      pp. 32–4). Macready ushered in another charge with 'Alarums, cannons, shouts etc.'
      (Macready pbk), but cut the scene's speeches entirely, thus clearing Henry of any blame
      around the uncomfortable order about the French prisoners while including the
      following scene's discovery of atrocities perpetrated by the enemy. Kean switched the
      order of events round, beginning the scene, set in 'The Field of Agincourt after the Battle'

[*Enter* EXETER *by another door*]

EXETER The Duke of York commends him to your majesty.
KING Lives he, good uncle? Thrice within this hour
    I saw him down, thrice up again and fighting.   5
    From helmet to the spur all blood he was.
EXETER In which array, brave soldier, doth he lie
    Larding the plain; and by his bloody side,
    Yoke-fellow to his honour-owing wounds,
    The noble Earl of Suffolk also lies.   10
    Suffolk first died, and York, all haggled over,
    Comes to him where in gore he lay insteeped,
    And takes him by the beard, kisses the gashes
    That bloodily did yawn upon his face.
    He cries aloud 'Tarry, my cousin Suffolk.   15
    My soul shall thine keep company to heaven.

with 'the bodies of the Duke of York and Earl of Suffolk . . . borne across the stage by soldiers'. Henry's first lines in this scene were 4.7.45–55, then lines 4–34. The mention of killing the prisoners (37–8) was cut. Calvert instructed 'all the super nobles enter and range across the stage' (Calvert pbk), and made the action retaliation, by moving 36–8 to 4.7.8, thus placing Henry's order as a response to the discovery of the murdered boys. This interpretation was followed by Mansfield. Olivier cuts all except lines 1–2, which he delivers to spur on his men in battle, before the sequence in which the boys are killed. 'A French knight rides into the English camp. Pan with him as he cuts down a tent and kills a boy', followed by the desperate attempts of another boy to escape and the torching of the camp (*Masterworks*, p. 286). BBC/Hayes cuts the entire scene. The BBC/Giles Henry begins the scene by planting a royal standard; Branagh begins the scene with the body of York draped over the cart, delivering lines 1–2 (the rest of the scene is cut) before returning to a slow-motion battlefield, where horses tumble heavily to the ground like buildings to the elegiac accompaniment of violin music and the stylised sound of clashing swords. Henry faces the Dauphin in single combat, but it is amid a muddy, inglorious rabble of a battle rather than the chivalric honour this suggests. The Boy is about to be mown down by a phalanx of French horsemen who are riding towards the English camp. There is 'the terrified screaming of children' (Branagh, p. 108), and Henry struggles through the mud and water back towards the devastated camp. Hands cut lines 1–34, and then interpolated Henry's expression of anger from 4.7.45–9 as a response to the death of the Boy, and then, on the instruction 4.6.37–8, Pistol slit Le Fer's throat.

Tarry, sweet soul, for mine, then fly abreast,
As in this glorious and well-foughten field
We kept together in our chivalry.'
Upon these words I came, and cheered him up.   20
He smiled me in the face, raught me his hand,
And with a feeble grip says 'Dear my lord,
Commend my service to my sovereign.'
So did he turn, and over Suffolk's neck
He threw his wounded arm, and kissed his lips,   25
And so, espoused to death, with blood he sealed
A testament of noble-ending love.
The pretty and sweet manner of it forced
Those waters from me which I would have stopped,
But I had not so much of man in me,   30
And all my mother came into mine eyes
And gave me up to tears.

KING   I blame you not,
For hearing this I must perforce compound
With wilful eyes, or they will issue too.
                         Alarm
But hark, what new alarm is this same?   35
The French have reinforced their scattered men.
Then every soldier kill his prisoners.
Give the word through.
                                            Exeunt

37 In Daniels' production, Henry seemed to revert to the mad brutality that gripped him
   before Harfleur: his order to kill the prisoners was greeted with disbelief by his men, and
   Le Fer was shot on his knees. Warchus had Henry force Pistol's sword across Le Fer's
   throat. At the Globe, killing a prisoner onstage was experimented with during rehearsal
   but ultimately rejected (Kiernan, p. 102). Branagh leaves killing as a French war crime
   rather than an English one, emphasising the pathos of the murdered English boys without
   mention of the fate of the French prisoners. The BBC/Giles production does not show
   prisoners killed onstage. In the Central Park production of 1984 directed by Wilfred Leach,
   Kevin Kline as Henry cut Le Fer's throat himself. In an interview, Kline explained: 'He
   wouldn't just give the order – he had to do it himself. He gets his hands quite dirty' (Loehlin,
   p. 156).

4.7   *Enter* LLEWELLYN *and* GOWER

LLEWELLYN Kill the poys and the luggage! 'Tis expressly against
the law of arms. 'Tis as arrant a piece of knavery, mark you now,
as can be offert, in your conscience now, is it not?
GOWER 'Tis certain. There's not a boy left alive, and the cowardly
rascals that ran from the battle ha' done this slaughter. Besides,   5
they have burned and carried away all that was in the king's tent,
wherefore the king most worthily hath caused every soldier to
cut his prisoner's throat. Oh, 'tis a gallant king!
LLEWELLYN Ay, he was porn at Monmouth. Captain Gower, what
call you the town's name where Alexander the Pig was born?   10
GOWER Alexander the Great.
LLEWELLYN Why, I pray you, is not 'pig' great? The pig, or the
great, or the mighty, or the huge, or the magnanimous, are all
one reckonings, save the phrase is a little variations.
GOWER I think Alexander the Great was born in Macedon. His   15
father was called Phillip of Macedon, as I take it.

4.7 Branagh begins the scene with the aftermath of the carnage: the boys' corpses are piled
on the cart from which Henry gave his speech at 4.3.40. In BBC/Hayes' production the boys
are playing dice in the camp when the French gallop in to kill them. In Noble's production
the boys' bodies were lying in a circle on the stage, and were carried off during the scene.
The BBC/Giles production begins the scene with an image of a bloodied blond corpse of
one of the boys; the Globe with a single scream offstage, and then the entry of the Boy,
staggering, to die. One reviewer felt this 'isn't nearly as chilling as it ought to be' (*T* 7 June
1997).

1 Olivier's Llewellyn enters 'with a dead boy in his arms' (*Masterworks*, p. 287); a review of
Noble's productions noted that Llewellyn 'delivers his most inconsequential observations
clasping the corpse' of one of the boys (*TLS* 13 April 1984).

1–44 Cut by Kean and by Hayes.

5–8 Calvert cut this, since his Henry only gave the order to kill the prisoners after the deaths
of the boys. Branagh's Gower merely confirms 'There's not a boy left alive': the rest of
the speech is cut, and Llewellyn breaks down in tears over the body of the Boy. The
moment is played for poignancy and emotional authenticity: thus Branagh, like Olivier
before him, cuts the remainder of Llewellyn and Gower's incongruous interchange to line
44.

7 Loehlin notes that Noble's production cut the significant 'wherefore', 'thus eliminating any
suggestion that Henry acted in revenge' (Loehlin, p. 95).

LLEWELLYN I think it is e'en Macedon where Alexander is porn. I
tell you, captain, if you look in the maps of the woreld I warrant
you sall find, in the comparisons between Macedon and
Monmouth, that the situations, look you, is both alike. There is   20
a river in Macedon, and there is also moreover a river at
Monmouth. It is called Wye at Monmouth, but it is out of my
prains what is the name of the other river. But 'tis all one, 'tis
alike as my fingers is to my fingers, and there is salmons in both.
If you mark Alexander's life well, Harry of Monmouth's life is   25
come after it indifferent well, for there is figures in all things.
Alexander, God knows, and you know, in his rages and his
furies and his wraths and his cholers and his moods and
his displeasures and his indignations, and also being a little
intoxicates in his prains, did in his ales and his angers, look you,   30
kill his best friend Cleitus.

GOWER Our king is not like him in that. He never killed any of his
friends.

LLEWELLYN It is not well done, mark you now, to take the tales out
of my mouth ere it is made and finished. I speak out in the   35
figures and comparisons of it. As Alexander killed his friend
Cleitus, being in his ales and his cups, so also Harry Monmouth,
being in his right wits and his good judgements, turned away the
fat knight with the great belly doublet. He was full of jests and
gypes and knaveries and mocks – I have forgot his name.   40

GOWER Sir John Falstaff.

LLEWELLYN That is he. I'll tell you, there is good men porn at
Monmouth.

GOWER Here comes his majesty.

Alarm. Enter KING *Harry,* [EXETER, GLOUCESTER, WARWICK, *and*
English HERALD,] *and* BOURBON *with prisoners. Flourish*

17 In the BBC/Giles production, Llewellyn turns an apple in his hand to signify the globe, and
Gower's intent stare at this prop is comic. Later in the speech, Llewellyn begins to munch on
the apple.

41 Despite producing the play as part of a sequence including Falstaff, Quayle's 1951
production cut this reference.

42-3 Noble's Llewellyn seemed 'to refer to the [dead] boy, whose hand he was holding, rather
than to Henry' (Loehlin, p. 95).

KING I was not angry since I came to France   45
              Until this instant. Take a trumpet, herald.
              Ride thou unto the horsemen on yon hill.
              If they will fight with us, bid them come down,
              Or void the field. They do offend our sight.
              If they'll do neither, we will come to them,   50
              And make them skirr away as swift as stones
              Enforcèd from the old Assyrian slings.
              Besides, we'll cut the throats of those we have,
              And not a man of them that we shall take
              Shall taste our mercy. Go and tell them so.   55
                                                        [*Exit English Herald*]

                              Enter MONTJOY

EXETER Here comes the herald of the French, my liege.
GLOUCESTER His eyes are humbler than they used to be.
KING How now, what means this, herald? Know'st thou not

---

45 Calvert set this on 'The Plains of Agincourt after the Victory'. Branagh's Henry is seen in
    close-up, his bloodstained and muddy face shouting lines 45–6a, but with no mention of the
    prisoners. Sheen's Henry, covered with blood, had his hand on the dead Boy (Daniels).
    Olivier's Henry speaks 45–6a, and immediately acts on his anger, seeking out the French
    Constable on the battlefield and besting him in single combat, unhorsing him with a blow to
    the chin from his mailed fist after losing his sword. After circling the Constable's body from
    horseback, Olivier delivers the remaining lines of the speech.

51–3 Cut by Noble.

53–5a Henry's retaliatory order was cut by Macready. In Hayes' production, there is an attempt by
    one of the nobles to remonstrate with Henry, but he is so angry he shakes off the argument.

53 Calvert had the bodies of York and Suffolk carried across by the soldiers, 'covered with a
    tribute flag'. The King's emotions almost got the better of him: he 'stoops and carries the
    hand of York then buries his face' (Calvert pbk).

56 At his entry, Kean's Montjoy 'uncovers and yields' (Kean pbk), showing that the English
    have the victory. In Daniels' production, Montjoy was covered with blood, feebly waving a
    bloody flag. His voice was broken and exhausted. The BBC/Giles Montjoy is similarly
    sombre, with no trace of his former arrogance. In Daniels' production, Montjoy spoke in
    front of a hastily erected Red Cross tarpaulin, where one soldier was holding an intravenous
    drip over a wounded comrade.

58 Branagh shouts lines 58 and 59 at Montjoy, pulling him from his horse, shaking him and
    yelling into his face. In Noble's production Henry dragged Montjoy over to the corpses of
    the boys, so that 'what means this?' referred to the massacre.

> That I have fined these bones of mine for ransom?
> Com'st thou again for ransom?

MONTJOY   No, great king.   60
> I come to thee for charitable licence,
> That we may wander o'er this bloody field
> To book our dead, and then to bury them,
> To sort our nobles from our common men,
> For many of our princes – woe the while –   65
> Lie drowned and soaked in mercenary blood,
> So do our vulgar drench their peasant limbs
> In blood of princes, while the wounded steeds
> Fret fetlock deep in gore, and with wild rage
> Yerk out their armèd heels at their dead masters,   70
> Killing them twice. Oh, give us leave, great king,
> To view the field in safety, and dispose
> Of their dead bodies.

KING   I tell thee truly, herald,
> I know not if the day be ours or no,
> For yet a-many of your horsemen peer   75
> And gallop o'er the field.

MONTJOY   The day is yours.

KING Praisèd be God, and not our strength, for it.
> What is this castle called that stands hard by?

MONTJOY They call it Agincourt.

KING Then call we this the field of Agincourt,   80
> Fought on the day of Crispin Crispianus.

67–73 The description of the dead was cut by Macready and Calvert. Branagh cuts 67–71a, in which
       the social confusion of dead bodies is stressed. In the film, Montjoy speaks with 'desperate,
       remote sadness' (Branagh, p. 109).

76b   Branagh lowers his head in relief, almost overcome with emotion. He falls to his knees,
       heavily, in the mud. Olivier's Henry removes his helmet to signal the end of the battle. Hayes
       has Henry kneel and the soldiers follow his lead, crossing themselves. Montjoy helps him
       up.

77   The BBC/Giles soldiers cross themselves and kneel in silence; in Noble's production they
       dropped their weapons.

78   Branagh's question is exquisitely weary, not at all triumphant.

81   This dedication was accompanied by a flourish of trumpets and drums in Macready's
       production. Kean's soldiers gave shouts and cheers. Olivier has Montjoy kneel and kiss
       Henry's hand. Robert Hardy delivers the lines to his kneeling troops in a slow, fatigued tone,
       his face smeared with blood (BBC/Hayes).

LLEWELLYN Your grandfather of famous memory, an't please your majesty, and your great-uncle Edward the Plack Prince of Wales, as I have read in the chronicles, fought a most prave pattle here in France.   85

KING They did, Llewellyn.

LLEWELLYN Your majesty says very true. If your majesties is remembered of it, the Welshmen did good service in a garden where leeks did grow, wearing leeks in their Monmouth caps, which your majesty know to this hour is an honourable badge of   90 the service. And I do believe your majesty takes no scorn to wear the leek upon St Tavy's day.

KING I wear it for a memorable honour,
For I am Welsh, you know, good countryman.

LLEWELLYN All the water in Wye cannot wash your majesty's   95 Welsh plood out of your pody, I can tell you that. God pless it and preserve it, as long as it pleases His Grace – and his majesty too.

KING Thanks, good my countryman.

LLEWELLYN By Cheshu, I am your majesty's countryman! I care   100 not who know it. I will confess it to all the world. I need not to be ashamed of your majesty, praised be God, so long as your majesty is an honest man.

KING God keep me so.

Enter WILLIAMS

Our heralds go with him.
Bring me just notice of the numbers dead   105
On both our parts.
            [*Exeunt Montjoy, Gower and English heralds*]
            Call yonder fellow hither.

82 In the BBC/Giles production, it is Llewellyn's speech which breaks a heavy silence where no one seems to know what to say. There is a sense that he is consciously cheering them all up in the BBC/Hayes version, too.

89 Llewellyn's leeks cause Branagh to smile amid his weariness. In Daniels' production, Henry was hardly listening to Llewellyn's chatter: he could scarcely take in the victory.

94 At this admission of shared heritage, Branagh has Henry and Llewellyn embrace, weeping.

106 Branagh cuts the trick played on Llewellyn and Williams, and interpolates 5.1.71–8, Pistol's bitter speech, 'contemplating his inevitably empty future' (Branagh, p. 111) as a cut-purse in

EXETER Soldier, you must come to the king.

KING Soldier, why wear'st thou that glove in thy cap?

WILLIAMS An't please your majesty, 'tis the gage of one that I
    should fight withal, if he be alive.   110

KING An Englishman?

WILLIAMS An't please your majesty, a rascal that swaggered with me
    last night, who if a live and ever dare to challenge this glove, I
    have sworn to take him a box o'th'ear; or if I can see my glove in
    his cap, which he swore as he was a soldier he would wear, if a   115
    live, I will strike it out soundly.

KING What think you, Captain Llewellyn, is it fit this soldier keep
    his oath?

LLEWELLYN He is a craven and a villain else, an't please your
    majesty, in my conscience.   120

KING It may be his enemy is a gentleman of great sort, quite from
    the answer of his degree.

LLEWELLYN Though he be as good a gentleman as the devil is, as
    Lucifer and Beelzebub himself, it is necessary, look your grace,
    that he keep his vow and his oath. If he be perjured, see you now,   125
    his reputation is as arrant a villain and a Jack Sauce as ever his
    black shoe trod upon God's ground and His earth, in my
    conscience, law.

KING Then keep thy vow, sirrah, when thou meet'st the fellow.

WILLIAMS So I will, my liege, as I live.   130

KING Who serv'st thou under?

WILLIAMS Under Captain Gower, my liege.

LLEWELLYN Gower is a good captain, and is good knowledge and
    literatured in the wars.

KING Call him hither to me, soldier.   135

WILLIAMS I will, my liege.   *Exit*

KING Here, Llewellyn, wear thou this favour for me, and stick it in
    thy cap. [*Gives him Williams's glove*] When Alençon and myself
    were down together I plucked this glove from his helm. If any

London. By emending 'Doll' (5.1.72) to 'Nell', Branagh makes Pistol refer to Mistress Quickly.
Coursen interpreted this version as 'the post-Vietnam veteran who also begged at the end of
the lane in Elizabethan England' (Coursen, p. 122). The Llewellyn and Williams exchange is
also cut in the BBC/Hayes production. Kean had Williams standing among the ranks and
dragged out of position for his audience with the King.

121–8 Cut by Hands.

man challenge this, he is a friend to Alençon and an enemy to   140
our person. If thou encounter any such, apprehend him, an thou
dost me love.

LLEWELLYN Your grace does me as great honours as can be desired
in the hearts of his subjects. I would fain see the man that has
but two legs that shall find himself aggrieffed at this glove, that   145
is all. But I would fain see it once, an't please God of His Grace,
that I might see.

KING Know'st thou Gower?

LLEWELLYN He is my dear friend, an't please you.

KING Pray thee go seek him and bring him to my tent.   150

LLEWELLYN I will fetch him.   *Exit*

KING My lord of Warwick, and my brother Gloucester,
　　　Follow Llewellyn closely at the heels.
　　　The glove which I have given him for a favour
　　　May haply purchase him a box o'th'ear.   155
　　　It is the soldier's. I by bargain should
　　　Wear it myself. Follow, good cousin Warwick.
　　　If that the soldier strike him, as I judge
　　　By his blunt bearing he will keep his word,
　　　Some sudden mischief may arise of it,   160
　　　For I do know Llewellyn valiant,
　　　And, touched with choler, hot as gunpowder,
　　　And quickly will return an injury.
　　　Follow, and see there be no harm between them.
　　　Go you with me, uncle of Exeter.   165

                                                    Exeunt

4.8 *Enter* GOWER *and* WILLIAMS

WILLIAMS I warrant it is to knight you, captain.

152 Calvert cut Henry's instructions; so too Hands, Noble and the BBC/Giles version.

4.8 Kean set this scene 'before King Henry's Pavilion', and the promptbook adds 'Picture of
gracious tent' (Kean pbk). By contrast, Hands' production began with the army clearing the
field of battle. BBC/Hayes and Branagh cut the scene up to line 64, thus omitting the
sequence of Williams' chastisement.

Enter LLEWELLYN

LLEWELLYN God's will and His pleasure, captain. I beseech you
now, come apace to the king. There is more good toward you,
peradventure, than is in your knowledge to dream of.

WILLIAMS [*To Llewellyn*] Sir, know you this glove?   5

LLEWELLYN Know the glove? I know the glove is a glove.

WILLIAMS I know this, and thus I challenge it.

Strikes him.

LLEWELLYN God's blood, an arrant traitor as any's in the universal
world, or in France, or in England!

GOWER [*To Williams*] How now, sir? You villain!   10

WILLIAMS Do you think I'll be forsworn?

LLEWELLYN Stand away, Captain Gower. I will give treason his
payment into plows, I warrant you.

WILLIAMS I am no traitor.

LLEWELLYN That's a lie in thy throat. I charge you in his   15
majesty's name apprehend him, he's a friend of the Duke
Alençon's.

Enter WARWICK *and* GLOUCESTER

WARWICK How now, how now, what's the matter?

LLEWELLYN My lord of Warwick, here is, praised be God for it, a
most contagious treason come to light, look you, as you shall   20
desire in a summer's day. Here is his majesty.

Enter KING *and* EXETER

KING How now, what's the matter?

LLEWELLYN My liege, here is a villain and a traitor, that, look your

---

14 Hands had the disagreement between Llewellyn and Williams turn into a 'general much-
enjoyed brawl', drawing in all the other soldiers, including Clarence and Gloucester
(Beauman, p. 208). Daniels had Henry enjoying the trick, and showed Williams and
Llewellyn exchanging blows before the joke was revealed. Williams was given his money
and bit a coin to check it was genuine, to everyone's amusement. All saluted, including
Henry, who winked affectionately at Llewellyn: it seems there were no hard feelings. In the
BBC/Giles version, the quarrel is stopped before blows are landed, and the stand-off ends in
laughter. In Warchus' version the sequence was presented as 'a vicious manipulation that
found Williams on the point of execution until the King apparently changed his mind'
(Coursen, p. 154).

grace, has struck the glove which your majesty is take out of the
helmet of Alençon.   25

WILLIAMS My liege, this was my glove – here is the fellow of it –
and he that I gave it to in change promised to wear it in his cap. I
promised to strike him if he did. I met this man with my glove in
his cap, and I have been as good as my word.

LLEWELLYN Your majesty, hear now, saving your majesty's   30
manhood, what an arrant, rascally, beggarly, lousy knave it is! I
hope your majesty is pear me testimony and witness and will
avouchment that this is the glove of Alençon that your majesty
is give me, in your conscience now.

[*Gives glove to king*]

KING Give me thy glove, soldier. Look, here is the fellow of it.   35
   'Twas I indeed thou promisèd to strike,
   And thou hast given me most bitter terms.

LLEWELLYN An't please your majesty, let his neck answer for it, if
there is any martial law in the world.

KING How canst thou make me satisfaction?   40

WILLIAMS All offences, my lord, come from the heart. Never came
any from mine that might offend your majesty.

KING It was our self thou didst abuse.

WILLIAMS Your majesty came not like yourself. You appeared to me
but as a common man – witness the night, your garments, your   45
lowliness. And what your highness suffered under that shape, I
beseech you take it for your own fault and not mine, for had you
been as I took you for, I made no offence. Therefore I beseech
your highness pardon me. [*Kneels*]

KING Here, uncle Exeter, fill this glove with crowns   50
   And give it to this fellow. Keep it, fellow,
   And wear it for an honour in thy cap
   Till I do challenge it. Give him the crowns.
   And captain, you must needs be friends with him.

LLEWELLYN By this day and this light, the fellow has mettle enough   55
in his belly. Hold, there is twelve pence for you, and I pray you
to serve God and keep you out of prawls and prabbles and
quarrels and dissentions, and I warrant you it is the better for
you.

WILLIAMS I will none of your money.   60

LLEWELLYN It is with a good will. I can tell you it will serve you to
mend your shoes. Come, wherefore should you be so pashful?

Your shoes is not so good. 'Tis a good silling, I warrant you, or I
will change it.

Enter HERALD

KING Now, herald, are the dead numbered?   65
HERALD Here is the number of the slaughtered French.
                    [*Gives him paper*]
KING What prisoners of good sort are taken, uncle?
EXETER Charles, Duke of Orléans, nephew to the king;
            John, Duke of Bourbon, and Lord Boucicault.
            Of other lords and barons, knights and squires,   70
            Full fifteen hundred, besides common men.
KING This note doth tell me of ten thousand French
            That in the field lie slain. Of princes in this number
            And nobles hearing banners, there lie dead
            One hundred twenty-six. Added to these,   75
            Of knights, esquires and gallant gentlemen,
            Eight thousand and four hundred, of the which
            Five hundred were but yesterday dubbed knights.
            So that in these ten thousand they have lost
            There are but sixteen hundred mercenaries.   80

67–71 Cut by Noble and Hayes.
72 Glen's delivery of the list of French dead (Warchus) was unusually slow, with 'shocked
pauses as the individual losses are taken in' (*TLS* 20 May 1994). This contrasts with
Kean's and Calvert's productions which cut lines 84–92, and the BBC/Hayes, which cut
73b–82. Branagh also cuts the names of the French noblemen, and keeps the focus on the
English losses through the speech by showing the bloodied corpse of the murdered Boy. In
Noble's production, Montjoy was present: his 'sudden urge to leave, as the list of French
dead is read out by the victorious king, is pregnant with shame and pity' (*ES* 17 May 1985).
Noble cut 79–82. That these lines might be greeted with chauvinistic delight rather than
piety is revealed by a performance at the new Globe, where a small group of audience
members cheered the announcement, only to be punished for 'a jingoistic, insensitive
cheapened response' by Mark Rylance as Henry, who turned his back on the audience to
deliver the rest of the speech: 'the disruptive playgoers were treated as if they were
despicable soldiers of Henry's army. When Rylance came to the end of the list, he turned
back to the audience, to find his disrespectful "soldiers" now suitably chastened' (Kiernan,
p. 20).

The rest are princes, barons, lords, knights, squires,
And gentlemen of blood and quality.
The names of those their nobles that lie dead:
Charles Delabret, High Constable of France;
Jacques of Châtillon, Admiral of France;   85
The Master of the Crossbows, Lord Rambures;
Great Master of France, the brave Sir Guiscard Dauphin,
John, Duke of Alençon; Antony, Duke of Brabant,
The brother to the Duke of Burgundy;
And Edward, Duke of Bar. Of lusty earls: 90
Grandpré and Roussi, Fauconbridge and Foix,
Beaumont and Marle, Vaudemont and Lestrelles.
Here was a royal fellowship of death.
Where is the number of our English dead?
          [*Takes another paper*]
Edward, the Duke of York, the Earl of Suffolk,   95
Sir Richard Keighley, Davy Gam, esquire.
None else of name, and of all other men
But five and twenty. O God, Thy arm was here!
And not to us, but to Thy arm alone
Ascribe we all. When, without stratagem,   100
But in plain shock and even play of battle,
Was ever known so great and little loss

95 Ron Daniels' Henry tearfully read the names of the English dead from the dogtags on
the body bags laid out on the stage. He unzipped the bag to look at Davy Gam, who
was revealed as the Boy. Kean gave lines 95–8a to Exeter. In the BBC/Hayes production,
the soldiers bow their heads, fearful of what they will hear. As Henry reads they look
up, disbelieving. Branagh reads slowly, dwelling on each name: there is a clap of thunder
in the background as the English are silent at the miracle of their delivery. Bogdanov
reintroduced the hooligan interpretation of the army, as a soldier was seen wrapped in
the Union Jack and a distant chorus of ' 'Ere we go' was heard (Loehlin, p. 121).
Michael Kahn's production dubbed this scene 'Ending Games. The Dead' and, as
Henry

recites the long roster, name by name, a score of men gradually come on stage
each wearing a ghostly white mask splotched with fresh blood. Finally the king
intones the incipit of the Te Deum and the ghostly choir picks it up in unison . . . and
moves downstage to face the audience in a long row, humming and swaying from
left to right – an inspired fusion of the quick and the dead. (Cooper, p. 151)

>   On one part and on th'other? Take it, God,
>   For it is none but Thine.
>
> EXETER   'Tis wonderful.
> KING   Come, go we in procession to the village,   105
>   And be it death proclaimèd through our host
>   To boast of this, or take that praise from God,
>   Which is His only.
> LLEWELLYN   Is it not lawful, an't please your majesty, to tell how
>   many is killed?   110
> KING   Yes, captain, but with this acknowledgement,
>   That God fought for us.
> LLEWELLYN   Yes, in my conscience, He did us great good.
> KING   Do we all holy rites.

104 Branagh's Exeter speaks in a low voice, quiet with wonderment at their delivery. Henry is close to tears as he leads the men to the village.

112 Daniels had Henry's voice breaking into sobs, as he knelt, stroking the face of Davy Gam. The soldiers began to sing 'Non nobis'.

114 Macready's 'rage for over-embellishing', as one reviewer saw it, was exemplified at this point: 'the actor literally kneels down with his soldiery and the curtain falls to the solemn strains of an organ, brought from England we suppose for the purpose' (*John Bull* 16 June 1839). Kean's production was even more susceptible to ridicule on this point: 'The Curtains of the Royal Pavilion are drawn aside and discover an Altar and Priests', and the act ends with 'organ music; all kneel and join in a song of thanksgiving' (Kean pbk). Phelps instructed 'when voices cease they all kneel in situations. Picture' (Sprague, p. 120). Calvert's Henry and his men all knelt to sing 'the Song of Thanksgiving' (Calvert pbk). Coleman interpolated a tableau of 'Thanksgiving after the Battle'. Olivier ends the scene with a 'Dissolve to the field of the dead', and a fade out on the long procession of the English army marching into the 'Agincourt village' (*Masterworks*, p. 291). Hayes has Henry in an emotional mood, half laughing and half crying, followed by the soldiers singing in prayer as they march off, hands clasped. Hands' soldiers resumed their 'Deo Gracias' marching song, as Llewellyn sang a Welsh 'Te Deum'. The scene closed with Henry and Montjoy looking silently back over the battlefield. Noble's production had the Chorus close a gauze curtain, covered with names suggesting the list of the dead, or a war memorial. The mood at the end of the scene in Branagh's film is sombre and low-key, as the procession includes soldiers shouldering the dead boys. In a piece of silent reconciliation, Henry returns Williams' glove taken before the battle in the challenge, followed by Williams' realisation that the hooded stranger was Henry himself. The soldiers sing 'Non nobis' over a long tracking shot as Henry carries the dead Boy through the battlefield's carnage, 'where men and women are pillaging the bodies

Let there be sung *Non nobis* and *Te Deum*,   115
The dead with charity enclosed in clay,
And then to Calais, and to England then,
Where ne'er from France arrived more happy men.

Exeunt

5.0 *Enter* CHORUS

[CHORUS] Vouchsafe to those that have not read the story

of the dead' (Branagh, p. 113). Ragpickers were a feature of Benson's productions, too. Branagh's English procession is a weary one which has sustained many losses: so too the French. It is a lengthy sequence as the King walks through the devastated field below Agincourt carrying the Boy's body, then kissing it as he rests it gently with the other corpses on a cart. 'We cut close on his blood-stained and exhausted face, the dreadful price they have all had to pay for this so-called victory clearly etched into his whole being. His head drops as if in shame' (Branagh, p. 114). The scene reprises, in a minor key, the choreography and editing of the speech before Agincourt: Branagh's tableau effects, akin to those favoured by Victorian producers, mark the contrast between the hopes before the battle and the price of victory.

5.0   The Chorus invites audiences to imagine the warmth of Henry's return to London after his victory. Macready used his dioramic staging effects to show the citizens of London as the Chorus invited such visualisation. This was not enough for Kean and his followers in the nineteenth century, when productions established a convention of interpolating an increasingly spectacular 'historical episode', filling the stage with returning soldiers and grateful citizens as if to read as an explicit challenge the rhetorical question of 'how many would . . . welcome him?' (33–4) Kean's pageant followed the Chorus' speech. Based 'upon the facts related by the late Sir Harris Nicholas, in his translated copy of a highly interesting Latin MS, accidentally discovered in the British Museum, written by a Priest, who accompanied the English army' (Kean, p. vii) and thus drawing on an impressive combination of national, scholarly, aristocratic, religious and historical authority, the description of the pageant was subsequently quoted by most Victorian acting texts:

> Extracts of King Henry's reception into L from the anonymous Chronicler who was an eye-witness of the events he describes: –
> And when the wished-for Saturday dawned, the citizens went forth to meet the King viz the Mayor and Aldermen in scarlet, and the rest of the inferior citizens in red suits, with party-coloured hoods, red and white. When they had come to the Tower at

the approach to the bridge, as it were at the entrance to the authorities to the city. Banners of the Royal arms adorned the Tower, elevated on its turrets; and trumpets, clarions, and horns sounded in various melody; and in front was this elegant and suitable inscription upon the wall, 'Civitas Regis justiciae' – (the City to the King's righteousness). And behind the Tower were innumerable boys, representing angels, arrayed in white and with countenances shining with gold, and glittering wings, and virgin locks set with precious sprigs of laurel, who at the King's approach, sang with melodious voices and with organs an English anthem. A company of Prophets, of venerable hoariness, dressed in golden coats and mantles, with their heads covered and wrapped in gold and crimson, sang with sweet harmony, bowing to the ground, a psalm of thanksgiving. Beneath the covering were the twelve kings, martyrs and confessors of the succession of England, their loins girded with golden girdles, sceptres in their hands, and crowns on their heads, who chanted with one accord at the King's approach in a sweet tune.

And they sent forth upon him round leaves of silver mixed with wafers, equally thin and round. And there proceeded out to meet the King a chorus of most beautiful virgin girls, elegantly attired in white, singing with timbrel and dance; and then innumerable boys, as it were an angelic multitude, decked with celestial gracefulness, white apparel, shining feathers, virgin locks, studded with gems and other resplendent and most elegant array, who sent forth upon the head of the King passing beneath minae of gold, with bows of laurel; round about angels shone with celestial gracefulness, chanting sweetly, and with all sorts of music.

And besides the pressure in the standing places, and of men crowding through the streets, and the multitude of both sexes along the way from the bridge, from one end to the other, that scarcely the horsemen could ride through them. A greater assembly, or a nobler spectacle, was not recollected, to have been ever before in London.

The scale and spendour of Kean's visualisation of this cavalcade was much remarked upon.

Calvert, too, interpolated a similar scene, followed by Mansfield, representing 'London Bridge at the Surrey end. Gaily decorated booths are banked against the fronts of the houses; banners, flags and garlands float in the air; a holiday throng crowds the ways, the booths and the windows.' The chimes of St Paul's accompanied a picture of busy merriment, including 'athletic antics' and pedlars selling ballads and gingerbread. The battle scenes are not quite forgotten, however, as 'two small boys get into a fight and anxious mothers separate them' (Calvert, p. 97). Sir Nicholas Wootton, the Lord Mayor, presents the King with the keys to the city, in an echo of the tableau in Act 3 in which Henry was given the keys to Harfleur. Then 'A Flourish of trumpets announces the head of the column. Company after company of bowmen, archers, pikemen, miners and sappers and other soldiers enter and pass through the crowds. Their ranks are broken and their files depleted through the fatalities of their victory', adding a twenty-one-gun salute at the entrance of the returning

That I may prompt them, and of such as have,
I humbly pray them to admit th'excuse
Of time, of numbers, and due course of things
Which cannot in their huge and proper life   5
Be here presented. Now we bear the king
Toward Calais. Grant him there. There seen,
Heave him away upon your wingèd thoughts
Athwart the sea. Behold the English beach
Pales-in the flood with men, with wives, and boys,   10
Whose shouts and claps out-voice the deep-mouthed sea,
Which, like a mighty whiffler 'fore the king,
Seems to prepare his way. So let him land,
And solemnly see him set on to London.
So swift a pace hath thought that even now   15
You may imagine him upon Blackheath,
Where that his lords desire him to have borne
His bruisèd helmet and his bended sword
Before him through the city. He forbids it,

army. Calvert's eye for those left behind, and for the individual stories within the pageant was acute:

> A mother kisses her returning son as he marches past. A young wife rushes to the embrace of her wounded husband and marches away with him. Another girl scans the faces of the passing troopers but seems not to find the one she seeks. She rushes to an officer. He shakes his head and whispers to her. She faints and is borne back into the crowd, her little tragedy unnoticed in the festivity.

Henry's entrance on his horse in Calvert's production prompted the Chorus' lines 6–28. Calvert's Chorus appeared in a 'crown of roses. Long garland over shoulder and leans on pedestal with a wreath in her hand. All the roses and foliage are white' (Calvert pbk). Hands' Chorus stood in front of a transparent scrim, behind which small candles burned among the bodies of the dead, still lying on the ground where they fell at Agincourt. This tableau remained visible throughout the final act. The BBC/Giles Chorus is set against a cliff face.

5.0 This speech was cut by Olivier, Branagh and Warchus. At the Globe, it was delivered by the roguish survivor, Pistol.

2b–6a Cut by Noble, whose Chorus stood in a spotlight for the speech.

15–22a Cut by Kean; 15–39a cut by BBC/Hayes.

Being free from vainness and self-glorious pride,   20
Giving full trophy, signal and ostent
Quite from himself to God. But now behold
In the quick forge and working-house of thought,
How London doth pour out her citizens,
The mayor and all his brethren in best sort,   25
Like to the senators of th'antique Rome,
With the plebeians swarming at their heels,
Go forth and fetch their conquering Caesar in –
As, by a lower but by loving likelihood
Were now the general of our gracious empress,   30
(As in good time he may) from Ireland coming,
Bringing rebellion broachèd on his sword,
How many would the peaceful city quit
To welcome him? Much more, and much more cause,
Did they this Harry. Now in London place him –   35
As yet the lamentation of the French
Invites the king of England's stay at home,
The emperor's coming in behalf of France
To order peace between them – and omit
All the occurrences, whatever chanced,   40
Till Harry's back return again to France.
There must we bring him, and myself have played
The interim, by remembering you 'tis past.
Then brook abridgement, and your eyes advance
After your thoughts, straight back again to France.   *Exit*   45

29–35a Cut by Kean; 29–32 cut by Hands and Noble.
36–45 Cut by Kean, and the following alteration to lines 40–1 inserted after 35b to introduce the 'historical episode': 'Show the occurrences, whatever chanc'd/Till Harry's back-return again to France.' Kean's replacement of the play's 'omit' with his own 'show' is a good symbol of his overall approach to the Chorus' statements of theatrical inadequacy. Hands had the Chorus stay on stage for his next scene, 5.2. Calvert's reordering of this act put 3.5, the language-lesson scene, as the first part of 5.2, which he ended after 252. 5.1 follows, with the remainder of 5.2 reserved for the finale in the Cathedral at Troyes: 'The ceremony of the espousal of King Henry the Fifth to the Princess Katherine of Valois' (Calvert pbk). This arrangement was followed by Mansfield, who added that the couple were attended by choristers, three archbishops, noblemen in full armour, six pages for Katherine and eight for Henry.

5.1 *Enter* LLEWELLYN *and* GOWER

GOWER Nay, that's right. But why wear you your leek today? St
     Davy's day is past.
LLEWELLYN There is occasions and causes why and wherefore in
     all things. I will tell you ass my friend, Captain Gower. The
     rascally, scald, beggarly, lousy, pragging knave Pistol, which you   5
     and yourself and all the world know to be no petter than a
     fellow, look you now, of no merits, he is come to me, and
     prings me pread and salt yesterday, look you, and bid me eat my
     leek. It was in a place where I could not breed no contention
     with him, but I will be so bold as to wear it in my cap till I see   10
     him once again, and then I will tell him a little piece of my
     desires.

                         Enter PISTOL

GOWER Why, here he comes, swelling like a turkey-cock.
LLEWELLYN 'Tis no matter for his swellings, nor his turkey-cocks.
     God pless you, Anchient Pistol, you scurvy, lousy knave, God   15
     pless you.
PISTOL Ha, art thou bedlam? Dost thou thirst, base Trojan, to have
     me fold up Parca's fatal web? Hence! I am qualmish at the smell
     of leek.
LLEWELLYN I peseech you heartily, scurvy, lousy knave, at my   20
     desires and my requests and my petitions, to eat, look you, this
     leek. Because, look you, you do not love it, nor your affections

---

5.1 Kean set this scene in 'France in the Neighbourhood of Troyes'; Macready in 'the English
     camp'. Coleman set this scene after 'an interval of five years' (pbk). The BBC/Giles version
     has no indication of the date of the scene, but it separates it from the previous act by
     introducing Llewellyn and Gower out of their armour; in the BBC/Hayes production they are
     in a tavern, sitting drinking at a table. Olivier introduces a scene strongly reminiscent of
     hourbook illustrations, fading in 'to a long shot of Agincourt village under snow. Dissolve to
     the gate to the village. Track forward to reveal Pistol flirting with village women inside a
     house. Pan to show three boys singing carols', and framing Llewellyn and Gower sitting on a
     wall (*Masterworks*, p. 291). The scene is cut by Branagh, having moved 5.1.71–8 to 4.7.104.
12 Macready's promptbook includes some business: 'Pistol swaggers without' (Macready pbk).
     Hayes has Pistol looking like a circus clown, his hair sticking out zanily.
15 Kemble instructed Llewellyn 'Draws the leek across his nose.'

and your appetites and your digestions does not agree with it, I
would desire you to eat it.

PISTOL Not for Cadwallader and all his goats.   25

LLEWELLYN There is one goat for you.

Strikes him [with cudgel]

Will you be so good, scald knave, as eat it?

PISTOL Base Trojan, thou shalt die!

LLEWELLYN You say very true, scald knave, when God's will is. I
will desire you to live in the meantime, and eat your victuals.   30
Come, there is sauce for it. [*Strikes him*] You called me yesterday
'mountain-squire', but I will make you today a squire of low
degree. I pray you, fall to. If you can mock a leek, you can eat a
leek.

GOWER Enough, captain. You have astonished him.   35

LLEWELLYN By Cheshu, I will make him eat some part of my leek,
or I will peat his pate four days. Bite, I pray you. It is good for
your green wound, and your ploody coxcomb.

PISTOL Must I bite?

LLEWELLYN Yes, certainly, and out of doubt and out of question   40
too, and ambiguities.

PISTOL By this leek, I will most horribly revenge – [*Llewellyn
threatens him*] I eat and eat, I swear!

LLEWELLYN Eat, I pray you. Will you have some more sauce to your
leek? There is not enough leek to swear by.   45

PISTOL Quiet thy cudgel, thou dost see I eat.

LLEWELLYN Much good do you, scald knave, heartily. Nay, pray
you throw none away. The skin is good for your broken
coxcomb. When you take occasions to see leeks hereafter, I pray
you mock at 'em, that is all.   50

PISTOL Good.

LLEWELLYN Ay, leeks is good. Hold you, there is a groat to heal your
pate.

---

26 The BBC/Giles Llewellyn trips Pistol up; Olivier's Llewellyn kicks Pistol's backside; Hayes has
Llewellyn knock him down bodily.

28 In Phelps' production, Pistol was 'affecting to be unable to draw his Sword' (Sprague, p.
120).

45 The BBC/Giles Llewellyn prolongs the torture, showing that he has another leek in his
pocket. At the Globe, Pistol was knocked to the ground and was made to eat the leek with
his head hanging over the edge of the stage.

PISTOL Me a groat?

LLEWELLYN Yes, verily, and in truth you shall take it, or I have   55
another leek in my pocket which you shall eat.

PISTOL I take thy groat in earnest of revenge.

LLEWELLYN If I owe you anything, I will pay you in cudgels. You
shall be a woodmonger, and buy nothing of me but cudgels. God
b'wi' you, and keep you, and heal your pate.   *Exit*   60

PISTOL All hell shall stir for this!

GOWER Go, go, you are a counterfeit cowardly knave. Will you mock
at an ancient tradition began upon an honourable respect, and
worn as a memorable trophy of predeceased valour, and dare
not avouch in your deeds any of your words? I have seen you   65
gleeking and galling at this gentleman twice or thrice. You
thought because he could not speak English in the native garb
he could not therefore handle an English cudgel. You find it
otherwise, and henceforth let a Welsh correction teach you a
good English condition. Fare you well.   *Exit*   70

PISTOL Doth fortune play the hussy with me now? News have I that
my Doll is dead i'th'Spital of a malady of France, and there my
rendezvous is quite cut off. Old I do wax, and from my weary
limbs honour is cudgelled. Well, bawd I'll turn, and something
lean to cutpurse of quick hand. To England will I steal, and   75
there I'll steal.

And patches will I get unto these cudgelled scars,
And swear I got them in the Gallia wars.   *Exit*

---

57 In Olivier's film, Pistol takes the proffered penny, and Llewellyn kisses his head. Lines 58–9
were cut. Hayes has Llewellyn flip the coin disparagingly into Pistol's helmet, as if he were a
beggar or street performer.

61 After Llewellyn's departure, Phelps' Pistol regained his composure, 'drawing his sword &
vaporing' (Sprague, p. 120). Many productions ended the scene here, including Mansfield,
who added the exit direction: Pistol 'struts boldly off, but, perceiving Fluellen, lowers his
sword and runs in the opposite direction' (Sprague, p. 121).

71–3 The mention of Doll's death was cut by Macready and Kean. In Bogdanov's production,
Pistol pulled a letter from his pocket and read of her death. Calvert cut 62–78. Hayes has
Pistol speak direct to camera, but finishing with a thumbs-up gesture to suggest that he is
unbeaten by the news. Olivier's Pistol substitutes 'present' for 'Gallia', and we see him
disappearing into a barn and re-emerging with a pig under one arm and a cockerel in the
other hand, before running away up the hillside.

5.2 *Enter at one door* KING *Henry*, EXETER, BEDFORD, WESTMORLAND *and other lords. At another*, QUEEN *Isabel, the* [FRENCH] KING, [*the Princess* KATHERINE *and* ALICE,] *the Duke of* BURGUNDY, *and other French*

KING Peace to this meeting, wherefore we are met.
　　　　　Unto our brother France and to our sister,
　　　　　Health and fair time of day. Joy and good wishes
　　　　　To our most fair and princely cousin Katherine.
　　　　　And as a branch and member of this royalty,　　　　　5
　　　　　By whom this great assembly is contrived,
　　　　　We do salute you, Duke of Burgundy.
　　　　　And princes French, and peers, health to you all.
FRENCH KING Right joyous are we to behold your face,
　　　　　Most worthy brother England, fairly met.　　　　　10
　　　　　So are you, princes English, every one.
QUEEN So happy be the issue, brother England,
　　　　　Of this good day, and of this gracious meeting,
　　　　　As we are now glad to behold your eyes,

5.2　The Folio stage direction suggests a clear visual symbol of the two opponents meeting: 'Enter at one doore, King Henry, Exeter, Bedford, Warwicke, and other Lords. At another, Queene Isabel, the King, the Duke of Bourgougne, and other French.' Macready set it in 'The French court in Troyes, Champagne' (Macready pbk); typically, Kean went one better in terms of spectacle with the 'Interior of the Cathedral of Troyes in Champagne', where 'the two parties, French and English, are divided by barriers' (Kean pbk). Branagh has the two sides line up on either side of a long table, with the Kings of France and England, wearing their crowns, facing each other at either end. This formal arrangement is a sharp contrast to the mud and confusion of the previous scene, as the strains of 'Non nobis' trail across the change of scene. The French, including Katherine and Alice (the film, like Hands' production, cuts the character of the French Queen), are in mourning: bands for the men, veils for the women. Burgundy serves as a chair or mediator. He stands in the centre of the frame in the BBC/Giles version, too. Daniels' production began the scene at a cenotaph decorated with a large circular poppy wreath. Three soldiers in greatcoats and dark dress uniforms saluted, as the French King and nobles, in dark tailcoats and top hats, with the women in mourning, entered.

4　A note in Calvert's promptbook instructs that Henry's greetings to Katherine are made 'rather pointedly'. In Daniels' production, Henry's demands were curt and businesslike.

8　Kean had 'all the French party bow to King Henry' (Kean pbk).

12–22　Cut by Noble, who cut the Queen's role entirely.

Your eyes which hitherto have borne in them   15
Against the French that met them in their bent
The fatal balls of murdering basilisks.
The venom of such looks we fairly hope
Have lost their quality, and that this day
Shall change all griefs and quarrels into love.   20

KING To cry amen to that, thus we appear.
QUEEN You English princes all, I do salute you.
BURGUNDY My duty to you both, on equal love,
Great kings of France and England. That I have laboured
With all my wits, my pains and strong endeavours,   25
To bring your most imperial majesties
Unto this bar and royal interview,
Your mightiness on both parts best can witness.
Since then my office hath so far prevailed
That face to face and royal eye to eye   30
You have congreeted. Let it not disgrace me
If I demand before this royal view
What rub or what impediment there is
Why that the naked, poor and mangled peace,
Dear nurse of arts, plenties and joyful births,   35
Should not in this best garden of the world,
Our fertile France, put up her lovely visage?
Alas, she hath from France too long been chased,
And all her husbandry doth lie on heaps,
Corrupting in its own fertility.   40
Her vine, the merry cheerer of the heart,
Unprunèd, dies. Her hedges, even-pleached,

22 Here, Kean reverses the earlier courtesy: 'all the English party bow to Queen Isabella' (Kean pbk).

23 Branagh uses Burgundy's long speech to review the losses of the battle – on both sides. As Burgundy speaks, there is a close-up on Henry's serious, set face, and through him, as if in his memory, we see the images: of the dead Constable in Orléans' arms, of York being carried by the other nobles, the Boy, Mistress Quickly, Nym, Bardolph, Scroop and Falstaff. Hands had the Chorus, still in his Chorus costume, act as Burgundy, whom Hands dubbed a 'deus ex machina' (Beauman, p. 227)

24–31a; 38–67 Cut by Bell, Macready and Kean: Burgundy's lengthy lament for France might swing the balance of audience opinion at this point.

Like prisoners wildly overgrown with hair
Put forth disordered twigs. Her fallow leas
The darnel, hemlock and rank fumitory   45
Doth root upon, while that the coulter rusts
That should deracinate such savagery.
The even mead, that erst brought sweetly forth
The freckled cowslip, burnet, and green clover,
Wanting the scythe, all uncorrected, rank,   50
Conceives by idleness, and nothing teems
But hateful docks, rough thistles, kecksies, burs,
Losing both beauty and utility.
And as our vineyards, fallows, meads and hedges,
Defective in their natures, grow to wildness,   55
Even so our houses, and ourselves, and children
Have lost, or do not learn for want of time
The sciences that should become our country,
But grow like savages, as soldiers will
That nothing do but meditate on blood,   60
To swearing and stern looks, diffused attire,
And everything that seems unnatural.
Which to reduce into our former favour
You are assembled; and my speech entreats
That I may know the let why gentle peace   65
Should not expel these inconveniences
And bless us with her former qualities.

KING If, Duke of Burgundy, you would the peace
Whose want gives growth to th'imperfections
Which you have cited, you must buy that peace   70
With full accord to all our just demands,
Whose tenors and particular effects
You have, inscheduled briefly, in your hands.

BURGUNDY The king hath heard them, to the which as yet
There is no answer made.

KING   Well then, the peace,   75
Which you before so urged, lies in his answer.

70 The surprised look on Exeter's face at this point in Branagh's film suggests that the deal with
Katherine is of Henry's own deciding; Exeter's grin at line 95 (Branagh cuts 83–94) shows he
understands just what that price will be. Katherine and Henry are left with only Alice as
chaperone, and they take up the places at either end of the table again.

FRENCH KING I have but with a cursitory eye
        O'er-glanced the articles. Pleaseth your grace
        To appoint some of your council presently
        To sit with us once more, with better heed   80
        To re-survey them. We will suddenly
        Pass our accept and peremptory answer.
KING Brother, we shall. Go, uncle Exeter,
        And brother Bedford, and you brother Gloucester,
        Westmorland, Huntington, go with the king,   85
        And take with you free power to ratify,
        Augment or alter as your wisdoms best
        Shall see advantageable for our dignity,
        Anything in or out of our demands,
        And we'll consign thereto. Will you, fair sister,   90
        Go with the princes or stay here with us?
QUEEN Our gracious brother, I will go with them.
        Happily a woman's voice may do some good
        When articles too nicely urged be stood on.
KING Yet leave our cousin Katherine here with us.   95
        She is our capital demand, comprised
        Within the forerank of our articles.
QUEEN She hath good leave.

Exeunt all but King and Katherine [and Alice]

KING   Fair Katherine, and most fair,
        Will you vouchsafe to teach a soldier terms

90 Kean removed the barriers between the two parties at this point so that the English lords
    could cross over to the French side. 90–4 were cut by Noble.

98 Cuts to this long scene are frequent, and establish it as another area in which the generally
    derived acting text of the play resembles Q. Macready and Kean cut 60 of the scene's 150
    lines; Calvert 30; BBC/Hayes 30; Noble 36. Daniels set the wooing scene in front of the
    cenotaph with the engraved names of the dead prominently lit, stressing the cost of the
    battle, as Hands did by retaining the tableau of the dead of Agincourt, lit by candles,
    upstage. Kahn's production entitled the scene 'The Deal'. Daniels' Katherine was two inches
    taller on her high heels than her wooer, a complex symbol of defeated France; by contrast a
    diminutive Dorothy Tutin was 'prettily placed on steps to give ear to her tall conqueror' in
    Glen Byam Shaw's 1951 production (Williamson, p. 58).

99 Hayes has Henry lead Katherine out of the court into a garden. He thinks they are alone and
    begins to woo her, but is interrupted by Alice's entry, ensuring a more formal courtship.

Such as will enter at a lady's ear   100
And plead his love-suit to her gentle heart?
KATHERINE Your majesty shall mock at me. I cannot speak your
England.
KING O fair Katherine, if you will love me soundly with your French
heart I will be glad to hear you confess it brokenly with your   105
English tongue. Do you like me, Kate?
KATHERINE *Pardonnez-moi*, I cannot tell vat is 'like me'.
KING An angel is like you, Kate, and you are like an angel.
KATHERINE [*To Alice*] *Que dit-il – que je suis semblable à les anges?*
ALICE *Oui, vraiment, sauf votre grâce, ainsi dit-il.*   110
KING I said so, dear Katherine, and I must not blush to affirm it.
KATHERINE *O bon Dieu, les langues des hommes sont pleines de
tromperies!*
KING What says she, fair one? That the tongues of men are full of
deceits?   115
ALICE *Oui*, dat de tongues of de mans is be full of deceits, dat is de
princess.
KING The princess is the better Englishwoman. I'faith, Kate, my
wooing is fit for thy understanding. I am glad thou canst speak
no better English, for if thou couldst thou wouldst find me such   120
a plain king that thou wouldst think I had sold my farm to buy
my crown. I know no ways to mince it in love, but directly to say
'I love you.' Then if you urge me farther than to say 'Do you in
faith?', I wear out my suit. Give me your answer, i'faith do, and
so clap hands and a bargain. How say you, lady?   125
KATHERINE *Sauf votre honneur*, me understand well.
KING Marry, if you would put me to verses, or to dance for your
sake, Kate, why, you undid me. For the one I have neither words
nor measure, and for the other I have no strength in measure, yet

102 Katherine's objections were presented in Hands' production as 'a speech obviously
prepared in advance' (*Moment*, p. 125).
114 In the BBC/Hayes production, Alice is still bearing the language book she and
Katherine were studying in 3.5, and here and at 168, Henry's question directs her to
check it.
125 Warchus' direction here 'made of the scene something dangerous, even as [Katherine]
copied [Henry's] gesture, holding out a hand for him to shake, learning the body language
of the conqueror' (Holland, p. 195).

a reasonable measure in strength. If I could win a lady at   130
leapfrog, or by vaulting into my saddle with my armour on my
back, under the correction of bragging be it spoken I should
quickly leap into a wife. Or if I might buffet for my love or
bound my horse for her favours I could lay on like a butcher and
sit like a jackanapes, never off. But before God, Kate, I cannot   135
look greenly, nor gasp out my eloquence, nor I have no cunning
in protestation, only downright oaths, which I never use till
urged, nor never break for urging. If thou canst love a fellow of
this temper, Kate, whose face is not worth sunburning, that
never looks in his glass for love of anything he sees there, let   140
thine eye be thy cook. I speak to thee plain soldier. If thou canst
love me for this, take me. If not, to say to thee that I shall die is
true, but for thy love, by the Lord, no. Yet I love thee too. And
while thou livest, dear Kate, take a fellow of plain and uncoined
constancy, for he perforce must do thee right, because he hath   145
not the gift to woo in other places. For these fellows of infinite
tongue that can rhyme themselves into ladies' favours, they do
always reason themselves out again. What? A speaker is but a
prater, a rhyme is but a ballad, a good leg will fall, a straight back
will stoop, a black beard will turn white, a curled pate will grow   150
bald, a fair face will wither, a full eye will wax hollow – but a
good heart, Kate, is the sun and the moon, or rather the sun and
not the moon, for it shines bright and never changes, but keeps
his course truly. If thou would have such a one, take me. And
take me, take a soldier. Take a soldier, take a king. And what   155
sayest thou then to my love? Speak, my fair, and fairly, I pray
thee.
KATHERINE Is it possible dat I sould love de *ennemi* of France?
KING No, it is not possible you should love the enemy of France,
Kate. But in loving me you should love the friend of France, for   160
I love France so well that I will not part with a village of it. I will

130 Branagh's Henry seems genuine – and self-conscious. After all that has passed, he
resembles the boyish figure of Act 1 more than the soldier and leader of the intervening
action. Michael Sheen seemed uncomfortably and inappropriately boyish, nervously filling
up Katherine's silence with more and more jerky conversation, as she sat impassive.
131 When Henry mentioned 'armour' in Warchus' production, a memory of her language lesson
stirred in Katherine and she touched her arm.

have it all mine; and, Kate, when France is mine and I am yours, then yours is France, and you are mine.

KATHERINE I cannot tell vat is dat.

KING No, Kate? I will tell thee in French, which I am sure will hang   165
upon my tongue like a new-married wife about her husband's neck, hardly to he shook off. *Je quand sur le possession de France, et quand vous avez le possession de moi* – let me see, what then? Saint Denis be my speed! – *Donc vôtre est France, et vous êtes mienne*. It is as easy for me, Kate, to conquer the kingdom as to speak so   170
much more French. I shall never move thee in French, unless it be to laugh at me.

KATHERINE *Sauf votre honneur, le français que vous parlez, il est meilleur que l'anglais lequel je parle.*

KING No, faith is't not, Kate. But thy speaking of my tongue and I   175
thine most truly falsely must needs be granted to be much at one. But Kate, dost thou understand thus much English? Canst thou love me?

KATHERINE I cannot tell.

KING Can any of your neighbours tell, Kate? I'll ask them. Come, I   180
know thou lovest me, and at night when you come into your closet you'll question this gentlewoman about me, and I know, Kate, you will to her dispraise those parts in me that you love with your heart. But good Kate, mock me mercifully, the rather, gentle princess, because I love thee cruelly. If ever thou   185
beest mine, Kate, as I have a saving faith within me tells me thou shalt, I get thee with scambling, and thou must therefore needs prove a good soldier-breeder. Shall not thou and I, between Saint Denis and Saint George, compound a boy, half French half English, that shall go to Constantinople and take the Turk   190
by the beard? Shall we not? What sayest thou, my fair flower de luce?

167 Henry's woeful attempts at French give Katherine and Alice the giggles in Branagh's film. The choreography of his movements and the editing of the scene focus the pair closer together, although Katherine keeps dodging his attempts to kiss her. Hands literalised this choreography, as Henry and Katherine began to dance 'a curious foxtrot', as one reviewer put it, characteristic of the production as a 'hybrid between realism and formalism' (David, p. 214). Anthony Davies observes that when Henry woos Kate in Olivier's film, 'the angular lines of Henry's body suggest the awkwardness of his invasion of the pictorial composition which typifies the spatial dispositions in the French palace' (Davies, p. 39).

KATHERINE I do not know dat.

KING No, 'tis hereafter to know, but now to promise. Do but now promise, Kate, you will endeavour for your French part of such a boy, and for my English moiety take the word of a king and a bachelor. How answer you, *la plus belle Katherine du monde, mon très cher et divin déesse?*   195

KATHERINE Your majesty 'ave *fausse* French enough to deceive de most *sage demoiselle* dat is *en France.*   200

KING Now fie upon my false French. By mine honour, in true English, I love thee, Kate. By which honour I dare not swear thou lovest me, yet my blood begins to flatter me that thou dost, notwithstanding the poor and untempering effect of my visage. Now beshrew my father's ambition! He was thinking of civil wars when he got me. Therefore was I created with a stubborn outside, with an aspect of iron, that when I come to woo ladies I fright them. But in faith, Kate, the elder I wax the better I shall appear. My comfort is that old age, that ill layer-up of beauty, can do no more spoil upon my face. Thou hast me, if thou hast me, at the worst; and thou shalt wear me, if thou wear me, better and better. And therefore tell me, most fair Katherine, will you have me? Put off your maiden blushes. Avouch the thoughts of your heart with the looks of an empress. Take me by the hand and say 'Harry of England, I am thine.' – which word thou shalt no sooner bless mine ear withal but I will tell thee aloud 'England is thine, Ireland is thine, France is thine, and Henry Plantagenet is thine', who, though I speak it before his face, if he be not fellow with the best king thou shalt find the best king of good fellows. Come, your answer in broken music, for thy voice is music, and thy English broken. Therefore, queen of all, Katherine, break thy mind to me in broken English. Wilt thou have me?   205   210   215   220

KATHERINE Dat is as it sall please de *roi mon père.*

KING Nay, it will please him well, Kate; it shall please him, Kate.   225

KATHERINE Den it sall also content me.

KING Upon that I kiss your hand, and I call you my queen.

KATHERINE *Laissez, mon seigneur, laissez, laissez! Ma foi, je ne veux point que vous abaissiez votre grandeur, en baisant la main d'une de*

---

225 Robert Hardy (in the BBC/Hayes production) chases a coquettishly shrieking Katherine around the pillar.

votre seigneurie indigne serviteur. Excusez-moi, je vous supplie, mon   230
très puissant seigneur.

KING Then I will kiss your lips, Kate.

KATHERINE *Les dames et demoiselles, pour être baisées devant leurs*
noces, il n'est pas la coutume de France.

KING Madam, my interpreter, what says she?   235

ALICE Dat it is not be de *façon pour les* ladies of France – I cannot tell
vat is *baiser en* Anglish.

KING To kiss.

ALICE Your majesty *entends* bettre *que moi.*

KING It is not a fashion for the maids in France to kiss before they   240
are married, would she say?

ALICE *Oui, vraiment.*

KING O Kate, nice customs curtsy to great kings. Dear Kate, you
and I cannot be confined within the weak list of a country's
fashion. We are the makers of manners, Kate, and the liberty I   245
that follows our places stops the mouth of all find-faults, as I will
do yours, for upholding the nice fashion of your country in
denying me a kiss. Therefore patiently, and yielding. [*Kisses her*]
You have witchcraft in your lips, Kate. There is more eloquence
in a sugar touch of them than in the tongues of the French   250
Council, and they should sooner persuade Harry of England
than a general petition of monarchs. Here comes your father.

Enter the French power [FRENCH KING, QUEEN *Isabel*, BURGUNDY],
and the English lords [EXETER, WESTMORLAND]

BURGUNDY God save your majesty. My royal cousin, teach you our
princess English?

KING I would have her learn, my fair cousin, how perfectly I love   255
her, and that is good English.

---

248 When Henry and Katherine do kiss in Branagh's film, they lean together across the throne,
symbolising the political implications of their union. This echoes a similar device in Olivier's
film: 'In close-up we see King Henry's hand clasping Katherine's. The heraldry of England
and France can be seen on the rings of their fingers' (O, Fol).

252 The couple's kiss is broken by the discreet coughing of Alice, indicating the arrival of the
royal party (BBC/Hayes). Trumpets sounded in Kean's production as 'the centre gates are
thrown open and reenter the French King and Queen etc.' (Kean pbk).

BURGUNDY Is she not apt?

KING Our tongue is rough, coz, and my condition is not smooth, so
  that having neither the voice nor the heart of flattery about me I
  cannot so conjure up the spirit of love in her that he will appear   260
  in his true likeness.

BURGUNDY Pardon the frankness of my mirth if I answer you for
  that. If you would conjure in her you must make a circle, if
  conjure up love in her in his true likeness he must appear naked
  and blind. Can you blame her then, being a maid yet rosed over   265
  with the virgin crimson of modesty, if she deny the appearance
  of a naked blind boy in her naked seeing self? It were, my lord, a
  hard condition for a maid to consign to.

KING Yet they do wink and yield, as love is blind and enforces.

BURGUNDY They are then excused, my lord, when they see not what   270
  they do.

KING Then, good my lord, teach your cousin to consent winking.

BURGUNDY I will wink on her to consent, my lord, if you will teach
  her to know my meaning; for maids well summered and warm
  kept are like flies at Bartholomew-tide, blind, though they have   275
  their eyes, and then they will endure handling which before
  would not abide looking on.

KING This moral ties me over to time, and a hot summer; and so I
  shall catch the fly, your cousin, in the latter end, and she must be
  blind too.   280

BURGUNDY As love is, my lord; before it loves.

KING It is so. And you may, some of you, thank love for my
  blindness, who cannot see many a fair French city for one fair
  French maid that stands in my way.

FRENCH KING Yes, my lord, you see them perspectively, the cities   285

257–92 The bawdy exchanges between the Kings and Burgundy are cut by Bell, Macready, Kean,
Olivier, BBC, Noble and Branagh, presumably in order to preserve the romance of the
foregoing courtship from the cynical misogyny of the noblemen. Hands also cut this section,
although the souvenir text is surely disingenuous when it describes the language of the
edited speeches as merely 'courtly circumlocutions' (Beauman, p. 228). More extensive
cuts, lines 257–309, are made by the BBC/Hayes production. Warchus' production kept the
innuendos, creating an uncomfortable juxtaposition with the foregoing wooing scene. Line
289 was delivered as a 'shouted threat . . . which emphasised that all of this was politics'
(Coursen, p. 154).

turned into a maid, for they are all girdled with maiden walls that war hath never entered.

KING Shall Kate be my wife?

FRENCH KING So please you.

KING I am content, so the maiden cities you talk of may wait on her, 290 so the maid that stood in the way for my wish shall show me the way to my will.

FRENCH KING We have consented to all terms of reason.

KING Is't so, my lords of England?

WESTMORLAND The king hath granted every article, 295
His daughter first, and then in sequel all
According to their firm proposèd natures.

EXETER Only he hath not yet subscribèd this:
where your majesty demands that the King of France, having
any occasion to write for matter of grant, shall name your 300
highness in this form and with this addition, in French: *Notre
très cher fils Henri, roi d'Angleterre, héritier de France*; and thus in
Latin: *Praeclarissimus filius noster Henricus, rex Angliae et heres
Franciae*.

FRENCH KING Nor this I have not, brother, so denied 305
But your request shall make me let it pass.

KING I pray you then, in love and dear alliance,
Let that one article rank with the rest,
And thereupon give me your daughter.

FRENCH KING Take her, fair son, and from her blood raise up 310
Issue to me, that the contending kingdoms
Of France and England, whose very shores look pale
With envy of each other's happiness,
May cease their hatred. And this dear conjunction
Plant neighbourhood and Christian-like accord 315
In their sweet bosoms, that never war advance
His bleeding sword 'twixt England and fair France.

LORDS Amen.

293 At this agreement, Branagh has the French King take a quill to sign the documents in front of him.
289–318 Cut by Macready; 295–309 cut by Branagh.
310 Branagh has the couple's hands joined by the French King.
310–1 Kean cut the rather explicit reference to child-bearing.

KING Now welcome, Kate, and bear me witness all
                That here I kiss her as my sovereign queen.   320

                                Flourish

QUEEN God, the best maker of all marriages,
                Combine your hearts in one, your realms in one.
                As man and wife, being two, are one in love,
                So be there 'twixt your kingdoms such a spousal
                That never may ill office or fell jealousy,   325
                Which troubles oft the bed of blessèd marriage,
                Thrust in between the paction of these kingdoms
                To make divorce of their incorporate league,
                That English may as French, French Englishmen,
                Receive each other. God speak this 'amen'.   330

ALL Amen.

KING Prepare we for our marriage; on which day,
                My lord of Burgundy, we'll take your oath
                And all the peers, for surety of our leagues.
                Then shall I swear to Kate, and you to me,   335
                And may our oaths well kept and prosperous be.

                                Sennet. Exeunt

320 When Branagh's Henry kisses Katherine, the remainders of his scratches and cuts from the battle are clearly visible. Kean's Henry placed a ring on her finger. Olivier cuts lines 320–37, following line 319 with a backwards tracking shot of Henry and Katherine on two thrones. A cut shows Henry turning round, revealing that 'He is wearing the crude Globe Theatre make-up. Applause is heard as we pan to show a boy made up as Katharine' (*Masterworks*, p. 304): the film has returned to the reconstructed Globe theatre with which it began. The Chorus steps forward to close the curtain on the scene and deliver his final speech.

320 Noble's promptbook indicates a lack of reciprocity in the note 'English clap' (Noble pbk).

321 Few productions have felt comfortable with a woman taking a major role in the espousal. Kean cut the Queen's speech. Calvert and Daniels (who, like Noble, cut the part of the Queen entirely) gave it to the French King, and Noble and Hands gave it to Henry, replacing 'your' with 'our'. In Branagh's film, too, Henry speaks these lines, as the camera pans back to reveal an emblematic, tableau-like picture of the pair holding hands. The Chorus steps into this frozen frame. Kean cut the Epilogue and ended on the wedding.

332–6 Cut by Noble and by Calvert, who replaced it with a tableau of the espousal itself. Hayes has the King in his regal robes and Katherine in her wedding clothes ascend separate stairways to come together for their marriage.

5.3 *Enter* CHORUS

CHORUS Thus far with rough and all-unable pen
    Our bending author hath pursued the story,
    In little room confining mighty men,
    Mangling by starts the full course of their glory.
    Small time, but in that small, most greatly lived   5
    This star of England. Fortune made his sword

5.3 Cut by Kean, Macready, Calvert and Mansfield. Coleman ended with 5.0, bringing the King back to London and so adapted Kean's 'historical episode' of Henry's triumphant return from Agincourt to a pageant welcoming 'Henry V and Katherine of Valois' (pbk). Quayle's production in 1951 ended with lines 1–7, with the remaining lines replaced by a concluding section intended to review and wind up the sequence, positing it as the end of a chain rather than as Shakespeare has it, the start of a new and bloody one:

> And nourished there the red rose of his blood
> Awakened from the self-despising dream
> Of tavern-victories hallowed by Sir John
> He moves in his true measure. So our theme
> From Richard's winter builds this summer throne:
> Which oft our stage hath told, and for our sake
> In your fair minds let this acceptance take. (Quayle pbk).

Olivier also cuts the speech, with lines 1–6 followed by 13b–14. The Chorus bows, and the camera tracks backwards and upwards to deliver a panoramic shot of London, as at the beginning of the film. Another playbill flutters in the wind, and is caught by the camera: it contains the film's credits. In the BBC/Hayes production, the confines of the play and the 'little room' are visualised in a small chamber with a coffin. The Chorus runs his fingers along the wood during the speech, and the programme's final image is the coffin with a crown and a sword on top. Branagh's Chorus finishes off the work begun in the Prologue, shutting the door on the action that he had opened in 1.0. His regretful, melancholic tone gives way to the 'Non nobis' refrain as the credits roll against a black background. Noble's Chorus ended by blowing out the candles lit for the dead of Agincourt. Bogdanov left the speech uncut, but ended the play with the hieratic image of the wedding picture, and the National Anthem playing through loudspeakers, gradually drowned out by the noise of helicopters and machine guns, and the lights came down. Daniels had the cast standing on stage as the Chorus spoke, with the houselights gradually rising. Hands notes: 'The play runs hot and cold, and so ends. The ambiguity is constant' (Beauman, p. 232).

By which the world's best garden he achieved,
And of it left his son imperial lord.
Henry the Sixth, in infant bands crowned king
Of France and England, did this king succeed,   10
Whose state so many had the managing
That they lost France and made his England bleed,
Which oft our stage hath shown – and for their sake,
In your fair minds let this acceptance take.   *[Exit]*

BIBLIOGRAPHY

Bate, Jonathan, *Shakespearean Constitutions: Politics, Theatre, Criticism 1730–1830* (Oxford: Clarendon Press, 1989).

Beauman, Sally, *The Royal Shakespeare Company's Production of Henry V for the Centenary Season at the Royal Shakespeare Theatre* (Oxford and New York: Pergamon Press, 1976).

    The Royal Shakespeare Company: A History of Ten Decades (Oxford: Oxford University Press, 1982).

Beerbohm Tree, Herbert, *Thoughts and Afterthoughts* (London: Cassell, 1915).

Bell's Edition of Shakespeare's Plays, As they are now performed at the Theatres Royal in London; Regulated from the Prompt Books of each House By Permission; with Notes Critical and Illustrative; By the Authors of the Dramatic Censor (London and York: 1774).

Berry, Ralph, *On Directing Shakespeare: Interviews with Contemporary Directors* (London: Hamish Hamilton, 1989).

Berry, Ralph (ed.), *Changing Styles in Shakespeare* (London: Allen and Unwin, 1981).

Bogdanov, Michael, and Michael Pennington, *The English Shakespeare Company: The Story of the Wars of the Roses 1986–1989* (London: Nick Hern Books, 1990).

Branagh, Kenneth, *Henry V by William Shakespeare: A Screen Adaptation* (London: Chatto and Windus, 1989).

British Broadcasting Corporation, *The BBC Shakespeare: Henry V* (London: British Broadcasting Corporation, 1979).

Burns, Landon, 'Three Views of King Henry V', *Drama Survey* 1.3 (1962), pp. 278–300.

Calvert, Charles, *Shakspere's historical play of Henry the fifth, arranged by C. Calvert, and produced under his direction at the Prince's theatre, Manchester* (Manchester, 1872).

Calvert, Mrs Charles [Adelaide Helen], *Sixty-Eight Years on the Stage* (London: Mills and Boon, 1911).

Coleman, John, *Memoirs of Samuel Phelps* (London, 1886).

Cook, Dutton, *Nights at the Play: A View of the English Stage* (London, Chatto and Windus, 1883).

Cooper, Roberta Krensky, *The American Shakespeare Theatre: Stratford 1955–85* (Washington D.C.: Folger, 1986).

Coursen, H.R., *Shakespeare in Production: Whose History?* (Athens, GA: Ohio University Press, 1996).

Crosse, Gordon, *Shakespearean Playgoing 1890–1952* (London: A.R. Mowbray & Co., 1953).

Darbyshire, Alfred, *The Art of the Victorian Stage: Notes and Recollections* (London and Manchester: Sherratt and Hughes, 1907).

David, Richard, *Shakespeare in the Theatre* (Cambridge: Cambridge University Press, 1978).

Davies, Anthony, *Filming Shakespeare's Plays: The Adaptations of Laurence Olivier, Orson Welles, Peter Brook and Akira Kurosawa* (Cambridge: Cambridge University Press, 1988).

Dover Wilson, John, and T.C. Worsley, *Shakespeare's Histories at Stratford, 1951* (London: Max Reinhardt, 1952).

Eckert, C.W. (ed.), *Focus on Shakespearean Films* (Englewood Cliffs, NJ: Prentice-Hall, 1972).

Fitter, Chris, 'A Tale of Two Branaghs: *Henry V*, Ideology, and the Mekong Agincourt' in *Shakespeare Left and Right*, ed. Ivo Kamps (London and New York: Routledge, 1991), pp. 259–75.

Foulkes, Richard, 'Charles Calvert's *Henry V*', *Shakespeare Survey* 41 (1989), pp. 23–34.

   The Calverts: Actors of Some Importance (London: Society for Theatre Research, 1992).

Geduld, Harry M., *Filmguide to Henry V* (Bloomington: Indiana University Press, [1973]).

Gould, Gerald, 'A New Reading of *Henry V*', *The English Review* 128 (1919), pp. 42–55.

Gurr, Andrew (ed.), *King Henry V* (Cambridge: Cambridge University Press, 1992).

   The First Quarto of Henry V (Cambridge: Cambridge University Press, 2000).

Healy, Thomas, 'Remembering with Advantages: Nation and Ideology in *Henry V*' in *Shakespeare in the New Europe*, eds. Michael Hattaway, Boika Sokolova and Derek Roper (Sheffield: Sheffield Academic Press, 1994), pp. 174–93.

Hill, Aaron, *King Henry the Fifth: Or, the Conquest of France, By the English. A Tragedy* (London, 1723).

Hogan, Charles Beecher, *Shakespeare in the Theatre 1701–1800* (2 vols., Oxford: Clarendon Press, 1952).

Holderness, Graham, *Shakespeare Recycled: The Making of Historical Drama* (Brighton: Harvester Wheatsheaf, 1992).

Holland, Peter, *English Shakespeares: Shakespeare on the English Stage in the 1990s* (Cambridge: Cambridge University Press, 1997).

Hortman, Wilhelm, *Shakespeare on the German Stage: The Twentieth Century*
(Cambridge: Cambridge University Press, 1995).

Kiernan, Pauline, *Staging Shakespeare at the New Globe* (Basingstoke and
London: Macmillan, 1999).

King, T.J., *Casting Shakespeare's Plays: London Actors and Their Roles
1590–1642* (Cambridge: Cambridge University Press, 1992).

Lee, Sidney, *Shakespeare and the Modern Stage* (London: John Murray, 1906).
Shakespeare's King Henry the Fifth: An Account and an Estimate (London:
Smith, Elder & Co., 1900).

Leiter, Samuel L. (ed.), *Shakespeare Around the Globe: A Guide to Notable
Postwar Revivals* (New York: Greenwood Press, 1986).

Loehlin, James N., *Shakespeare in Performance: Henry V* (Manchester:
Manchester University Press, 1996).

Macready, William, *The Diaries of William Charles Macready, 1833–1851*, ed.
William Toynbee (London: Chapman and Hall, 1912).

Mazer, Cary, *Shakespeare Refashioned: Elizabethan Plays on Edwardian Stages*
(Ann Arbor, MI: UMI Research Press, 1980).

Odell, George C.D., *Shakespeare: From Betterton to Irving* (London: Constable,
1963).

Olivier, Laurence, *Confessions of an Actor* (London: Weidenfeld and Nicolson,
1982).

On Acting (London: Weidenfeld and Nicolson, 1986).

Payne, Ben Iden, *Life in a Wooden O* (New Haven and London: Yale University
Press, 1977).

Pilkington, Ace G., *Screening Shakespeare from Richard II to Henry V* (Newark
and London: University of Delaware Press, 1991).

Rabkin, Norman, *Shakespeare and the Problem of Meaning* (Chicago and
London: Chicago University Press, 1981).

Schoch, Richard W., *Shakespeare's Victorian Stage: Performing History in the
Theatre of Charles Kean* (Cambridge: Cambridge University Press,
1998).

Shattuck, Charles H., *The Shakespeare Promptbooks: A Descriptive Catalogue*
(Urbana and London: University of Illinois Press, 1965).

Shaughnessy, Robert, *Representing Shakespeare: England, History and the RSC*
(New York and London: Harvester Wheatsheaf, 1994).

Sprague, Arthur Colby, *Shakespeare and the Actors* (Cambridge, MA: Harvard
University Press, 1994).

Shakespeare's History Plays: Plays for the Stage (London: Society for Theatre
Research, 1964).

Taylor, Gary, *Moment by Moment by Shakespeare* (London and Basingstoke:
Macmillan, 1985).

'We Happy Few: the 1600 Abridgement' in Stanley Wells and Gary Taylor, *Modernising Shakespeare's Spelling, with Three Studies in the Text of 'Henry V'* (Oxford: Clarendon Press, 1979).

Taylor, Gary (ed.), *The Oxford Shakespeare: Henry V* (Oxford: Oxford University Press, 1984).

Trewin, J.C., *Benson and the Bensonians* (London: Barrie and Rockliff, 1960). *Shakespeare on the English Stage 1900–1964* (London: Barrie and Rockliff, 1964).

Williams, John Ambrose, *Memoirs of John Philip Kemble Esq. With an Original Critique on his Performance* (London, 1817).

Williamson, Audrey, *Old Vic Drama 2* (London: Rockliff, 1957).

Young, John W., 'Henry V, the Quai D'Orsay and the Well-being of the Franco-British Alliance, 1947, *Historical Journal of Film, Radio and Television* 7 (1987), pp. 391–21.

INDEX

Bold type indicates illustration